**FIORE'S**

# SUMMER LIBRARY READING PROGRAM HANDBOOK

*Carole D. Fiore*

## Neal-Schuman Publishers, Inc.
New York                    London

Published by Neal-Schuman Publishers, Inc.
100 William St., Suite 2004
New York, NY 10038

Printed and bound in the United States of America.

The paper used in this publication meets the minimum requirements of American National Standard for Information Sciences – Permanence of Paper for Printed Library Materials, ANSI Z39.48–1992.

**Library of Congress Cataloging-in-Publication Data**

Fiore, Carole D.
    Fiore's summer library reading program handbook / Carole D. Fiore.
        p. cm.
    Includes bibliographical references and index.
    ISBN 1-55570-513-8
  1. Children's libraries—Activity programs—United States. 2. Children—Books and reading—United States. 3. Young adults' libraries—Activity programs—United States. 4. Teenagers—Books and reading—United States. 5. Reading promotion—United States. I. Title: Summer library reading program handbook. II. Title.
    Z718.2.U6F54 2005
    027.62'5'0973—dc22
                                                                                    2004031104

For all my yesterdays —

My mentors — Carolyn Field, Helen Mullen, and Susan Roman —

thank you for inspiring me;

For today —

My colleagues and friends who support these efforts;

And for my tomorrows —

To the youth of today who will be the readers and library users of tomorrow.

# Contents

## PART I
## SUMMER READING PROGRAM ESSENTIALS

## PART II
## SERVING THE COMMUNITY OF USERS (AND NONUSERS)

## PART III
## ORGANIZING AND PROMOTING YOUR PROGRAM

## PART IV
## DESIGNING AND EVALUATING YOUR PROGRAM

# Contents

# Contents

## APPENDICES

# List of Figures

# Foreword

For over a century, public libraries have played a critical role in providing summer learning opportunities to young people across the United States. At a time of year when many public institutions close their doors to children and families, our nation's 117,000 public libraries provide a rich array of summer reading programs and educational activities designed to enrich our communities. These services are particularly valuable in light of recent research about the impact of learning losses over the summer in reading and mathematics on young people who do not have access to high-quality learning experiences over the summer months.

*Fiore's Summer Library Reading Program Handbook* is an important resource for librarians as they look for ways to strengthen and expand their role in supporting learning over the summer months. The manual was designed to serve as a comprehensive program-planning and implementation tool. It begins with a thorough description of the origins of summer library reading programs and examines the current context for such programs. The first part of the manual gives librarians the powerful information they need to make the case for increased investment and participation in their programs.

Part II covers all of the elements of planning a successful summer library reading program. Both experienced librarians and those who are just starting new programs will find valuable resources in this section on topics such as planning outcomes, designing programs for teens, and meeting the needs of students with disabilities.

Part III of the manual focuses on strategies for organizing and promoting programs. This section offers important insights into how libraries can build partnerships with other agencies and market their services to their communities. From working with the media to establishing relationships with the local business community, marketing often plays a crucial role in determining the long-term success and sustainability of summer programs.

Part IV explores the myriad themes and programming ideas that can be used to increase participation in summer reading programs. This section contains a wealth of creative ideas for libraries, such as contests, festivals, and poetry slams, that can be used to generate increased excitement and interest in summer programs.

*Fiore's Summer Reading Program Handbook* concludes with a compendium of successful summer reading program models offered by public libraries across the country. While the list is certainly not exhaustive of every noteworthy program, those featured are representative of the excellent work of libraries of all sizes from all regions of the country. One of the most distinguishing characteristics of these programs is the importance of energetic and knowledgeable staff in developing and implementing high-quality programs.

I encourage you to follow the examples of your colleagues and take full advantage of the resources in *Fiore's Summer Library Reading Program Handbook.* The manual will assist you greatly in meeting the needs of children and families in your community over the summer months.

Ron Fairchild
Executive Director
Center for Summer Learning, Johns Hopkins University

# Preface

When my new editor, Charles Harmon, asked that I do a revision of my 1998 book, *Running Summer Library Reading Programs*, I was somewhat reluctant. Would there be enough new material to warrant a second edition?

Instead I proposed a new book focusing on promising practices and model programs of summer reading programs. I wanted to create a complete handbook to meet the needs of today's libraries. In the years since the first edition, I had become aware of some important "disconnects" in this area. Why had some libraries pushed the envelope and developed cutting-edge programs, while many other libraries still provided the same services that they did years ago. While most libraries have computers available for patron use, few incorporate Web-based services in their summer programs. The *No Child Left Behind* Act called the public's attention to the crisis in students' reading skills and the *Reading at Risk* report of the National Endowment for the Arts notes a decline in literature reading by adults, but few libraries have formed effective partnerships with the education community. Nor has the education community recognized the important and vital support summer library reading programs can make in creating a new generation of readers. *Fiore's Summer Library Reading Program Handbook* is the new resource that I anticipated would answer these needs and more.

I read, researched, and talked with many people involved in the education community, especially those involved in reading instruction and libraries. One potent fact emerged. Libraries play a vital role in creating a new generation of readers and library users. Many of us have heard the phrase or seen the bumper sticker, "If you can read, thank a teacher." But, reading is more than just mastering phonics and decoding skills. Reading is comprehension. Reading is understanding. Reading is escape and compassion. Therefore, I counter and offer another phrase for a bumper sticker, "If you love to read, thank a librarian!"

Librarians, especially through summer library reading programs, can focus on the outcome of reading instruction. Summer library reading programs

- emphasize the joy reading brings to life,
- combine the solitary activity of reading with the social aspects of literacy, and
- center on the way reading expands knowledge and experience.

This handbook shows how libraries can, should, and *do* enhance children's, teens', and families' language and literacy experiences through imagination and summer programs.

*Fiore's Summer Library Reading Program Handbook* brings together practical how-to guidance. Chapters include educational, technological, and social potential of reading programs and examples of how libraries implement their summer programs. It also provides a sampling of emerging best practices and successful programs.

Part I, "Summer Reading Program Essentials," provides readers with the basics. Chapter 1, "Defining Summer Library Reading Programs," helps readers understand the nature of this service by offering a background and history. It points out some of the forerunners to our modern summer library reading programs and explains the difference between a reading program and a library program—and how these separate and distinct offerings can be melded for the greater benefit of the communities served.

Chapter 2, "Exploring the Literacy/Learning Value of Summer Library Reading," condenses and updates the research on how summer library programs positively affect reading retention of students over the traditional summer vacation. This information can be used as justification to develop grant applications and budget requests. This chapter also discusses the connection of summer reading programs with the 2004 National Endowment for the Humanities report, *Reading at Risk*, and the *No Child Left Behind* Act. I discovered several new studies that expand the research base and provide more data on why these programs need to be an integral part of library programming, no matter what size the library is or the population it serves.

Part II, "Serving the Community of Users (and Nonusers)," looks at the library user base—both patrons already visiting the library and the mass potential audience outside the library. Chapter 3, "Planning the Program," discusses goals, objectives, long-range plans, outcome-based planning, and more. Chapter 4, "Designing the Summer Reading Program," explores traditional and nontraditional audiences for these programs, such as preschoolers, young adults, and children with various types of disabilities. Programs for families and even adults are also included.

Part III, "Organizing and Promoting Your Program," gets into implementation. Chapter 5, "Beginning Your Program," helps organize your summer library program, including time frames and themes for planning. Promotion is important, so numerous examples of how to promote your program are included in Chapter 6, "Promoting Your Summer Program." This chapter also includes information on partnering with pre-existing organizations in your community and educational institutions.

For many people, Part IV, "Designing and Evaluating Your Program," is of great importance. Since many summer library programs are literature based, Chapter 7, "Exploring the A to Z of Summer Reading Programs," provides advice for navigating and complying with copyright law; an inventory and discussion of various types of programs that can be developed (video and film festivals, writing programs, booktalks, read-to-me programs, library sleepovers, and more); and suggestions for adapting books into other formats utilizing Web-based services and programs. This greatly expanded chapter includes many examples that have been shared with the author by numerous librarians from all over the United States and other nations the world over.

Evaluation is an often-overlooked aspect of the summer library program. Chapter 8, "Evaluating Program Success," covers measures, questionnaires, focus groups, and other methods of evaluation. The emphasis is on how these tools can be used to appraise the summer library program.

Chapter 9, "Summer Reading Programs in the Spotlight," gathers some of the best programs and promising practices from around the nation, including programs that focus on different audiences or have special aspects that show new directions libraries could take to better serve their communities. As communities and technology change, libraries need to as well. These best practices build on traditional programs and forecast the future of summer library reading programs.

I hope reading this book, *Fiore's Summer Library Reading Program Handbook,* and applying the knowledge will help you to plan a summer library program that is responsive to the needs of your community and that helps build a nation of readers.

# Acknowledgments

I would like to thank the following people and organizations for their help in bringing this publication to fruition:

Everyone who provided information that was included in the first edition and those who helped make the first book a success;

The staff in the Office of Information Access Services, State Library and Archives of Florida, especially Louise Brown and Linda Pulliam, for helping me locate the many resources needed to research this book and for processing all my interlibrary loan requests;

The staff in the Office of Library Community Development, State Library and Archives of Florida, for lending support, reading drafts of the manuscript, making suggestions for improvement, and helping in all the many ways that you all do;

The youth-serving librarians in Florida for working so hard to make the Florida Library Youth Program a model summer library program, and especially to all who have contributed to the Florida Library Youth Program and Florida Summer Library Program manuals over the past 30+ years. There are too many of you to name individually, but without your support, I never would have had so many wonderful ideas to include in this book;

The members of the Association of State and Cooperative Library Agencies, State Library Agency Section, Consultants for Library Service for Children and Young People Discussion Group for so freely sharing information about your states' summer library programs and the manuals and allowing me to include the list of summer library program themes by state;

Michael G. Gunde, Chief, Bureau of Braille and Talking Book Library Services, Division of Blind Services, Florida Department of Education, for helping me update the section on working with children and teens with disabilities;

The many children's and YA librarians from around the world who responded to requests for information on several electronic discussion lists, and who discussed many aspects of summer programs on numerous listservs; especially Kapila Sankaran, Youth Services Librarian, Springfield (N.J.) Free Public Library, and Monica Anderson, Youth Services Librarian, Grace A. Dow Memorial Library, Midland, Michigan, for sharing the information they gathered about how summer library reading programs *really* operate; and

Friend and colleague Sue McCleaf Nespeca for providing support and encouragement; I would like to thank the following for granting permission to use their materials in my book:

- Ron Fairchild, Executive Director, Johns Hopkins Center of Summer Learning, for sharing information and sources and allowing me to use *The Impact of Summer Learning Loss on the Achievement Gap in Reading* chart in Chapter 2;
- The Search Institute<sup>SM</sup>. The list of Developmental Assets is reprinted with permission from the Search Institute<sup>SM</sup> Web page, www.search-institute.org/assets/ (Minneapolis, Minn.: Search Institute). © Search Institute<sup>SM</sup>, 2004. www.search-institute.org. All rights reserved;
- The American Library Association for allowing me to use several items. The List of Service Responses is from *The New Planning for Results: A Streamlined Approach,* by Sandra Nelson for the Public Library Association, ©2001, and is reprinted with the permission of the American Library Association. The Decision Chart in Chapter 3 is adapted from *The TELL IT! Manual,* copyright © 1996 and reprinted with permission of the American Library Association. "The Teen Library Bill of Rights" from Virginia A. Walter and Elaine Myers, *Teens and Libraries: Getting It Right* (Chicago: American Library Association, ©2003), page 86, created by the Public Libraries as Partners in Youth Development project's Youth Partnership Council, July 28, 2002. The ALSC/Book Wholesalers Summer Reading Program Grant Application form in Chapter 5 is adapted with permission of the Association for Library Service to Children;
- The Forum for Youth Investment for granting permission to use in Chapter 3 "Libraries as Positive Developmental Settings," from Nicole Yohalem and Karen Pittman, *Public Libraries as Partners in Youth Development: Lessons and Voices from the Field* (Washington, D.C.: The Forum for Youth Investment, 2003) page 12. Available online at www.forumeforyouthinvestment;
- The State Library and Archives of Florida for permission to use the LSTA Outcomes Plan that appears in Chapter 3; the public service announcements, sample press releases, and reading and read-to-me logs from the FLYP 2004 program that appear in Chapter 6, and the parent pages that appear in chapter 7;
- Berkeley (Calif.) Public Library for allowing me to include information about their "Cover to Cover" program in Chapter 4;
- Clearwater (Fl.) Public Library System, Youth Services Department, especially Jana Fine, Youth Services Manager, for allowing me to include their Teen Volunteer Form and Teen Volunteer Guidelines in Chapter 4;
- Seminole County (Fl.) Public Library System for providing their System Volunteer Application Form that can be found in chapter 4;
- Gene DelVecchio, author of *Creating Ever-Cool: A Marketer's Guide to a Kid's Heart* (Gretna, La.: Pelican, 1998), for giving me permission to use information from his March 2004 Public Library Association presentation in Chapter 6;
- Georgia Public Library Service, for granting permission to include the Media-

Alert Template, Photo-Opportunity Alert, and the Public Service Announcements that are included in Chapter 6;

- New York State Library, for allowing me to use the fliers targeted to trustees and educators that appear in Chapter 6;
- The Indianapolis-Marion County (Ind.) Library, for providing promotional materials from their ALSC/NASA-based summer program that is found in Chapter 6;
- The Idaho State Library for allowing me to use the sample letters to the school district superintendent, parents, and school principals that are included in Chapter 6. They are reprinted with permission from the 1995 Idaho Summer Reading Manual, *Read around the World*;
- The Connecticut State Library, for materials that appear in Chapter 6;
- The parent survey in Chapter 8 is adapted with permission and was originally developed under a Library Services and Construction Act Title 1 grant from the State Library of Pennsylvania;

And all the many librarians who shared their ideas and concerns about summer library programs in journal articles and over the Internet.

A special thanks also goes to my supportive and tolerant husband Stan, for his understanding and patience while I worked on what seemed to be the never-ending project.

# I

# Summer Reading Program Essentials

# 1

# Defining Summer Library Reading Programs

## The Early Years

Summer library programs have long been a staple of public libraries in providing services to children and young adults. Summer library programs first emerged as public library services for children during the latter part of the nineteenth century. These services burgeoned almost simultaneously in several communities in the United States as aspects of influencing children to use the library, to read during the summer leisure time, and to develop a lifelong reading habit.

Today, 95 percent of all public libraries in the United States offer summer programs.[1] Many of the summer library programs that are flourishing today owe their success to the solid base that was laid at the end of the nineteenth and start of the twentieth centuries.

One of the earliest summer library programs in the United States was initiated by Carolyn Hewins at the public library in Hartford, Connecticut. Prior to school being dismissed for summer vacation in 1898, Hewins invited school children who were staying in town for the summer to come to the library once a week for an organized program of booktalks. She provided displays of books as she told about them; she also read aloud to the children who came to the library. Hewins was a believer in neighborhood library services; she advocated for clubs for children who lived in the same neighborhood, were of similar ages, and had similar interests. Because they relied on available resources (materials, space, and personnel) and the children's interests, these clubs were not always focused on reading.[2] Likewise, many of the summer library programs offered today also are not strictly focused solely on reading.

The Carnegie Library of Pittsburgh was also a leader in providing summer programs for children in the communities it served. In 1898, these programs began as an experiment by providing deposit collections at selected neighborhood playgrounds for six weeks during the summer. In addition to providing access to materials in places where the children had a tendency to congregate anyway, the library also conducted storytimes at these recreation centers. As staff who had trained at the Carnegie Library of Pittsburgh moved to other communities and found employment in other libraries, these other libraries followed the lead that the Carnegie Library of Pittsburgh had taken. Vacation playground-deposit collections were developed at the Seattle Public Library as well as at the Boston Public Library.[3]

Another early model for summer library programs for children was developed by the Library League in Cleveland, Ohio. Begun in 1897, the purpose of the league was to stress book care, to advertise the library to children, and to direct the reading of the city's young people.[4] Children's librarian Linda Eastman, director of this turn-of-the-century project commented, "It would be a fatal thing in this league work to merely stop at the taking care of books; that is just the beginning."[5] As with the youth-serving librarians of today, Eastman wanted to do more than just teach children how to take care of books.

When Eastman was unable to contact the children before the school year ended to interest them in reading over the summer, the library director sent school children a letter urging them, among other things, to use the library in the summer and discover how books add to the pleasure of vacation. The director also urged the children to compile a list of six or more of the best books they read to share with other children. In this simple request, we see the birth of what today librarians and readers alike call reading logs.

As the Library League of Cleveland and summer library programs in other communities grew and developed, additional materials and methods of attracting children were added. Bookmarks with booklists were distributed to encourage reading. Eastman reported in an article in *Library Journal* in 1897 that library use did increase in the summer because of the Library League. She also reported that children were being reached who had not been reached by ordinary methods.[6] This is one of the most prevalent reasons today for providing summer library programs: to turn non-library users into lifelong library users.

## Why Summer Programs?

In 1898, Cleveland Public Library Director W. H. Brett sent a letter to the teachers of the Cleveland Public Schools urging them to be aware of the library's mission to provide books for children. While reminding them that many children did not read enough over the summer, he asked teachers to:

Impress upon such of your pupils as have little home care the fact that the Public Library and its branches will be open all summer, and that here they can always find a good book to take home—that it is a good place to go when it is too hot and dusty to stay on the street.[7]

Even in 1898, libraries were reaching out to provide a safe and comfortable harbor to "latchkey children," long before they were so named by society.

Other library administrators saw additional values in providing summer programs for children. John Cotton Dana, for whom the H. W. Wilson/Library Administration and Management Association (LAMA) Library Public Relations Award is named, suggested in a 1901 editorial that children needed to know certain books so that they had a common cultural heritage. As a result of Dana's suggestion, the Michigan City (Indiana) Library used this idea as the basis for their 1901 vacation reading club. Children were given graded checklists of books and were asked to write about the book they enjoyed the most and why.[8]

Even though these programs were developing almost simultaneously in different regions of the United States, they all were concerned with children's reading and using the library year round, but most especially during summer vacation. During the early decades of the twentieth century, vacation reading clubs and similar projects were mentioned frequently in the library literature and in the histories of children's departments of many large public library systems. Even as far back as the 1927 *Survey of Libraries in the United States* conducted by the American Library Association, contests were used to encourage vacation reading by young people in cities throughout the United States. While some libraries used rolls of honor, certificates, diplomas, and honorary awards to stimulate interest in the clubs and reading, others expressed disapproval of all contests. This controversy regarding awards, incentives, and other manner of recognition is still under debate today. Other methods that were used to influence reading included personal contact, booklists, school visits, bookmarks, and prizes—which many times was a book.[9]

From these scattered beginnings, libraries across the United States and in many other parts of the world began to understand the need for summer library reading programs. But why exactly are summer library reading programs desirable and necessary in a world of electronic communication and other emerging technologies? Why are summer library reading programs necessary as we find ourselves at the dawn of a new century and a new millennium?

The youth of today will be the workers of the twenty-first century. Even with the emergence of new technologies, they will need reading and literacy skills that rival and exceed the skills of today's students and workers. While schools and other educational agencies diligently work to provide reading instruction and other literacy skills, there is seldom time in the school day, or even through homework assignments, to provide experiences that emphasize the social aspects of reading and literacy. At-risk students, most of whom do not gain a full year of achievement in reading during the academic year, are also the most at-risk to lose what little gain they have made if they do not participate in summer programs where reading and literacy skills are included. [10] All children need to have experiences that show reading as an integral part of life, not just a skill that is needed in school. Summer library reading programs provide experiences through which children, their parents, teachers, and caregivers can delight in sharing perceptions gained from literature. Group activities that are today an integral part of most summer library reading programs help dispel the myth that reading is a lonely pursuit. Activities that promote cooperation rather than competition help establish reading and literacy activities as ones in which everyone who participates becomes a winner.

Many state library agencies and some state library associations sponsor summer library programs. Many of the goals of these statewide programs are the same as when these types of programs originated over one hundred years ago. These programs, sponsored on a statewide basis, provide the foundation upon which local libraries can build and customize their program offerings and make them truly neighborhood programs, just as Carolyn Hewins had encouraged back in 1898. These statewide offerings are planned in such a way as to eliminate repetitive tasks, and because they are planned on such a large scale, they minimize the need for individuals throughout the state to reinvest the same activities. Statewide planning also allows for economy of scale and, therefore, monetary savings when materials such as posters, bookmarks, and reading logs are designed and produced.

Carol Gill writes about the benefit of statewide programs for library users. As children travel or their families relocate within a state, they can find a summer library reading program where the general structure is familiar. As many families relocate during the summer, when it interrupts schooling less, it is comforting for the child to find something familiar in the new location. Gill also writes of the benefits to the libraries when they participate in statewide programs:

> Small libraries without staff specifically responsible for youth services can take advantage of the expertise of their specialist colleagues. Larger libraries can dedicate staff to other needed programs. Even well established programs can expand their intended audience to include pre-readers and young adults if they can draw on the experiences of other libraries. With the Library for the Blind and Physically Handicapped as a member of the planning team, physically challenged children can participate in the same program as their friends. All libraries can take advantage of shared ideas and resources. It is the perfect symbiotic relationship. [11]

Summer library programs provided by local public libraries in partnership with other youth-serving agencies have beneficial effects on the children and teens who join or participate; their families and the community in general also benefit. It is generally assumed that the children who participate learn something about the general theme of the program. For example, children and teens who participated in the 2004 Cooperative Summer Library Program, Discover New Trails @ Your Library, learned about the Lewis and Clark expedition and the opening of the West. Many librarians today believe, as did the founders of the summer library program movement, that a summer library program promotes the development of reading interests and habits. Carolyn Field, former head of the Office of Work with Children, Free Library of Philadelphia states:

> The value of the club to child development varies according to its organization and the quality of its supervision. . . . Some librarians admit frankly that the VRC [vacation reading club] is a "gimmick" to keep up circulation statistics during the summer. Others use it as an opportunity to work with the individual child and guide his reading when he has more time.[12]

Many youth-serving librarians use summer library program activities to provide individualized reader guidance. However, in many libraries, so many children participate in these programs that librarians are limited in the amount of time they have to provide that guidance.

Goals of statewide programs vary slightly from local programs, but they serve as the basis for most of these local offerings. In my recent survey of state library agencies, 64 percent of statewide summer library programs sponsored by state library agencies or state library associations have clear goals.[13] These goals range from promoting library services to the public to assuring adequate library service in all areas of the state, from providing training for local library staff to encouraging children to read and use the local library and its resources when school is not in session. While making non-library users into lifelong library users and instilling a love of reading was often a stated or implied goal, rarely did a statewide program have as a stated goal maintaining students' reading skills over the school hiatus period.

## Reading versus Library Programs

Even though most statewide programs do not have maintaining students' reading skills as a specific goal, this turns out to be one of the benefits, and many summer programs do in fact have reading in their names. Whether known as the vacation reading club, summer reading club, vacation reading program, summer library program, or by some other name, these programs are similar. Having the word "reading" in the program name, however, does promote some expectations, and possible misconceptions, on the part of the library user, whether adult or child, and the community as a whole.

Reading programs, as the name implies, emphasize reading. Upon hearing that a local library is sponsoring a reading program, many parents may think that the library is going to teach their child the skills needed to read. Libraries are devoted to promoting the lifelong love of reading, and the fact is that enjoyment is the chief motivator for learning skills. Today, there are numerous libraries throughout the United States that are actively involved in adult and family literacy projects. Adult literacy programs are skills oriented; however, most family literacy programs are geared toward reading motivation rather than teaching reading skills for children still of school age. Having reading as the key word in the program title may also lead to misinterpretation by library staff, the education community, and parents as well unless they come to understand the many aspects of reading and its relation to meaning, experience, imagination, interest, and discussion.

Library programs emphasize the many and varied resources that libraries have. Rather than focusing just on reading skills, library programs can focus on the clients' introduction to thinking, learning, and sharing experience's with literature and they can provide the welcome atmosphere where a child who does not excel in other areas can succeed. As the American Library Association National Library Week theme of several years ago says, "Kids who read succeed!" Library programs can instill in children the love of reading for reading's sake rather than for the reward of a grade or a prize. Library programs, when designed as noncompetitive activities, promote reading as an activity in which everyone can win.

Library programs are more diverse in nature than reading instruction or skills programs. They may feature new and developing technologies that libraries are adopting and the youth of our country are embracing. Since they are not as book centered as a reading program, summer library programs are able to help participants develop their visual literacy and language skills as well as give them practice in reading. Library programs tend to utilize the innate curiosity and information-seeking behavior of the participants rather than just prescribing a set list of books from which to read. Whether through a reading program or a library program, instilling a love of reading and providing participants with the skills necessary to survive in an information-saturated society is one of the end results of these programs. By allowing the youth of our communities to see the value that a full-service library has to offer, not only are we creating the next generation of library users, but we are also creating the next generation of library supporters.

In addition to instilling the love of reading in children and young adults, library programs also promote cultural literacy, one of the goals John Cotton Dana suggested in 1901. Not only are youth and their families exposed to a variety of materials through summer library programs, they are exposed to the cultural resources of the community. For example, Dunedin, Florida, is a community that has as part of its cultural heritage Scottish life, including the Highland Games and the food, music, dance, literature, and language of Scotland. The unofficial city mascot is a kilt-clad Highlander; the high school music program includes a bagpipe band. The high school bagpipe band provides musical programs and demonstrations at the local library that entice younger children into joining the band when they enter high school. These programs also give the community the opportunity to gain an appreciation for the city's cultural heritage. If the teens of the community act as a resource, they are able to demonstrate that they have valuable skills; they also gain self-confidence from participating in the programs. In addition, the band provides similar programs for other libraries in the geographic region, thus promoting better understanding throughout a larger area.

Today, few libraries have the required reading list of Dana's prescription. While many schools still rely on a required reading list, many are discovering that library staff can recommend many other age- and developmentally-appropriate books for students to read during summer vacation time. The education community is now realizing that having students participate in library programs in which the youth and their families are exposed to literature, folk and fairy tales, art, music, sports, food, languages, and other aspects of cultures that are both familiar and unfamiliar to them and their families, develops well-rounded citizens of the world. While the social and cultural aspects of summer library programs are important, the educational value of these programs cannot be denied.

## Endnotes

1.  National Center for Education Statistics. 1995. *Services and Resources for Children and Young Adults in Public Libraries*. Washington, D. C.: U. S. Department of Education, Office of Education Research and Improvement.
2.  Jill L. Locke. 1988. "The Effectiveness of Summer Reading Programs in Public Libraries in the United States." Ph.D. diss. University of Pittsburgh, 6.
3.  Locke. 1998, 6–7.
4.  Sarah Cody. 1958. "A Study of the Summer Reading Club as a Recreational Reading Guidance Method with Children at the East 131st Street Branch of the Cleveland Public Library." Master's thesis. Cleveland, Ohio: Western Reserve, 9.
5.  "Philadelphia Conference: The Cleveland Children's Library League." 1897. *Library Journal* 22 (October): 151–152.
6.  Linda A. Eastman. 1897. "Methods of Work for Children—Cleveland Library League." *Library Journal* 22 (November): 687–688.
7.  "The Library in Vacation Days." 1898. *Library Journal* 23 (July): 279.
8.  Marilla Waite Freeman. 1901. "Summer Reading for Children: An Experiment." *Bulletin of the Iowa Library Commission* 1 (October): 57.
9.  Jill L. Locke. 1992. "Summer Reading Activities—Way Back When." *Journal of Youth Services in Libraries* 6, no. 1 (Fall): 72–78.
10. Larry Mikulecky, 1990. "Stopping Summer Learning Loss among at-Risk Youth." *Journal of Reading* 33 (1990): 516–521.
11. Carol Gill. 1993. "State Wide Summer Reading Program: CAYAS in Action!" *Aliki: The Washington Library Association Journal* 9, no. 3 (December): 14.
12. Carolyn W. Field. 1963. "To Reward or Not to Reward—That Is the Question!" *Wilson Library Bulletin* 37 (June): 885.
13. Carole D. Fiore. 1999. Survey of member of the Association of State and Cooperative Library Agencies, State Library Agency Section, Consultants for Library Service for Children and Young People Discussion Group.

# 2

# Exploring the Literacy/Learning Value of Summer Library Reading

## Effect of Summer Reading Programs

Summer library programs are a key to creating a nation of readers. And, as such, summer library programs are a key to creating a nation of literate citizens. In the aggregate, summer library programs are an integral part of public library services. "Virtually all public libraries (95.2 percent) provide summer reading programs for children. More children participate in public library summer reading programs than play Little League baseball. Moreover, these programs have been shown to play a definite role in children improving reading skills over the summer."[1]

There have been numerous studies, most of them within the education field, that explore the value of reading over the summer. Judith Menoher reported in her 1984 doctoral dissertation the results of several previous studies. Previous research indicates there is a direct relationship between ownership or availability of books to students and their reading scores. Menoher also reports that other studies found students who read more than ten books during the summer vacation made significant gains in reading ability over those who read less. Her own research found that reading of books and magazines was among the top three choices of activities that students in the fourth, sixth, and eighth grades perceived helped them improve their reading ability.[2]

Even before Menoher's study, others had found similar results. In 1959, William Harmer studied the effects of a summertime library training program on the reading abilities of fourth-grade children randomly selected from the Minneapolis (Minn.) Public Schools. Harmer reports, "Only five out of 230 summer participants showed a loss while only eight of 170 non-participants made a gain. The library plan was superior to all other plans in average gain of participants but the number of participants was somewhat smaller."[3]

Other researchers endorse summer reading, in whatever form it may take, as a significant manner to improve students reading performance. Ruth Cook reports: "It was found that any of the plans described was better than no plan. Whenever children engage in some systematic plan for summer reading, test results indicated significant improvement over their gain when they participated in no reading plan." Of special interest to librarians is the fact that membership in a summer reading club proved the most beneficial experience of all. Cook reports that children who joined the reading clubs made greater progress than those who took part in any of the other reading programs used.[4]

There are other studies that document how summer library programs positively affect students' reading ability. According to Lesley Mandel Morrow, voluntary reading correlates with high levels of reading achievement, increased comprehension, and vocabulary development. She states that correlation studies have found that children who read voluntarily or show an interest in books in early childhood or elementary and middle grades achieve higher levels of reading on standardized tests. Children with early and frequent exposure to literature tend to develop sophisticated language structures and develop a sense of story structure. Literature-based summer library programs provide this exposure. These activities also help increase interest in learning to read. For many children, this exposure also leads to early reading.[5] Morrow also cites Dr. William Teale's writings. Teale, professor at the University of Chicago and a recognized authority on emergent literacy, sees literacy "resulting from children's involvement in reading and writing activities mediated by literate others; it is the interaction that is most significant to the child's development."[6]

While all this research provides much information upon which librarians can base their programs, seeing these theories work in real situations is even more important. In 1984, Vivian Carter, children's librarian at the Normal (Ill.) Public Library, studied the effects of participation in public library summer reading programs on children's reading skills.[7] To establish children's reading levels prior to the summer, Carter used one version of the Gates-MacGinitie Reading Tests. This standardized reading-assessment test is easily administered and is available in two versions, thus allowing for a second administration of the test at the close of the summer library program. The study design resulted in 279 children being given the test both before and after the summer; this group included both participants and nonparticipants in the summer library program. Analysis of the data gathered by Carter during the study supports the following findings:

- Children who participate in the summer reading program show an increase in vocabulary scores on the post-test, whereas those who do not participate show a decrease.

- Children who participate in the summer reading program show an increase in comprehension scores, whereas those who do not participate show a decrease.
- No correlation seems to exist between improvement in scores for either vocabulary or comprehension and the number of books participants read. In other words, there is no statistical difference between scores of those children who read more books and those who read fewer books.

While this study is important, there are certain limitations. One of the most significant limitations is that no information was available on the summer reading activities of the nonparticipants group, since nonparticipation did not necessarily mean that these children did not read.

Mary Howes also investigated the extent to which participation in a summer library program affects the reading achievement of students at the beginning of second grade. Her study concludes that while "summer school children showed a significant gain across all categories . . . summer library program children gained significantly over all categories, almost half a year."[8] In other words, even though all children who participated in some type of structured summer program, such as summer school, had gains in reading skills, those children that participated in summer library reading programs showed more improvement. Howes' study showed that "total reading achievement was increased for each group of students who participated in the Public Library Summer Reading Program."[9] "If the choice has to be made between summer school and the public library summer reading program," concludes Howes, "then the library program can be considered more successful and cost effective. It is true that summer school attendees are often low achievers, but there is a reason to believe that properly motivated, a library program would be at least equally effective."[10]

The implications of Howes' study are important as librarians revise old and design new programs and work in partnership with other educational and youth-serving agencies. As Howes' study shows, library programs are more effective and should, perhaps, be combined with a skill-oriented summer school. This is one of the hallmarks of summer reading camps that have been created in response to the *No Child Left Behind* Act. Additional information on these camps is presented later in this chapter.

Stephen Krashen states that while direct instruction will teach the mechanics of reading, voluntary reading of literature is a powerful means of developing literacy, reading comprehension, writing style, vocabulary, grammar, and spelling.[11,12] Krashen defined "literature" as "any text that improves the lives of our students and helps them grow." He continues saying, "Literature is applied philosophy. It includes ethics, how we are supposed to live, and metaphysics, speculations on why we are here. Fiction is a very powerful way of teaching philosophy. Good stories help us reflect on our behavior and our lives."[13] A combined effort in which schools and libraries have separate yet distinct roles could help alleviate the problem of parents' misperceptions that summer library programs provide formal instruction.

Encouraging children to read is in the current and future interest of individual children, their families, the community, and the nation as a whole. Time spent reading would probably increase if the child enjoyed reading. Since research shows that good reading attitudes and skills are developed when children are young, it implies that parents and other primary caregiving adults should take an active interest in children's reading activities. Krashen states:

> An important goal of literature is to encourage more reading and a wider range of reading among children.... Reading stories aloud to children is an important part of a literature program. There is strong and consistent evidence that reading to children builds language and literacy competence. ... Reading stories helps directly by providing comprehensible and interesting texts, thereby helping in the acquisition of the grammar and vocabulary of printed English. Reading stories helps indirectly as well, by stimulating an interest in reading.[14]

Encouraging children to read begins with reading aloud to children at the earliest age and discussing the books and then continuing to do so even when they have acquired skills to read independently. "The most recently available data (2001) indicate that 58 percent of 3- to 5-year olds were read to daily by a family member. This percentage has fluctuated since 1993, ranging from 53 to 58 percent. Females (61 percent) were more likely to have been read to than males (55 percent).[15] Children who spend more time reading develop larger vocabularies and rank higher on standardized tests than their peers who spend less time reading. A study reported in the *Reading Research Quarterly* finds that 90 percent of fifth-grade students devoted only one percent of their free time to reading. 50 percent read for an average of four minutes or less per day, while ten percent read nothing at all.[16]

Children who spend approximately one minute per day (less than seven hours per year) reading are being exposed to 0.05 million words per year; they score in the 10th percentile on standardized tests. Children who spend approximately 11 minutes per day (less than 70 hours per year) reading are being exposed to 0.6 million words per year; they score in the 50th percentile. Children who spend approximately 38 minutes per day (more than 225 hours per year) reading are being exposed to more than two million words per year; they score in the 90th percentile.[17]

Unfortunately, most children spend more time in front of a television set than they do in front of a book. American children, ages 2–17, watch television on average almost 25 hours per week, or 3.5 hours per day. Almost one child in five watches

| Figure 2–1 Reading Times Per Day | | |
|---|---|---|
| Reading Times Per Day (Minutes) | Words Per Year (Millions) | Reading Rank— Percentile |
| 37.8 | 2.3 | 90th |
| 19.5 | 1.1 | 70th |
| 11.1 | 0.6 | 50th |
| 5.3 | 0.25 | 30th |
| 1.1 | 0.05 | 10th |

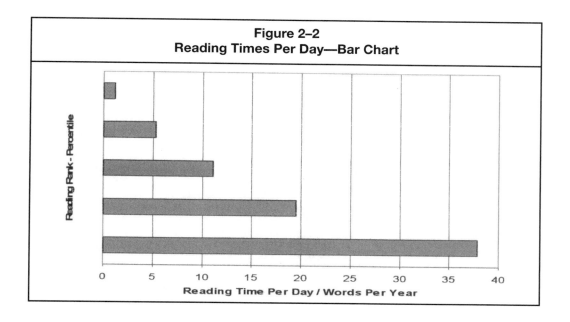

**Figure 2–2**
**Reading Times Per Day—Bar Chart**

more than 35 hours of TV each week.[18] If children were to spend more time reading and less time in front of a television set, one could anticipate that reading scores would go up. Encouraging children to become readers is what summer library reading programs are about.

Another related study, conducted by Linda Walker Thompson, found that inactive adult readers report:

> . . . significantly more reading-related problems and fewer reading experiences during childhood. . . . Data from adults who describe themselves as "active readers" or regular users of the public library indicated that their reading patterns were established early. . . . If all readers can be encouraged to read and learn to like reading as children, there is an increased likelihood that they will become adults who read and like to read. Such adults will be better prepared to participate as employable, contributing citizens.[19]

Becoming part of an organized group of readers may, in and of itself, be one of the key factors in motivating children to read.

In a March 1996 article in *School Library Journal,* G. Kylene Beers writes about three types of aliterates.[20] Aliterates are defined as people who can read but do not. As defined by Beers, the three types are

- dormant readers—these people like to read but don't often find the time to do it,
- uncommitted readers—they don't like to read but say they may read at some future date, and
- unmotivated readers—these people don't like to read and don't ever expect to change their minds.

Beers contends that avid and dormant readers:

> . . . joined book clubs, reading groups, libraries, and play groups. They
> had concrete items such as membership cards to prove they were members
> of a club whose purpose was reading.
>
> Students who did not value reading, who perceived it only as a
> functional skill, did not have these experiences. None of them had ever
> received their own library cards; they had never been a part of any group
> that focused on reading; they had not joined summer reading clubs.[21]

## Summer Learning and the Effects of Schooling

The most definitive study of the effects of summer library programs on the
education of students was done by Dr. Barbara Heyns, professor at New York
University. Her landmark study, *Summer Learning and the Effects of Schooling,* was
the first thorough investigation of summer learning. She followed sixth- and seventh-
grade students in the Atlanta, Georgia, public schools through two academic years
and an intervening summer.[22]

Structured summer programs, Heyns states, are, in many ways, similar to school
in that they require, and perhaps teach, many of the same social skills. Participants
are expected to attend regularly and arrive promptly at scheduled times and places.
Many times, participants must work cooperatively in a group situation. For younger
children especially, many of the activities are to a large extent planned, directed, and
supervised by adults. While older children and teens have more say in the activities,
they still work within limits set by supervising adults. Groups, whether in recreation
centers, churches, or libraries, tend to be composed of children of roughly similar
ages, backgrounds, and skill levels. This is similar in nature to what Hewins advocated
nearly a century earlier.

Heyns studied sex differences in summer activities. Boys clearly dominated the
more active and gregarious unstructured activities, such as playing with friends,
pursuing hobbies, and playing outside.

> The two activities in which girls averaged more time than boys were reading
> and watching television, both fairly sedentary domestic activities. Both boys
> and girls were reported to spend nearly 6 hours a day playing; boys, however,
> spent almost all of this time outside and away from home. Girls read nearly
> an hour more than boys each day and watched 30 minutes more television.[23]

While the study of sex differences was interesting, Heyns concluded that these activity
patterns do not seem to be related to summer learning.

> Moreover, when a particular activity is associated with gains, it tends to be
> equally effective for both males and females. Reading, for example, is
> positively related to summer learning, but watching television is not. Yet
> both males and females are positively benefited by reading books, and

both tend to be negatively influenced by large amounts of television viewing."[24]

"Reading and the use of public libraries are highly related to summer gains irrespective of parental status. The results also suggest that such behavior should be taken into account in formulating policy."[25]

The most significant finding from the Heyns study is that the single summer activity that is most strongly and consistently related to summer learning is reading. Reading during the summer, whether measured by number of books read, time spent reading, or even by the regularity of library usage, systematically increases the vocabulary test scores of children. "Although unstructured activities such as reading do not ordinarily lend themselves to policy intervention," Heyns writes, "I will argue that at least one institution, the public library, directly influences children's reading. Educational policies that increase access to books, perhaps through increased library services, stand to have an important impact on achievement, particularly for less advantaged children."[26]

Heyns specifically found that socioeconomic status had little impact on reading achievement over the summer. Although reading tends to be patterned by family situation, the increases in summer learning are largely independent of a child's social class. She found that "each additional hour spent reading on a typical day, or every four books completed over the summer, are worth an additional vocabulary word, irrespective of socioeconomic status, for both black and white children."[27] She also found that children in every income group who read six or more books during the summer consistently gained more than children who read fewer books.[28] Heyns found that there are many reasons for achievement over the summer. This is in direct contradiction to Carter's study previously mentioned in which she found that the number of books read did not make a significant difference; participation in a summer library reading program, not the quantity of books read, was the important factor in the Carter study. Carter found that "the number of books read by children during the summer does not seem to be as important as the fact that those children are enrolled in a summer reading program."[29] A conclusion from the Heyns study is, "The unique contribution of reading to summer learning suggests that increasing access to books and encouraging reading may well have substantial impact on achievement."[30] Both the number of books read and participating in a group in which reading and literacy activities are valued add significantly to improved reading abilities, achievement, and attitudes.

According to Heyns, the major determinants of reading are, in order of importance:

- whether the child uses the public library
- the child's sex—girls read more than boys
- the child's socioeconomic status
- the distance between a child's home and the library

Socioeconomic status was more important and sex less so for white children. Girls read almost two books more than did boys during the summer; Heyns found this difference even greater among black children. "Insofar as library use influences summer learning, this effect operates entirely through reading. As one might surmise, library use is of little importance unless a child reads there."[31]

Heyns makes several statements based on her research regarding the effectiveness of the public library on summer learning. Since libraries facilitate reading, they also promote reading achievement. "More than any other public institution, including the schools, the public library contributed to the intellectual growth of children during the summer. Moreover, unlike summer school programs, the library was used regularly by over half of the sample and attracted children from diverse backgrounds."[32]

Attracting children to the library during the summer, and getting them involved in an organized reading program appears to be a significant way that libraries can increase the summer learning of the young people in their service area.

## Summer Learning, Summer Learning Loss, and Summer Learning Day

Within the past decade, more attention has been focused on finding out what happens to children's learning over the summer. According to Anne McGill-Franzen and Richard Allington, "Regardless of other activities, the best predictor of summer loss or summer gain is whether or not a child reads during the summer. And the best predictor of whether a child reads is whether or not he or she owns books."[33] And the traditional school calendar also has an impact on children's summer learning.

Harris Cooper cites the challenge issued in 1993 by the National Education Commission on Time and Learning for school districts to develop school calendars that acknowledge differences in student learning and how the antiquated agrarian-related school calendar adversely affects students.[34] Cooper's research has helped the education community learn more about summer learning and summer learning loss. According to Cooper, students appear, at best, to demonstrate no academic growth over the summer when there is no intervention. At worst, students appear to lose the equivalent of one month of grade-level skills relative to national norms.[35]

Cooper and Ronald A. Fairchild, executive director for the Center for Summer Learning, Johns Hopkins University, subscribe to the "faucet theory." During the school year, while the "faucet" is open and students are exposed to various types of educational and enhancement opportunities, all students, regardless of socioeconomic status, experience learning at a parallel rate, no matter where they begin. The difference in learning occurs during the summer, when the educational-experience "faucet" is different for children of different socioeconomic status. Children who attend summer camp, summer school, travel to visit relatives, or participate in structured summer reading programs do not have their learning interrupted. This mirrors Heyns' findings. Multiyear programs have a greater cumulative effect than short-term interventions. The following chart shows the impact on learning of continuing educational and enhancement programs on students in kindergarten though fourth grade.[36–39]

McGill-Franzen and Allington also talk about summer setback. According to their research, children from low-income families are more prone to summer learning loss

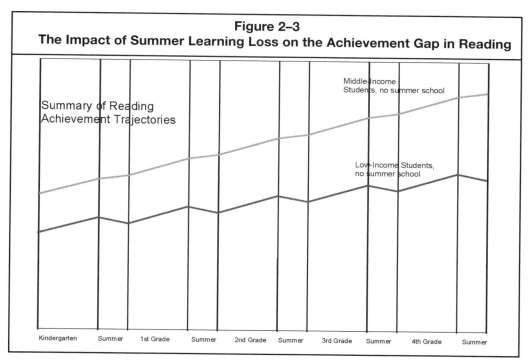

Figure 2–3
The Impact of Summer Learning Loss on the Achievement Gap in Reading

Summary of Reading Achievement Trajectories

Middle-Income Students, no summer school

Low-Income Students, no summer school

Kindergarten    Summer    1st Grade    Summer    2nd Grade    Summer    3rd Grade    Summer    4th Grade    Summer

Used by permission of Ron Fairchild. 2004. Handout, American Library Association Conference.

than children in middle- and upper-income families. They contend, as does Fairchild, that summer learning loss is cumulative. "Summer reading loss of three months accumulates to a crucial two-year gap by the time kids are in middle school, even if their schools are equally effective. It suggests that focusing all of our efforts on improving schools isn't going to work."[40]

To call attention to the impact summer learning has on student achievement and to attract public attention to this, the John Hopkins Center for Summer Learning initiated Summer Learning Day in 2004. Camps, schools, libraries, and other educational entities were invited to use July 15 as a day to promote the value of summer programs. The purpose of the day is to "send young people back to school ready to learn, support working families, and to keep kids healthy and safe." One of the ideas suggested recognizing summer learning is to plan a community event to "focus on reading." What better place to host such an event than local public library. The Center plans to sponsor this observance every summer.[41] Libraries should adopt this day in the middle of their summer library reading programs to promote the idea that libraries are part of the education community.

Summer learning is affected by the activities that children engage in during the summer. Documenting this summer learning has been tracked as early as the summer after kindergarten. According to the National Center for Education Statistics:

Children in households with low SES were the least likely to participate in each of the nine activities listed in table 1 [library; bookstore; state or national parks; art, science, or discovery museums; zoo, aquarium, or petting farm; historic sites; concerts or plays; vacation; day or overnight camp] during the summer after their kindergarten year, while children in households with high SES were the most likely to do so. . . . Some 46 percent of low SES children went to a library over the course of the summer compared to 66 percent of middle SES children and 80 percent of high SES children).[42]

This report from the National Center for Education Statistics provides insight into the use of libraries by children in various socioeconomic groups. "Of those children that visited a library—low SES library visitors went, on average, less often (4 times) than middle or high SES visitors (7 times each). However, among those children who visited a library over the summer, low SES and middle SES library visitors were more likely to attend story time at a library than high SES library visitors (27 percent and 26 percent compared to 20 percent."[43]

As with the conclusions from the Heyns study, this National Center for Education Statistics report reinforces the concept that proximity to a library is important, especially for children in low socioeconomic status.

Among children whose parents report no neighborhood library, low SES children were the least likely to visit the library (31 percent) while high SES children were the most likely to do so (72 percent). In addition, when no neighborhood library was reported, low SES library visitors went less frequently, on average, than middle or high SES library visitors (4 times compared to 5 and 6 times respectively). These relationships also held among children whose parents reported having a neighborhood library. However, the difference between the percentage of low and high SES children who visited the library was smaller in neighborhoods with a library than those without one (26 percentage point gap compared to 41 percentage point gap). Among children whose parents reported no neighborhood library, low SES library visitors attended storytime at higher levels than high SES library visitors (28 percent compared to 15 percent).[44]

McGill-Franzen and Allington also find that lack of transportation affects how children in low-income families use public libraries. "Even when public libraries are open, poor children may lack transportation. Research shows that public library use among poor children drops off when a library is more than six blocks from their home, compared with more than two miles for middle-class children."[45]

Other researchers have also found that summer library reading programs enhance children's learning and literacy development. Donna Celano and Susan B. Neuman conducted research on the summer reading programs in Philadelphia. They studied four groups of children who came from low-income, working families; the children all had low-reading scores. Two groups of children attended summer reading programs and the other two groups attended day camps. After a few weeks in their respective programs, it was found that the children in the summer reading program read significantly better than those children who attended the camp. Other significant findings from this study include:

- Reading programs encourage children to spend increased time with books.
- Public library summer reading programs play an important role in the reading achievement of children who lack access to books and other reading materials in their lives.
- Literacy-related activities and events (such as those provided in summer library reading programs) enhance reading experiences. These activities and events encourage children to read themselves, hear stories read aloud, and write about what they read.
- Public library reading programs encourage parents to become involved in their children's reading.[46]

## *No Child Left Behind* Act

The lynchpin in President George W. Bush's education program is the *No Child Left Behind* Act (NCLB). School districts are required to use instructional methods based on scientifically based reading research. One aspect of this all-encompassing educational-reform legislation stresses that students perform at certain levels before they can be promoted.

Research shows that children who read well in the early grades are far more successful in later years; and those who fall behind often stay behind when it comes to academic achievement. . . . Reading opens the door to learning about math, history, science, literature, geography and much more. Thus, young, capable readers can succeed in these subjects, take advantage of other opportunities (such as reading for pleasure) and develop confidence in their own abilities. On the other hand, those students who cannot read well are much more likely to drop out of school and be limited to low-paying jobs throughout their lives. Reading is undeniably critical to success in today's society.[47]

Part of the NCLB uses definitions based on the *Report of the National Reading Panel (2000)* and has adapted them to relate directly to reading instruction.

- *Phonemic awareness:* the ability to hear, identify, and play with individual sounds—or phonemes—in spoken words.
- *Phonics:* the relationship between the letters of written language and the sounds of spoken language.
- *Fluency:* the capacity to read text accurately and quickly.
- *Vocabulary:* the words student must know to communicate effectively.
- *Comprehension:* the ability to understand and gain meaning from what has been read.[48]

The library community is responding to the *No Child Left Behind* Act. The Public Library Association and the Association for Library Service to Children, both divisions of the American Library Association, have partnered to develop a program that supports *No Child Left Behind.* The program, "Every Child Ready to Read @ Your Library," though designed primarily to support programs for infants and toddlers and their parents and caregivers, supports and enhances the library role in emergent literacy and reading instruction. The main concepts developed in the "Every Child Ready to Read @ Your Library" relate to definitions in NCLB:

- *Print Motivation* is a child's interest in and enjoyment of books.
- *Phonological Awareness* is the ability to hear and play with the smaller sounds in words.
- *Vocabulary* is knowing the names of things.
- *Narrative Skills* is the ability to describe things and events, and to tell stories.
- *Print Awareness* is noticing print everywhere; knowing how to handle a book; knowing how we follow the words on a page.
- *Letter Knowledge* is knowing that letters are different from each other, that they have different names and sounds.[49]

In addition to incorporating these concepts into infant and toddler programs, libraries can incorporate these concepts into programs and services for children of other ages. It is especially important to incorporate these concepts when designing programs for parents and caregivers.

## Summer Reading Camps

One program established through NCLB designed specifically to assist third-grade students perform at a level that will enable them to be promoted to fourth grade is summer reading camps. While not citing the work of the Center for Summer Learning, communications from the U.S. Department of Education cites the need for summer reading camps to counteract summer learning loss.[50] While school districts have used summer schools for many years, the success of students enrolled in these programs has not been at the desired level. Summer school was looked on as punitive. Many of the children who attend mandatory summer school have few opportunities to read extensively in books that are

> . . . at their level and about topics that truly interest them. Our work [McGill-Franzen and Allington] suggests that if children have opportunities to listen to, discuss, and read books on topics they select, or books about the characters they love, they develop extensive background knowledge that can scaffold their independent reading and sustain their engagement. Summer school must provide interventions that can accomplish these goals.[51]

In Los Angeles in 2000, the Milken Family Foundation developed an eight-week reading summer day camp intervention program where disadvantaged first-grade children attend reading camp instead of summer school. Within the context of summer camp, credentialed teachers taught reading to the campers for two hours per day. The remaining time was devoted to regular summer camp fun activities. These were supplemented with enrichment activities, such as field trips to museums, aquariums, and cultural centers.

In 2003, this program was adapted to become the Summer Reading Achievers Project. The first Summer Reading Achievers program was offered through the auspices of the Atlanta Fulton Public Library. The public library reports that the central piece that is core to the success of the program is the collaboration with the public schools.[52] In 2004, this program was expanded to 11 diverse locations around the country. While most of the programs are school based, they incorporate many of the activities that public libraries use in their summer library reading programs—reading logs, access to books, and parental involvement.[53,54]

At the same time that the U.S. Department of Education was developing their first summer reading camp in 2003, the State Library and Archives of Florida was developing the Summer Library Reading Partnership Program (SLRPP). Public libraries participating in this statewide program receive federal Library Services and Technology Act grant funds based on the population of their service areas. Libraries partnered with local school districts, and together they targeted low-achieving third-grade students. Libraries provided extra summer library activities both in the library and at the summer reading camp location. While the schools focus on reading skills, libraries provide reading enrichment activities and materials. For additional information about how this program was implemented in Florida, see Chapter 9, "SLRPP, Alachua County Library District."

## *Reading at Risk*—and Its Implications

While not specific to the reading habits of children and teens, *Reading at Risk: A Survey of Literary Reading in America,* the 2004 report of the National Endowment of the Arts (NEA), reported that literary reading has shown a dramatic decline over the past 20 years. The report defines literary reading as reading novels, short stories, plays, and poetry during leisure time. Reading to meet informational needs is not included, nor is required reading for school or work.

The report documents an overall decline of 10 percentage points in literary reading from 1982 through 2002. This represents a loss of 20 million potential readers. According to NEA Chairman Dana Gioia:

This report documents a national crisis: Reading develops a capacity for focused attention and imaginative growth that enriches both private and public life. The decline in reading among every segment of the adult population reflects a general collapse in advanced literacy. To lose this human capacity—and all the diverse benefits it fosters—impoverished both cultural and civic life."[55]

The report also states that reading affects lifestyle. Literary readers are much more likely to be involved in cultural, sports, and volunteer activities; nonreaders are less likely to be so involved. The report documents that the most important factor in literary-reading rates is education. Only 14 percent of adults with a grade school education read literature in 2002; by contrast, 74 percent—more than five times as many respondents with a graduate school education—read literary works.

The report also details the correlation between literary reading and other leisure activities. Literature readers watched an average of 2.7 hours of television each day; nonreaders of literature watched an average of 3.1 hours daily. The report concluded that adults who do not watch TV in a typical day are 48 percent more likely to be frequent readers. These frequent readers consume from 12 to 49 books each year. This report correlates with, parallels, and reinforces the information presented earlier in this chapter from *Get **Media** Wise* about children's television viewing versus their reading habits.

While the drop in literary reading is alarming, this report does not track all the reading that adults do. It does not track other types of literary behavior—especially the type of reading and literacy activities in which teens engage. The report does indicate that older adults, those with more leisure time, read more than their younger counterparts. It does not include online reading and writing, reading magazines or 'zines, blogging, or journaling.[56]

## Incentives—Prizes or Punishment

Encouraging children and young people to read can be a difficult task. Many children and teens are motivated to participate in summer reading programs through the use of incentives and contests. However, caution in this area is urged.

Library programs, especially during the summer or other school vacation periods, should be viewed as enjoyable and noncompetitive. The number of books read should not be considered the goal; rather, the enjoyment of books and the camaraderie found in sharing books with peers and significant adults should be of prime importance. Contests where only one child wins for reading the greatest number of books creates a situation in which only one child is the winner, and the other children, no matter how many books they have read, how long they have spent reading, or whether they have enjoyed their reading, are all considered losers. "Opponents castigate it as competitive, charging that children and their parents become interested in how many more books Johnny reads than Jimmy and in 'who wins,' rather than in if Johnny's reading is spontaneous and pleasurable, contributing to his mental and emotional growth."[57]

One series of books more than any other has turned numerous children on to reading and into readers. The length of the Harry Potter books has not discouraged these young readers. Many children, regardless of their reading ability, read these lengthy books. Good readers will devour them quickly, while struggling readers may take the entire summer to read one of these several hundred–page volumes. Are we to reward the voracious reader for reading more books than the struggling reader? Or should the struggling reader be rewarded for reading, period? And why are they reading Harry? One of the reasons is social—the ability to discuss the books with their peers. Sharing the literary experience provides added value.

Incentives have become the focus of some summer library programs. During the summer of 1990, the Indianapolis-Marion (Ind.) County Public Library conducted a summer reading program for the residents of the greater Indianapolis area. While the goal of the summer program has remained the same for almost the entire 80 plus years this program has been in existence (to instill a love of reading in those who participate), the format of the Indianapolis program changed significantly in the 1980s. Since 1919, the program had focused on school-age readers accomplishing a prescribed amount of book reading; in 1985 participation was expanded to include parents and preschool children as well as school-age readers. In addition, a menu of incentives was added to reward *all* reading rather than only those who met an externally established goal.

Parents could register with their preschool children. Parents earned points for reading to their preschoolers, and the preschoolers earning points for listening to their parents read those very same books aloud. School-age children earned points for independent reading as well as reading to and with others.

The changes in the summer library program in Indianapolis resulted in dramatic increases in participation, from fewer than 3,500 participants in 1984 to 44,273 in 1990. There were 34,689 children under 18 years of age participating in 1990, representing an almost 1,000 percent increase in children's participation in the summer reading program. During the same six-year period, "summer circulation of children's books increased more than 25-fold, in 1990 individual participants checked out, on the average, three times the number of books than the average participant in the 1984 summer program."[58]

There are varying opinions regarding the use of incentives to promote reading and participation in summer library programs. Librarians need to be cognizant that all children are different and that various forms of reward and competition are appropriate so long as everyone who participates becomes a winner in his or her own eyes. Zacharie Clements, a reading educator at the University of Vermont in Burlington, talks about reading incentives. "The emerging reader has not yet developed the understanding of the value of reading is in the reading itself."[59]

Basing their summer library program on ones in the United States, the Napier Public Library in New Zealand also uses incentives. In planning their program and establishing their goals, they decided that incentives would be given as reinforcements for success. As with Clements, staff at the Napier Public Library feel that reluctant readers especially need reinforcement. "Pleasant rewards make the process palatable and teach the children to relish reading and to perceive libraries as purveyors of pleasure."[60]

Other people believe that tangible rewards and incentives are not appropriate. Alfie Kohn challenges a basic strategy for raising children, teaching students, and managing workers that says "Do this, and you'll get that." Kohn writes that while manipulating people with incentives seems to work in the short run, it is a strategy that ultimately fails and even does lasting harm. Programs that use rewards to change people's behavior are also ineffective over the long run. Promising prizes and rewards to children for reading can only produce a temporary change.[61]

Kohn relates the story of a nine-year-old boy from Philadelphia who, as his mother said, had not learned to love books. As with many other reluctant readers, he read only what was required. When the child learned that the summer library program was offering baseball cards and other prizes for reading books, he checked out six books. He checked the books out not really to read, but because he wanted the baseball cards. The reward purchased a temporary change in behavior. When the library ran out of baseball cards, this child, as did many others, stopped reading.[62] Sharing books with others and being part of the sharing should be rewarded, not just borrowing the books from the library. The switch from external rewards to internal incentives takes time and exposure. As Clements writes, "You've got to prime the pump; later, the internal gratification will come."[64]

Librarians and others who care about the youth of our nation and the world need to instill in them an intrinsic love of reading. Voluntary free reading as promoted in summer library programs means reading because you want to, not because you are required to. But lacking built-in motivation, something must spur children and young adults to want to read. It means no book reports, no questions at the end of each and every chapter. It does mean telling other people, especially your peers, about the books that you enjoy. It also means sharing books and personal reactions to literature with significant adults—parents, teachers, caregivers, and library staff. It means being introduced to books by a variety of methods. It means reacting to books through various means—through the arts, movement activities, writing experiences. It means being able to put down a book you don't like and choosing another one instead. Summer library programs promote all these behaviors, behaviors that highly literate people demonstrate instinctively all the time.

## Conclusions

What can be concluded from the NEA study; the research by Morrow, Carter, Kohn, Trelease, Krashen, Beers, Heyns, Cooper, Fairchild, and others who have been discussed in this chapter? We can conclude that students who read succeed, and successful students read more than those who do not succeed in school. Leisure reading occurs more frequently when readers, including dormant readers, have more leisure time. We know that access to books plays an important part not only in whether but also in how frequently people read. People will read when it is not a chore. And if we make reading fun from the beginning, people will become lifetime readers. The goal of summer library reading programs is to create a new generation of readers and library users. We need to use the research to design programs that enhance children's, teens', and their families' language and literacy experiences and turn them into readers. Summer library reading programs in public libraries must be designed and promoted so that they are accepted by the education community as an integral part of the methodology to create readers and lifelong learners. Summer library reading programs must be well planned, fit into the overall plan of the library, be promoted to nonusers as well as library users, and must be evaluated. The subsequent chapters will provide insight into how do to that.

## Endnotes

1. F. William Summers, et al. 1999. "Florida Libraries Are Education: Report of a Statewide

Study on the Educational Role of Public Libraries." Tallahassee, Fl.: School of Information Studies, Florida State University, iv.

2. Judith A. Menoher, 1984. Factors Affecting Reading Achievement Retention over Summer Vacation. Ph.D. diss. Salt Lake City, Utah: Brigham Young University.

3. William R. Harmer, 1959. "The Effect of a Library Training Program on Summer Loss or Gain in Reading Abilities." Ph.D. diss. Minneapolis: University of Minnesota.

4. Herbert Goldhor and John McCrossan. 1966. "An Exploratory Study of the Effect of a Public Library Summer Reading Club on Reading Skills." *Library Quarterly* 36 (January): 17–18.

5. Lesley Mandel Morrow. 1987. "Promoting Innercity Children's Recreational Reading." *Reading Teacher* 41, no. 3 (December): 266–274.

6. Morrow, 272.

7. Vivian Carter. 1988. "The Effect of Summer Reading Program Participation on the Retention of Reading Skills." *Illinois Libraries* 70, no. 1 (January): 56–60.

8. Mary Howes. 1989. "Intervention Procedures to Enhance Summer Reading Achievement." Ph.D. diss. Dekalb: Northern Illinois University: 99–100.

9. Howes, 102.

10. Howes, 103–104.

11. Stephen Krashen. 1993. *The Power of Reading: Insights from the Research.* Englewood, Colo.: Libraries Unlimited.

12. Stephen Krashen. 2004. *Free Voluntary Reading: New Research, Applications, and Controversies.* Paper presented at PAC5 (Pan-Asian Conference), Vladivostok, Russia, June 24, 2004. Available: www.sdkrashen.com/articles/pac5/01.html. Accessed June 8, 2004.

13. Stephen D. Krashen. 1996. *Every Person a Reader: An Alternative to the California Task Force Report on Reading.* Culver City, Cal.: Language Education Associates: 6–7.

14. Krashen. 1996, 7.

15. *America's Children in Brief: Key National Indicators of Well-Being, 2004.* 2004. Washington, D.C.: Federal Interagency on Child and Family Statistics, 12. For further information go to http://childstats.gov.

16. Richard Anderson, Linda Fielding, and Paul Wilson. 1988. "Growth in Reading and How Children Spend Their Time Outside of School." *Reading Research Quarterly* 23(3), (Summer): 285–303. doi: b.1598/RRQ.23.3.2

17. Jim Trelease. 2001. *The Read Aloud Handbook,* 5th ed. New York: Penguin: 108–109.

18. *Get Media Wise: Watch What Your Kids Watch.* Available: www.mediafamily.org/facts/facts_childandtv.shtml. Accessed October, 28, 2004.

19. Linda Walker Thompson. 1991. "A Study of Low-Achieving Students' Recreational Reading." Ph.D. diss. Bloomington: Indiana University.

20. G. Kylene Beers. 1996. "No Time, No Interest, No Way! The 3 Voices of Aliteracy." *School Library Journal* 42, no. 3 (March): 110–114.

21. Beers, 1996. 111.

22. Barbara Heyns. 1978. *Summer Learning and the Effects of Schooling.* New York: Academic Press.

23. Heyns, 146.

24. Heyns, 149.

25. Heyns, 160.

26. Heyns, 161.

27. Heyns, 168.

28. Heyns, 169.

29. Carter, 57.

30. Heyns, 172.

31. Heyns, 172.

32. Heyns, 177.

33. Anne McGill-Franzen and Richard Allington. 2003. "Bridging the Summer Reading Gap." *Instructor* 112 (May–June): 17–20.

34. Harris Cooper. 2003. *Summer Learning Loss: The Problem and Some Solutions.* ED475391. Champaign, Ill.: ERIC Clearinghouse on Elementary and Early Childhood Education. Available: www.ericfacility.net/ericdigests/ed475391.html. Accessed June 17, 2004.

35. Harris Cooper, et. al. 1996. "The Effects of Summer Vacation on Achievement Test Scores: A Narrative and Meta-Analytic Review." *Review of Educational Research* 66, no. 66 (Fall): 227–268.

36. Geoffrey Borman, Laura T. Overman, Ron Fairchild, et. al. 2004 "Can a Multiyear Summer Program Prevent the Accumulation of Summer Learning Losses?" In *Summer Learning: Research, Policies, and Programs*. Mahwah, New Jersey: Lawrence Erlbaum Associates, 223–253.

37. Ron Fairchild. 2004. "Summer Learning: Research and Best Practices." Handouts, American Library Association Annual Conference, June 29, 2004. Chart used with permission of Ron Fairchild, Center for Summer Learning, Johns Hopkins University.

38. Ronald A. Fairchild and Matthew Boulay. 2002. "What If Summer Learning Loss Were an Education Policy Priority?" Unpublished paper, Assessing the Public Policy and Management Research Conference, November 9, 2002.

39. Fairchild, "Summer Learning," Handouts.

40. McGill-Franzen and Allington. 2003. American Library Association Annual Conference. "Bridging the Summer Reading Gap." Instructor. Volume 12 (May-June): 17–20.

41. Promotional Materials for Summer Learning Day 2004 from the Center for Summer Learning, Johns Hopkins University. Information is also available at www.summerlearning.org.

42. National Center for Education Statistics (NCES). 2004. "The Summer after Kindergarten: Children's Activities and Library Use by Household Socioeconomic Status." *Issue Brief*. Washington, D.C.: National Center for Education Statistics, U.S. Department of Education, (September), 1.

43. NCES, 2.

44. NCES, 2.

45. McGill-Franzen, Allington.

46. Donna Celano and Susan B. Neuman. 2001. *The Role of Public Libraries in Children's Literacy Development: An Evaluation Report*. Harrisburg, Penn.: Pennsylvania Library Association.

47. *Questions and Answers on* No Child Left Behind—Reading. Washington, D.C.: U.S. Department of Education. Available: www.ed.gov/print/nclb/methods/reading/reading.html. Accessed October 28, 2004.

48. Ibid.

49. *Every Child Ready to Read @ Your Library*. Chicago, American Library Association. Available: www.ala.org/ala/pla/plaissues/earlylit/earlyliteracy.htm. Accessed October 28, 2004.

50. *The Achiever: No Child Left Behind*. Washington, D.C.: U.S. Department of Education, June 1, 2003. Available: www.ed.gov/print/news/newsletters/achivere/2003/06012003.html. Accessed October 28, 2004.

51. McGill-Franzen and Allington.

52. "Pilot Summer Reading Program in Atlanta Sponsored by the U.S. Department of Education." E-mail from Barbara Huntington, 2003 Collaborative Summer Library Program Chair, August 14, 2003.

53. *No Child Left Behind: Summer Reading Achievers*. 2004. Washington, D.C.: U.S. Department of Education.

54. "Summer Reading Program Launched in 10 Cities, One State." Press Releases. Washington, D.C.: U.S. Department of Education, 2004. Available: www.ed.gov/news/pressreleases/2004/04/04082004a.html. Accessed August 3, 2004.

55. "Literary Reading in Dramatic Decline, According to National Endowment for the Arts Survey." Washington, D.C.: National Endowment for the Arts, July 8, 2004. Available: www.arts.gov/news/news04/ReadingAtRisk.html. Accessed July 9, 2004.

56. Mary Ellen Vogt. 2004. "Book Reading Drops, Says New Survey." *Reading Today*. Newark, Del. International Reading Association, 22, no. 1, (August/September): 6.

57. Elizabeth Henry Gross and Gene Inyart Namovicz. 1963. *Children's Services in Public Libraries: Organization and Administration*. Chicago: American Library Association, 81.

58. Thompson.

59. "An Interview with Two Hip Reading Educators on How Librarians and Others Can Put the Zing Back into Sleepy-Time and Year-Round Reading Programs." 1973. *Wilson Library Bulletin* 47, no. 8 (April): 689.

60. Su Scott. "Kids and Libraries: Improving the Connection: The Summer Reading Programmes of Napier Public Library." 1993. *New Zealand Libraries* 47, no. 8 (December): 158.
61. Alfie Kohn. 1993. *Punished by Rewards: The Trouble with Gold Stars, Incentive Plans, A's, Praise, and Other Bribes.* Boston: Houghton Mifflin.
62. Kohn, 73–74.
62. "An Interview with Two Hip Reading Educators. . . ." 687–690.

## Recommended Reading

Connor, Jane Gardner. 1990. *Children's Library Services Handbook.* Phoenix, Ariz.: Oryx.
Kim, Jimmy. 2004. "Summer Reading and the Ethnic Achievement Gap." *Journal of Education for Students Placed at Risk* 9, no. 2: 169–189.
Minkel, Walter. 2002. "Study: Summer Reading Helps Students." *School Library Journal* 48, no. 2: 24.
Walter, Virginia A. 2001. *Children & Libraries: Getting It Right.* Chicago: American Library Association.

# II

# Serving the Community of Users (and Nonusers)

# 3

# Planning the Program

Traditionally, vacation reading clubs and other similar library programs were open to children who already had acquired some reading skills. From the 1950s through the early 1980s, many summer programs, such as the Vacation Reading Club of the Free Library of Philadelphia, were open to children who had completed third through eighth grades. Other library systems also had similar grade or reading-level restrictions on membership in the summer library programs they sponsored. Most programs were targeted at school-age children who were enrolled in regular, not special education, classes. Prior to the 1970s, libraries provided minimal service to children with learning, emotional, mental, or physical disabilities. Services for preschoolers were provided to those children whose parents brought them to the library during the day throughout the school year; most summer library programs did not have a component for pre-readers. As with other types of library services, the audience for summer library programs has changed as both society and the educational system have changed.

As we have already seen, summer library programs are not only a major activity that entices children into becoming literate citizens and library users, they are also the best predictors of academic success the following year. Libraries have traditionally been the common factor that have provided "everyone the opportunity to enhance their civic, language, and literacy skills. Librarians and libraries have historically played a great part in initiating and supporting literacy efforts."[1]

Additional studies show that "Reading enhances literacy development lead[ing] to an uncontroversial conclusion: Reading is good for you. . . . Reading is the only way we become good readers, develop a good writing style, an adequate vocabulary, advanced grammar, and the only way we become good spellers."[2] Knowing these things, librarians, schools, and the communities they serve must devise methods of working together to accomplish the long range goal of helping children and young adults become joyous, enthusiastic, self propelled, and motivated readers and library users. But when should these programs begin, how long should they run, and who should participate? More importantly, what do you, the library administration, the library users, parents, schools, and the community as a whole expect from a summer library program?

## Goals and Objectives of Summer Library Programs

Whether talking about the summer library program, the youth services program as a whole, or the library program in general, librarians along with the communities they serve must go through some type of planning process and make many important decisions along the way. Whether using *The TELL IT! Manual: The Complete Program of Evaluating Library Performance* by Douglas Zweizig, Debra Wilcox Johnson, Jane Robbins, and Michele Besant (Chicago: American Library Association, 1996); *The New Planning for Results: A Streamlined Approach* by Sandra Nelson for the Public Library Association (Chicago: American Library Association, 2001); outcomes-based evaluation; or another planning tool, the basic steps in the planning process and the vocabulary associated with these processes are similar.

One of the first steps in the planning process is for the library and the community the library serves to establish a *vision* for the library program. This vision is a desired state of affairs and has a societal rather than a library focus. From the vision, the *mission* of the library is generated. The mission is a statement of the library's business, its purpose, and priorities. Once the mission of the library is established, several roles may be established. A *role* or *service response* is a concrete image for library service. Whether your library has selected as primary or secondary roles either *formal learning support,* where the library "helps students who are enrolled in a formal program of education or who are pursuing their education through a program of homeschooling to attain their educational goals"; or *commons,* where the library creates an environment that "addresses the need of people to meet and interact with others in their community . . . "; or has selected *current topics and titles,* where the library "helps to fulfill community residents' appetite for information about popular culture and social trends and their desire for satisfying recreational experiences," a summer program can fit within these and several other roles. The needs of the community must be kept at the forefront when roles are established.[3]

Once your library has selected its primary and secondary roles, you must develop goals. A *goal* is something that will take years to achieve—if ever. Goals are directions in which the library wants to proceed; they provide the framework from which objectives will be developed. *Objectives* are specific, measurable, attainable outcomes that can be accomplished within a definite time frame. They indicate how far the library intends to proceed towards its goals within a limited period of time. As librarians establish objectives and establish the scope of a specific program, they must be aware of the potential audience, and the cost, space, personnel, and materials that will be required to accomplish the objective. It is essential to know that you have in mind the *entire* potential audience, not just that portion of which you are aware. Every community has members who, though fully entitled to library service, never have demanded it and, therefore, remained invisible.

As you and your library's administrators establish the objectives, you will also need to determine what level of effort you are willing to invest in achieving your goals. In other words, you will need to make choices, sometimes some very hard choices, as you work to establish your program. You will also need to explore alternative approaches as you design your program.

## How Summer Library Reading Programs Fit into the Long–Range Plan

Today, planning is an important administrative task for most libraries. As previously discussed, this planning involves looking at the community of users as well as nonusers, people who are potential users of library services. Most of the service responses described in Nelson's *New Planning for Results* are flexible enough so that service to children and young adults can be included. Summer library reading programs can easily be incorporated into many of those service responses.

The discussion in Chapter 1 clearly establishes the educational and literacy value of summer library reading programs. This supports both the *Basic Literacy* and *Formal Learning Support* service responses. Since many summer library reading programs provide programs that provide information about the cultural diversity in their communities, these summer programs would support the *Cultural Awareness* service response. For summer programs to be adopted by teens, they must take advantage of popular culture and the fads of the moment. Programs should be designed to take advantage of popular books, characters, movies, and toys and games. Even though planning a summer library program can take up to two years, selecting the theme and the designing the art needs to take advantage of what children and teens are currently attracted to. Programs that rely heavily on this relationship to pop culture fit into the *Current Topics and Titles* service response.

Many summer library reading programs bring students from different areas of the community together and provide them opportunities to meet and interact in a nonthreatening setting. While most of the interaction is centered on books and other library materials, discussions that are part of the programs allow participants to talk about their feelings and philosophies. Having parents participate in book discussions with their children in programs such as PRIME TIME Family Reading Time© allows multiple generations to participate in a library program that meets the intent of the *Commons* service response.

While the library may not actually be referring program participants to community

**Figure 3–1**
**Library Service Responses**

### Basic Literacy

A library that offers Basic Literacy service addresses the need to read and to perform other essential daily tasks.

### Business and Career Information

A library that offers Business and Career Information service addresses a need for information related to business, careers, work, entrepreneurship, personal finances, and obtaining employment.

### Commons

A library that provides a Commons environment helps address the need of people to meet and interact with others in their community and to participate in public discourse about community issues.

### Community Referral

A library that offers Community Referral addresses the need for information related to services provided by community agencies and organizations.

### Consumer Information

A library that offers Consumer Information service helps to satisfy the need for information to make informed consumer decisions and to help residents become more self-sufficient.

### Cultural Awareness

A library that offers Cultural Awareness service helps to satisfy the desire of community residents to gain an understanding of their own cultural heritage and the cultural heritage of others.

### Current Topics and Titles

A library that provides Current Topics and Titles helps to fulfill community resident's appetite for information about popular culture and social trends and their desire for satisfying recreational experiences.

### Formal Learning Support

A library that offers formal learning support helps students who are enrolled in a formal program of education or who are pursuing their education through a program of homeschooling to attain their educational goals.

### General Information

A library that offers General Information helps meet the need for information and answers to questions on a broad array of topics related to work, school and personal life.

### Government Information

The library that offers Government Information service helps satisfy the need for information about elected officials and government agencies that enables people to participate in the democratic process.

### Information Literacy

A library that provides Information Literacy service helps address the need for skills related to finding, evaluating, and using information effectively.

### Lifelong Learning

A library that provides Lifelong Learning service helps address the desire for self-directed personal growth and development opportunities.

### Local History and Genealogy

A library that offers Local History and Genealogy service addresses the desire of community residents to know and better understand personal or community heritage.

Used by permission of the American Library Association. Figure 9 from *The New Planning for Results*.

agencies as part of the summer library reading program, many libraries invite other service providers to participate in their activities by presenting programs. Educating community members about the other services that are available to them is part of the services provided by libraries that select *Community Referral* as one of their service responses.

Whichever service responses a library selects, the design of their summer programs need to support the long-range plan of the library.

## Incorporating Developmental Assets

"Libraries build communities" was the theme Sara Long chose for the American Library Association for the year she was president. Building communities is also the purpose of the Search Institute, an independent, nonprofit organization whose mission is to provide leadership, knowledge, and resources to promote healthy children, youth, and communities. To accomplish this mission, the institute generates and communicates new knowledge, and brings together community, state, and national leaders.

At the heart of the institute's work is the framework of 40 Developmental Assets. Making communities better places to grow up is part of this mission. The 40 Developmental Assets are concrete, common sense, positive experiences and qualities essential to raising successful young people. While these assets have the power during the critical adolescent years to influence choices that young people make and help them to become caring, responsible adults, they are applicable for younger children as well.

The Developmental Asset framework is categorized into two groups of 20 assets. External assets are the positive experiences young people receive from the world around them. These 20 assets are about supporting and empowering young people, about setting boundaries and expectations, and about positive and constructive use of young people's time. External assets identify important roles that families, schools, congregations, neighborhoods, and youth organizations can play in promoting healthy development.

The twenty internal assets identify those characteristics and behaviors that reflect positive internal growth and development of young people. These assets are about positive values and identities, social competencies, and commitment to learning. The internal Developmental Assets will help these young people make thoughtful and positive choices and, in turn, be better prepared for situations in life that challenge their inner strength and confidence.[4]

Libraries need to consider these assets when developing their summer library reading programs. Several of the assets can be enhanced when youth participate in summer library reading programs. For example, of the external assets, libraries can contribute to asset number 3: "Other Adult Relationships—Young person receives support from

## Figure 3–2
## 40 Developmental Assets

Practical research
benefiting children
and youth

# 40 Developmental Assets™

Search Institute℠ has identified the following building blocks of healthy
development that help young people grow up healthy, caring, and responsible.

| Category | Asset Name and Definition |
|---|---|

**External Assets**

**Support**
1. **Family Support**-Family life provides high levels of love and support.
2. **Positive Family Communication**-Young person and her or his parent(s) communicate positively, and young person is willing to seek advice and counsel from parents.
3. **Other Adult Relationships**-Young person receives support from three or more nonparent adults.
4. **Caring Neighborhood**-Young person experiences caring neighbors.
5. **Caring School Climate**-School provides a caring, encouraging environment.
6. **Parent Involvement in Schooling**-Parent(s) are actively involved in helping young person succeed in school.

**Empowerment**
7. **Community Values Youth**-Young person perceives that adults in the community value youth.
8. **Youth as Resources**-Young people are given useful roles in the community.
9. **Service to Others**-Young person serves in the community one hour or more per week.
10. **Safety**-Young person feels safe at home, school, and in the neighborhood.

**Boundaries & Expectations**
11. **Family Boundaries**-Family has clear rules and consequences and monitors the young person's whereabouts.
12. **School Boundaries**-School provides clear rules and consequences.
13. **Neighborhood Boundaries**-Neighbors take responsibility for monitoring young people's behavior.
14. **Adult Role Models**-Parent(s) and other adults model positive, responsible behavior.
15. **Positive Peer Influence**-Young person's best friends model responsible behavior.
16. **High Expectations**-Both parent(s) and teachers encourage the young person to do well.

**Constructive Use of Time**
17. **Creative Activities**-Young person spends three or more hours per week in lessons or practice in music, theater, or other arts.
18. **Youth Programs**-Young person spends three or more hours per week in sports, clubs, or organizations at school and/or in the community.
19. **Religious Community**-Young person spends one or more hours per week in activities in a religious institution.
20. **Time at Home**-Young person is out with friends "with nothing special to do" two or fewer nights per week.

**Internal Assets**

**Commitment to Learning**
21. **Achievement Motivation**-Young person is motivated to do well in school.
22. **School Engagement**-Young person is actively engaged in learning.
23. **Homework**-Young person reports doing at least one hour of homework every school day.
24. **Bonding to School**-Young person cares about her or his school.
25. **Reading for Pleasure**-Young person reads for pleasure three or more hours per week.

**Positive Values**
26. **Caring**-Young person places high value on helping other people.
27. **Equality and Social Justice**-Young person places high value on promoting equality and reducing hunger and poverty.
28. **Integrity**-Young person acts on convictions and stands up for her or his beliefs.
29. **Honesty**-Young person "tells the truth even when it is not easy."
30. **Responsibility**-Young person accepts and takes personal responsibility.
31. **Restraint**-Young person believes it is important not to be sexually active or to use alcohol or other drugs.

**Social Competencies**
32. **Planning and Decision Making**-Young person knows how to plan ahead and make choices.
33. **Interpersonal Competence**-Young person has empathy, sensitivity, and friendship skills.
34. **Cultural Competence**-Young person has knowledge of and comfort with people of different cultural/racial/ethnic backgrounds.
35. **Resistance Skills**-Young person can resist negative peer pressure and dangerous situations.
36. **Peaceful Conflict Resolution**-Young person seeks to resolve conflict nonviolently.

**Positive Identity**
37. **Personal Power**-Young person feels he or she has control over "things that happen to me."
38. **Self-Esteem**-Young person reports having a high self-esteem.
39. **Sense of Purpose**-Young person reports that "my life has a purpose."
40. **Positive View of Personal Future**-Young person is optimistic about her or his personal future.

Used by permission of the Search Institute℠.

three or more nonparental adults." Especially during the summer, library staff can establish a supportive relationship with the children and teens participating in library programs. In addition, library staff provide a positive adult role model; when other community leaders are involved in summer library reading programs they serve as additional positive adult role models (asset number 14). Many libraries have teen volunteer programs; these activities support the empowerment assets 7, 8, and 9. Participation in library programs supports the constructive use of time assets.

Summer library reading programs also enhance internal assets. Commitment to learning is encouraged by library programs. As previously discussed, success in reading encourages children and teens to read more. Reading for pleasure three or more hours per week is one way that youth can show their commitment to learning. For young children, parents should read aloud to their children an average of 30 minutes a day; older children should read independently or to younger children for that time.

As libraries establish the goals for their summer library reading programs and develop activities to meet those goals, they need to incorporate activities that enhance the developmental assets for the youth of their communities. Libraries have already been incorporating this asset-based philosophy into their programs and services. A four-year, $6 million effort sponsored by the Wallace-Reader's Digest Funds provided the Urban Libraries Council with the opportunity to work collaboratively with ten libraries and their teens and community partners to understand and strengthen library commitment to the positive development of young people. The study found that, "It is in the best interest of libraries themselves and of communities and your organizations to take a fresh look at libraries as settings that can and do support young people's development. Like schools, youth organizations, community centers, parks and other settings, libraries contribute in significant ways to the positive development of young people."[5] The project developed a grid that builds on the Search Institute's Developmental Assets and emphasizes the library's place in youth development. See Figure 3–3 for "Libraries as Positive Developmental Settings." For those libraries that selected "commons" as one of their service responses as described in the Public Library's Association's *Planning for Results*, this has great importance.

Another document that came out of the Public Libraries as Partners in Youth Development project is the "Library Teen Bill of Rights." This document, Figure 3–4, shows how youth development affects library services not just during the summer, but year round.

## Outcome Planning

You need to determine where you want to be at the end of your project at the very beginning. If you don't know where you are going, you will never know if you got there. Therefore, plan your evaluation at the beginning so you can determine the effectiveness of your program. But there is more to determining success than just counting the number of programs you offer or the number of books that are circulated, things libraries have traditionally used as the basis for program evaluation.

In 1993, Congress passed the Government Performance and Results Act of 1993.

**Figure 3–3**
**Libraries as Positive Developmental Settings**

| BENEFITS ZONE | FEATURES | DANGER ZONE |
|---|---|---|
| Physical space is safe; youth feel comfortable and welcome; building is open weekends and evenings. | *Physical and Psychological Safety* | Physical hazards are present; youth feel unwelcome; building hours are inconsistent. |
| Some spaces and activities are designed with teens' needs in mind; activities managed consistently with mutual respect for youth and adults. | *Appropriate Structure* | Spaces and activities are too restrictive (e.g., not allowing for groups to meet, talk); activities are inconsistent, unclear or change unexpectedly. |
| Designated areas are available for youth to interact with peers; youth feel supported by staff. | *Supportive Relationships* | Youth do not have opportunities to interact with peers; youth feel ignored or not supported by staff. |
| Youth are encouraged to join groups and activities; programs, activities and materials reflect youth interests. | *Opportunities to Belong* | Youth are excluded from activities; programs, activities and materials do not reflect youth interests. |
| Library staff have high expectation of youth and encourage and model positive behaviors. | *Positive Social Norms* | Library staff allow negative behaviors to go unaddressed or make some teens feel unwelcome, rather than helping them understand expectations. |
| Youth-focused programs and activities are challenging and based on youth input; youth are encouraged to take active roles in the overall functioning of the library. | *Support for Efficacy and Mattering* | Youth is not considered; activities are not challenging; youth are not offered leadership roles. |
| Staff help youth identify interested and opportunities to develop and practices skills in the library and community. | *Opportunities for Skill Building* | Youth do not have opportunities to develop and practices skills in areas of interest. |
| Library offers opportunities for families; homework help is available; space is available for youth and community meetings and activities; library works with schools and maintains information on local resources. | *Integration of Family, School, Library, and Community Efforts* | Library does not offer opportunities for family activities; homework help is not available; library does not partner with schools and community organizations; no information on local resources available. |
| Library offers information on health and social service resources, helps access option, may make referrals; transportation, snacks, and small stipends are available for special programs | *Basic Care and Services* | Library is not equipped to make social service referrals; snacks, transportation are never available. |

From Nicole Yohalem and Karen Pittman. *Public Libraries as Partners in Youth Development: lessons and Voices from the Field.* Washington, D.C.: The Forum for Youth Investment, 2003, page 12. Available online at www.forumforyouthinvestment.org. Used with permission.

**Figure 3–4**
**Library Teen Bill of Rights**

- Teens have the right to choose materials for teens at the library.

- Teens have the right to use the library despite origin, background, and views.

- Teens have the right to use all library materials for the purposes or interest, information, and enlightenment.

- Teens have the right to a space and exhibits just for them, and within this space teens should be allowed to have freedom.

- Teens have the right to have access to all technology in the library.

- Teens have the right to access information as quickly and efficiently as possible.

- Teens have the right of offer an opinion for change in the library.

- Teens with disabilities should be able to move just as freely as everyone else throughout the library.

- Teens have the right to a safe environment.

- Teens should be respected as responsible young adults.

- All teens should be open-minded to all types of learning.

- Libraries should cooperate with all teens and teens should cooperate with adults and peers.

- Teens have the right to respect all library materials.

- Teen should be treated equally and fairly and not stereotyped.

- Teens have the right to have representation in library administrative roles.

- All patrons reserve the right to fight censorship of any and all books and media.

Source: Virginia A. Walter and Elaine Myers. *Teens and Libraries: Getting It Right.* Chicago: American Library Association, 2003, page 86. Created by the Public Libraries as Partners in Youth Development project's Youth Partnership Council, July 28, 2002. Used with permission.

This law required the Institute of Museum and Library Services (IMLS) to document the results of grant activities to show that grants from this federal agency make a "vital contribution to museum and library audiences and their communities."[6] This "contribution" to library audiences and their communities is the benefits people derive from the program. Specifically, the benefits are the "achievements or changes in skill, knowledge, attitude, behavior, condition, or life status for program participants."[7] Outcome-based evaluation, or OBE, is the measurement of results. OBE systematically collects information about indicators that demonstrate these changes. Funders, boards of directors, and community members want to know what happened as a result of a program of service. OBE helps human service professionals, including library staff, to document the benefits of a program.

The United Way has been the leader in developing OBE for the human services field; the State Library and Archives of Florida has been a leader in adapting this process to the library field. In 1998, IMLS sought participation of state library agencies in a pilot project that would test the feasibility of applying an outcomes measure approach to the evaluation of projects funded under the Library Services and Technology Act (LSTA). Florida was one of five states selected to pilot the approach.

Since evaluation is most effective when it is included in project planning from the very beginning, the outcomes approach is also used as a planning tool. To know what the outcome is, we need to know what resources are being brought to the project and how the service is to be delivered. The planning portion of OBE will be discussed here; the outcomes and evaluation segment of this process will be discussed in Chapter 8, "Evaluating Your Success."

The State Library and Archives of Florida has adapted forms and definitions developed by the United Way and now utilizes this process with all federal LSTA Grants they subgrant. The LSTA Outcome Plan is a one-page outline of the entire project and includes the key components of every project.

In addition to identifying the project and the library's planning the project, the Outcome Plan provides a concise *summary* of the project. It states what you plan to do and who will benefit from the project. Persons reading this summary will get a clear overview of what the project is about.

The first column in the Outcome Plan is used to indicate the *inputs,* or resources, that will be used to implement this project. These ingredients include money, staff, volunteers, partners, and facilities. Each input should be listed as a single input.

*Activities* comprise the second column of the Outcome Plan. Activities are the verbs of the project. These are what the project coordinators will actually do and coordinate during the project to achieve the stated purposes. By listing all the major activities, project planners can anticipate what needs to be coordinated to get the desired results. The most difficult part of listing the activities is to make certain that they are client centered—focusing on the end users and the benefits to them rather than the benefits to the library.

Outputs are really nothing new for libraries, but the terminology is. The things entered in the *Outputs* column are the results of the project. They measure "how many." They are tallies of the programs and services offered through this project. It does *not* reflect the change in the customer's knowledge, skill, behavior, or condition that you are hoping will result from their participation in the library's project.

The final part of the outcomes plan that needs to be completed as part of planning is the outcome statement itself. Each *outcome* statement should tell why this project is important. The outcome statement identifies who achieves the outcome. It describes a change in knowledge, status, or condition of the client or patron who is receiving the service. An outcome for a summer library reading program could be "Youth increase the time spent reading independently," or "Parents read to their children every day." The evaluation segments of the Outcomes Plan, *Indicators* and *Sources/ Methods*, will be discussed in Chapter 8.

**Figure 3–5**
**State Library and Archives of Florida LSTA Outcomes Plan**

Project Name: _____     Library: _____
Project Summary / Program Purpose:

| | | | | EVALUATION | |
|---|---|---|---|---|---|
| INPUTS | ACTIVITIES | OUTPUTS | OUTCOMES | INDICATORS | SOURCES/ METHODS |
| | | | | | |

Used by permission of the State Library and Archives of Florida.

## Explore Alternative Approaches

After you have established your objectives and know what changes you want to make in the lives of your customers, you will need to brainstorm the various ways that the library can work towards the vision. These alternatives will become the activities referred to in the section on outcomes planning. In Chapter 7, you will find a number of approaches that can be used in designing your summer library program. While all the approaches may work, it is up to each librarian in each local library to select those methods that are most appropriate for their community and considering the resources that are available. The question then becomes one of how to decide which alternative is the best to use in your library.

As suggested in *The TELL IT! Manual*, librarians need to think of the process that *Consumer Reports* uses in evaluating new cars, computers, or any other product or service. The report lists the various brands of the item or the purveyors of the specific service and compares each of them against the same criteria. Similarly, when trying to decide what approach to use, librarians need to list the criteria against which each approach will be judged and evaluated. The alternative approaches are listed along one side of a decision matrix and the criteria for judging them along the other axis.[8]

You can use the following criteria to evaluate what program approach to use, or use other standards depending on your library and the activities you are planning:

- cost of providing this service or approach;
- number of youth to be reached by this activity;
- number of youth with disabilities who will be reached by this service;
- number of youth from at-risk families and neighborhoods to be reached by this program;
- ages of youth to be reached by this program;
- number of families to be included in this service;
- number of staff needed to implement this approach;
- space needed to implement this program; and
- cooperation of other agencies needed to ensure the success of this service.

Not all of these criteria will be used to evaluate every program; nor will each criterion have equal weight. At times, it will be difficult to make these judgments, but by evaluating the many options in advance you will be better prepared to justify your decision to your supervisor, administrator, your funding agency, and your community.

Figure 3–4 is a decision chart adapted from *The TELL IT! Manual.* It provides a method of evaluating some of the possible programs and services that might be offered during a summer library program.

By using this type of decision matrix, you might see that while a kick-off party will attract large numbers of children, the effectiveness may be offset by the number of staff needed to monitor and properly supervise this program, or the high cost of the entertainment, prizes, and refreshments at such an event. If one of the goals of your program is to encourage individual participation and sharing of literature, booktalks, and "booknics" (see Chapter 7 for details about booknic) may be ranked high. If, on the other hand, your goal is to reach large numbers of children, puppet shows that can accommodate large groups may be appropriate. If you desire to involve parents and grandparents in the programs, then starting an intergenerational book discussion program may be what is needed. Library staff need to know the goals of the program, the desired outcomes, and the inputs that are available to make informed decisions. Even before you make decisions as to what activities you will use in your action plan, you need to decide what audience you want to attract.

**Figure 3–6**
**DECISION CHART**

| Possible Approaches | Criteria | Cost | Number of Children | No. of Children with Disabilities | Ages of Children | Number of Families | Number of Staff Needed | Space Needed | Cooperation of Other Agencies |
|---|---|---|---|---|---|---|---|---|---|
| | | High/ Low | High/ Low | High/ Low | High/ Low | High/ Low | High/ Low | High/ Low | High/ Low |
| Bedtime story time | | | | | | | | | |
| Booknic | | | | | | | | | |
| Booktalks | | | | | | | | | |
| Decorating children's section of library | | | | | | | | | |
| Deposit collection at juvenile justice facility | | | | | | | | | |
| Kick-off party | | | | | | | | | |
| Puppet shows by staff or other adults | | | | | | | | | |
| Puppet shows by teens | | | | | | | | | |

Used by permission of the American Library Association.

# Endnotes

1. Douglas Fisher, Diane Lapp, and James Flood. 2001. "The Effects of Access to Print through the Use of Community Libraries on the Reading Performance of Elementary Students." *Reading Improvement* 38, no. 4 (Winter): 176.
2. Stephen Krashen. 1993. *The Power of Reading: Insights from the Research.* Englewood, Colo.: Libraries Unlimited, 23.
3. Sandra Nelson for the Public Library Association. 2001. *The New Planning for Results: A Streamlined Approach.* Chicago: American Library Association, 65.
4. "Introduction to Developmental Assets." 2004. Minneapolis, Minn.: Search Institute. Available: www.search-institute.org/assets/. Accessed November 7, 2004.
5. Nicole Yohalem and Karen Pittman. 2003. *Public Libraries As Partners in Youth Development: Lessons and Voices from the Field.* Washington, D.C.: The Forum for Youth Investment. Available: www.forumforyouthinvestment.org.

6. "New Directives, New Directions: Documenting Outcomes in IMLS Grants to Libraries and Museums." n.d. Washington, D.C.: Institute of Museum and Library Services. Available: www.imls.gov/grants/current/crnt_obebasics.htm. Accessed October 31, 2004.

7. "New Directives, New Directions."

8. Douglas Zweizig, Debra Wilcox Johnson, Jane Robbins, with Michele Besant. 1996. *The TELL IT! Manual: The Complete Program for Evaluating Library Performance.* Chicago: American Library Association.

## Recommended Reading

Durrance, Joan C., Karen E. Fisher, with Marian Bouch Hinton. 2005. *How Libraries and Librarians Help: Assessing Outcomes in Your Library.* Chicago: American Library Association.

Lance, Keith Curry, et al. 2004. *Counting on Results: New Tools for Outcome-Based Evaluation of Public Libraries.* Denver, Colo.: Library Research Service.

*The LSTA Outcome-Based Evaluation Toolkit: September 2004.* 2004. Tallahassee, Fla: Florida Department of State, Division of Library and Information Services. Also available at www.lstatoolkit.com.

McClure, Charles R., Amy Owen, Douglas L. Zweizig, Mary Jo Lynch, and Nancy A. Van House. 1978. *Planning and Role Setting for Public Libraries: A Manual of Options and Procedures.* Chicago: American Library Association.

Van Orden, Phyllis, and Patricia Pawelak-Kort. 2005. *Library Service to Children: A Guide to the History, Planning, Policy and Research Literature.* Lanham, Md.: Scarecrow.

Wallace, Linda K. 2004. *Libraries, Mission and Marketing: Writing Mission Statements That Work.* Chicago: American Library Association.

# 4

# Designing the Summer Library Reading Program

If the goal of the summer library reading program is to develop a new generation of readers and lifelong library users, we need to reach out to all members of our communities, especially those who currently are not library users. Many segments of the communities we serve do not have a history of library usage. Those adults who themselves are poor readers may not feel comfortable using a library or bringing their children to library programs. Recent immigrants to our country may be hesitant to frequent public/government buildings, especially if they have left their native land because of political unrest. These newcomers to our communities may also be faced with a language barrier. Libraries may need to provide translation services so people whose primary language is not English can participate in the programs and services the library offers. Economically deprived families may not want to grant permission for their children to borrow books from the library, fearing the financial consequences if a book they check out is lost, damaged, or returned late. Libraries need to establish policies and procedures that will attract the varied members of their communities and put to rest these fears and anxieties. Summer library reading programs, through their noncompetitive, recreational nature, can do much to dispel this apprehension. Children from single-parent families, and even those in which both parents work, may not be able to attend library programs at traditional times. Libraries need to adapt programs and services to the needs of all potential library users.

## Children

As we have already seen, one of the overarching goals of most summer library programs is to turn children onto reading and have them become lifelong library users. The basic philosophy of many of these programs is similar to that of the Florida Library Youth Program.

> We want children to learn about the library and the services it offers, to understand that there is a wealth of information and fun waiting for them in a friendly, encouraging atmosphere. Especially during school breaks and vacation periods, we want the experience to be relaxing, pleasurable, and free of stress. For that reason, we downplay numbers of books read. "How many" is not nearly as important as "how good." No prizes should be given for number of books read **unless** it is an agreed upon contract between child and librarian. We want children to share books and stories in the company of others and discover the satisfaction of reading alone or being read to. That's why we have group programs and individual guidance.[1]

This philosophy encourages inclusion, rather than exclusion, of all children, regardless of social or economic circumstances or educational or physical abilities, and provides a basis upon which local libraries can build their programs in response to the needs of their communities.

As previously noted, many libraries have designed their summer library programs to focus on children who are already reading, the very same elementary school–age children who have already discovered the joys of reading and, more than likely, are already library users. However, if your vision really does include turning nonreaders into readers and non–library users into lifelong library users, then limiting your summer program to those whom you know to be readers will prevent you from reaching those who really need this service the most.

Summer library programs should have components that will attract readers and non-readers of all ages. With so many libraries turning their attention towards family literacy, it is desirable, even necessary, for summer library programs to change their focus from just school-age programs to programs that include all members of the family—from infant and toddler through elementary school age–children who have traditionally been served to young adults who can participate in various ways, to parents and other adults, all the way through to senior citizens. All these people can benefit from participating in your summer library program.

Since research has shown that access to public libraries and reading are highly related to learning over the summer regardless of parental status,[2] and since all children start learning from the day they are born, libraries should assist in getting young children ready to enter school by providing opportunities for them, their parents, and their caregivers to participate. This assistance should not be limited to storytimes for toddlers and preschool children or lapsit storytimes for infants and toddlers and their parents and caregivers; they need to be included in some manner in summer programs as well. By making reading enjoyable, libraries can make learning easier for children. Dr. William Teale of the University of Chicago and his colleagues maintain that providing a print-rich environment for children from the very start will lead them to better literacy development.[3] By providing opportunities for parents and primary caregivers to share literature experiences and read aloud with their young charges, libraries are helping to establish the parent as the child's first teacher.

Reading aloud has several beneficial effects on literacy development. Hearing and discussing stories encourages reading. This, in turn, promotes literacy development. Even after listening to new stories only a few times and hearing new and unfamiliar words in the books that are read aloud, children learn this new vocabulary. In other words, just reading aloud to children promotes language, vocabulary, and literacy development.[4]

One of the easiest ways to include young children and their parents in your summer library reading program is to provide "Read to Me" Logs. These folders encourage parents and other caregivers to keep track of what they read to their young children and can take many formats. Whether single sheets of paper or more elaborate booklets, reading logs or read-to-me logs provide spaces where children can note the title and author of the books they have read or listened to. Depending on the goal of your summer library reading program, the logs could have places to record the child's or caregiver's reactions to the books as well as to record either number of pages read or listened to or amount of time spent reading or listening. Both children and parents should be recognized for this activity. To read more about Read to Me and Reading Logs, see Chapter 6.

## Teens in the Summer Library Reading Program

Adolescence is one of the most difficult periods of life. It is the time when the body experiences one of the two most rapid periods of changes, the other being the first five years of life. Not only is adolescence a time of extraordinary physical changes, it is a time of significant social and emotional change. During adolescence, children are making the sometimes treacherous passage from childhood to adulthood. During that time, young adults are trying to achieve social, emotional, and intellectual growth and maturity. In addition to becoming independent, they are testing themselves in terms of what their vocations will be. As they are developing their own ethical systems or philosophies of life, they are testing and applying those ethics to all aspects of their lives. All of this is occurring while they are trying to find a true self, a personality, an identity. Adolescence is also a time when adults and society in general try to put labels on these growing children. But who, exactly, is a young adult?[5]

In many circles, a young adult is someone who is 13 through 19 years of age. In other libraries, young adults are children in middle school. In other aspects of society, young adults are considered the under-25 set. Many people say that a young adult is a person who does not consider her or himself to be a child but who is regarded by society as not yet an adult. For the purpose of our discussions here, we will use the definition of the Young Adult Library Services Association (YALSA), a division of the American Library Association. This national association defines young adults as those individuals 12 through 18 years of age.

Sixteen is a very important milestone in the life of a young adult. While children are "transportationally disadvantaged" and at the mercy of adults to get them to the library and other places they need or want to go, once they reach 16 years of age they are eligible, in many states, to qualify for a driver's license. It is also the time at which many youth can legally start working. What with part-time jobs, school, and social responsibilities and pressures, many teens avoid the library except for school assignments.

As many people working in libraries know, getting teens involved in library programs is one of the hardest things to accomplish. One reason for this may be the lack of specially trained staff. According to a 1995 report from the National Center for Educational Statistics, only 11 percent of all public libraries in the United States have a young adult specialist librarian.[6] Without staff who have the proper training and who can relate to the special needs of this underserved client group, many efforts, though well intentioned, may fall short of their goals.

When planning any type of program, regardless of the age of the patron, the needs of the client or patron must be kept in the forefront. Because of the developmental needs of young adults, not only must their needs be met, but they must actually and genuinely be involved in developing the program. YALSA strongly believes and advocates that youth participation is vital to the success of any program or service for young adults. They have shown their commitment to encouraging young adults to become actively involved in the library decision-making process through the publication of *Youth Participation in School and Public Libraries: IT WORKS.*[7] Their vision reflects the advice given by the Carnegie Council on Adolescent Development: program designers (including librarians) need to actively seek the advice of young adults and involve them in planning and implementing programs that are aimed at this age group.[8] This, too, is a reiteration of the *empowerment assets* developed by the Search Institute, discussed in Chapter 3. No matter how well intentioned adults are, young people tend to avoid and dodge programs that adults plan for them without their input.[9] "Libraries do not, should not, and cannot develop services for young adults because it is good for the library, but rather because these services will make an affirmative impact leading to positive outcomes for teens. Healthy youth create healthy communities in which libraries can thrive."[10]

Since many teens will shy away from the traditional storytime, craft, and booktalk programs that are well received by preschool and elementary school–age children, these may not be the most appropriate alternatives to entice teens to actively participate in your summer library program. However, many libraries do report success with luring teens into the library during vacation periods with reading games.

The Enoch Pratt Free Library in Baltimore, Maryland, has been using reading games with their young adults since the early 1980s and has had much success with these programs. The benefits to the library system and the teen patrons are many.

- The programs show the young adults in the community that the young adult librarians are resource people for school assignments, recreational reading, and more.

- They provide library staff with an opportunity to work closely with teens, thus they have the chance to see teens, up close and personal, as real people and can learn more about teenagers' needs, interests, reading habits, and opinions on books. This knowledge then can be used in selecting additional YA materials and designing new programs with the young adults in mind.
- They build a cadre of teens to serve on young adult advisory boards.
- In addition to extending the use of the library to YAs, they expand the image of the library in the eyes of the teens and the community in general.
- They increase circulation of young adult materials.
- They enhance each player's self-image through positive interaction with peers and adults, while allowing them to accomplish something.[11]

The Berkeley (Calif.) Public Library also reports success with their reading game for teenagers. During the summer of 1991, the library initiated "Cover to Cover," a board game that was planned and promoted by the Young Adult Advisory Council (YAAC). In an attempt to make the game as easy as possible to play, self-service registration stations were set up with posters explaining the rules and procedures for the game. Teens 13 to 18 years of age had to read a total of ten books, or 1,500 pages, to qualify for "a great prize"; the books had to be from the YA or adult area of the library. For each book read, the player completed a brief review form, which included his or her name, the title and author of the book, a few sentences about the book, and most importantly, a rating from one (dud) to four (great!). The great prizes required lots of leg work on the part of the library staff and YAAC to solicit prize donations from local merchants. As many librarians have found out, the prizes do not have to be expensive, but they must have appeal to the teens in your community.[12] The library continues to provide this program, although it has changed slightly over the years. The reading requirement remains at ten books or 1,500 pages. The writing requirement has taken on a new twist. Teens have to figure out a "password" by answering a book-related question. Once they find out the password, they need to incorporate that word into their reviews of the book. To make it even more challenging, teens are offered the opportunity to write their reviews in the writing style of the author. Reviews may also be submitted in the style of a graphic novel, as a poem, or as a recipe. Since materials in languages other than English are available and eligible for the "Cover to Cover" contest, reviews for these books should be written in the same language as the book. See Figure 4–1, which shows the library's fact sheet on this program.

Another community found yet another way of incorporating teens into their summer program and providing yet another literacy experience for the community. The Chappaqua (N.Y.) Library offered beginning readers a lifeline by recruiting preteens and teens to read aloud to younger children during the summer. The library wanted to attract YAs who were too young to work, were home during most of the summer, and were bored with just hanging out with their friends. To recruit the readers, or lifeguards as they were called, library staff visited sixth-grade classes in the local elementary schools and seventh- and eighth-grade classes at the middle schools.

**Figure 4–1**
**Berkeley Public Library—"Cover to Cover"**

## Berkeley Public Library
### Cover to Cover
### June 14 - August 14, 2004
win prizes; participate in weekly drawings; get published
anyone 13-19 welcome!

### how it works

1. Register at any (but only one) of the Library locations. Go to the Teen area of the Library. Fill out the registration form you find there. Read the board giving you directions about where to put your registration card and how to find the materials you need to enter contests.
2. Read or listen to any 10 books or 1500 pages. Anything you want! In any language or genre you want!
3. For each book you complete, write the title and number of pages on the **Cover to Cover** playing card and turn in a completed book comment form. You need to do both these things for your work to count toward prizes!

For more detailed instructions, ask a librarian at your branch.

### two special contests!

**Password**
Each Monday of the game, check the Teen area for the Password Question of the Week.
1. The answer to that question is the "password" you are looking for.
2. Next, figure out a way to use the password in one or more of your comment forms that week.
3. We'll put the comment forms in the hat, and pull one out in a weekly raffle.
4. Check the following week to see if you won the drawing.

| |
|---|
| Password question: What kind of fairy tale does Lawrence Marvit write about in his graphic novel **Sparks** |

Sample Password ?

Answer: *urban*

How did you find the answer? You looked up the author "Marvit, Lawrence," in the catalog, and found the book **Sparks: an Urban Fairytale**.

Now, imagine you are reading the book **Drinking Coffee Elsewhere**. Include the word *urban* in your review of this book: "ZZ Packer's stories show that racism isn't limited to urban areas…"

**Write in Style**
For the review, imitate the author's writing style. You can submit graphic-novel style reviews, reviews as poems, recipes, etc. If you are reading a book in a language other than English, write your review in that language.

| |
|---|
| **Dancing in My Nuddy-Pants**<br><br>Georgia Nicolson is becoming boring, predictable, and unbelievably shallow (like a three day old puddle). I'm completely sick of reading her whining, pointless tale of her boy escapades. Georgia needs a life and a new personality, because she is horrible to almost everyone (except the boys she chases constantly). P.S. Georgia is too much of a snotty gossip. |

Write in Style sample

**about those prizes…**
Most prizes are awarded during several raffles on Sunday, August 22, 2004. That's the date for the annual **Cover to Cover** party. Everyone who finishes the program is eligible. When you enter the special contests, you become eligible to win additional prizes. And don't forget the weekly drawings at each library site for the Password contest. See **Our Sponsors** for a list of prize donors.

Used by permission of the Berkeley (Calif.) Public Library.

Interested lifeguards were required to attend three training sessions at the public library; the sessions included an orientation to the children's room and collection, tips on how to read aloud to children, and recommendations of picture books that are appropriate to read aloud to preschoolers. This intergenerational program (and it was one because of the difference in ages of the readers and listeners) attracted 20 students as lifeguards; they contributed 285 hours of their time during the summer of 1989. The preschoolers especially like sharing stories and books with "big kids" rather than with their parents. For the parents of the preschoolers, it gave them 15 to 30 minutes of free time in the library during which they could search for books for themselves or read a magazine without being interrupted. Today, that time could be used to perform an online search or surf the Internet. Again, the teens were rewarded with the knowledge that they were contributing a valuable service to the community. At the end of the summer, the teens were recognized in many ways. The teen lifeguards received a T-shirt as a thank-you from the library, a long lasting, tangible reminder for themselves and something that showed others they had been part of this program. They were also treated to a pizza party, a more immediate reward. The Book Buddies program ended in 1995 because the library was unable to match up readers' and listeners' schedules. This type of program provides ways to enhance the Search Institute's developmental assets previously discussed.

As we have already seen from this book, having teens furnish community service is a valuable method for involving them in the library program. This benefits not only the library and the community as a whole, but, especially, and almost more importantly, the individual teen.

One library that has designed a teen-volunteer program that has gained a national reputation as a model program is the Clearwater (Fla.) Public Library. The staff of the Clearwater Public Library speak about the benefits to the teens of participating in a volunteer program in glowing terms:

> For the teens, the chance to learn about the library profession and all the materials that are available, first views of work in a non-threatening setting, preparation for a paid job as a page or library assistant, and a place to socialize are all beneficial. Letters of reference for future interview situations and fulfilling requirements for community service commitments are perhaps more tangible advantages. Something more than baby-sitting as work experience will help the resume.[13]

The Clearwater Public Library has developed several methods to recruit teens into their teen-volunteer program. Letters to school district officials and local school principals and fliers to middle and high schools help spread the word, especially where community service is required for graduation. Information about the program is included in the library's calendar of events; the calendar is widely distributed throughout the community. News releases to school and local media, PTA, and other youth-serving agencies are basic publicity tools, as are school visits when time permits. Once your program is somewhat established, word of mouth from former volunteers to prospective ones can be one of the best tools for recruitment. Speaking with other groups, such as church groups, scouts, clubs, and other service organizations, is a viable way to spread the word. A PowerPoint presentation or a video of what the library has to offer teens as well as appearances by library staff and current and former teen volunteers on local talk shows, including broadcast, cable, and closed circuit in the schools, may result in additional volunteers.

Once you have advertised this program to the teens and some of them have become interested, you need to keep track of who wants to volunteer, when each volunteer wants to work, what jobs each teen wants, and in which of your libraries they want to perform this service. Figure 4–2, Teen Volunteer Form, is used as part of the application procedure at the Clearwater Public Library. It is recommended that these application forms be available at least four to six weeks prior to the start of your summer volunteer program.

The Seminole County (Fla.) Public Library System also utilizes teen volunteers. So that the treatment of teen volunteers is similar to that of adult volunteers, this system uses the same volunteer application form for teens and adults. In addition, the county's human resource department performs a newly required background check.

As with any new employee, teen volunteers need a thorough orientation to your program. It is recommended that all new volunteers attend this session. Occasionally parents of first-time or prospective volunteers attend these sessions; do not discourage this interaction. Remember, parents are our allies. At this first official meeting, library staff has the opportunity to inform perspective volunteers of their responsibilities and to remind them of the benefits they will accrue by working in the library. The typical agenda for a volunteer orientation includes a discussion of the type of work that is available, equipment used (projectors, computers, copy machines, etc.), work rules and guidelines, and a tour of the library. It is also a good idea to let the teens know what other programs the library has to offer them as well as other volunteer opportunities that are available in the community. Clearwater Public Library has established guidelines that are given to each volunteer at this orientation meeting. See Figure 4–4 for this handout. If you have a large number of "volunteens" joining after the program has begun, you may want to hold a second orientation three or four weeks into the summer.

Once the teen volunteers have been recruited and they have made the decision that volunteering at the library is really for them, it is time to start training them. Training any new employee is crucial; for your volunteer program to be successful and for each individual teen to have a positive sense of accomplishment, training is especially important. Be specific about what is expected of each volunteer. Instructions must be clear and concise. Some teens are more focused than others and can work with a certain amount of independence once they have completed their training and orientation; others need reminders to keep them on task. Awareness of each teen's knowledge, skills, and abilities and making assignments based on this knowledge will lead to success and increased self-esteem. Continuous monitoring of the volunteens' performance is necessary; work with the teens on a continuous basis to help them develop skills and expertise. Encourage them with praise and catch minor difficulties before they become major problems.

**Figure 4–2**
**Clearwater Public Library—Teen Volunteer Form**

## Clearwater Public Library System Youth Department
### *2004 Volunteer Form*

Last Name _____ First Name _____

Address _____

City _____ Zip _____

Home phone _____ Birthday _____

School _____ Current Grade _____

E-Mail address_____

Parent/Guardian name(s) _____

Home Address (if different from above) _____

City _____ Zip _____

Home Phone _____ Work Phone _____

Emergency Contact name _____

Emergency Phone Number _____

**Availability** (Please check when you are available to volunteer)

|           | MON | TUE | WED | THUR | FRI | SAT |
|-----------|-----|-----|-----|------|-----|-----|
| Morning   |     |     |     |      |     |     |
| Afternoon |     |     |     |      |     |     |
| Evening   |     |     |     |      |     |     |

I hereby assume complete responsibility for any injury of damage sustained by the applicant and release the Clearwater Public Library System and the City of Clearwater and all sponsoring agencies of any and all liability for such injury or damages occurred during volunteer work for the Clearwater Public Library System.

_____          _____
Signature of Parent or Guardian                            Date

**Figure 4–3**
**Seminole County Public Library System Volunteer Application Form**

### SEMINOLE COUNTY PUBLIC LIBRARY SYSTEM
### VOLUNTEER APPLICATION

Youth or Adult    _____
(Circle One)                    (Branch)

Name_____

Address_____

City_____    Zip_____

Home Phone_____    Business_____

Email address_____    Are you employed?_____

POSITION(S) IN WHICH YOU ARE INTERESTED (please check one or more):

_____Circulation Unit Aide

_____Youth Services Aide

_____Technical Services Aide

Number of hours per week you are available to work (not less than 4):_____

Are you available to work:

_____ Saturdays    _____ Sundays    _____ Evenings    _____ Afternoons    _____ Mornings

Do you:_____Type?  Words per minute?_____

_____Operate a copy machine?

_____Speak OR read a foreign language?  Which ones?_____
_____

Other skills or talents useful to the library?_____
_____

Can you:    _____Lift up to 25 pounds?

_____Stand for up to 4 hours at a time?

EDUCATION:  Are you a high school graduate?_____

College (number of years completed?)_____    Degree earned?_____

Other training or certification?_____

**Figure 4–3**
***Continued***

WORK EXPERIENCE: Please list position worked that you consider useful to a library volunteer, most recent first.

Position Title:______________________ Dates worked______________

Employer Name:______________________________________________

Employer Address:____________________________________________

Nature of duties:_____________________________________________

---

Position Title:______________________ Dates worked______________

Employer Name:______________________________________________

Employer Address:____________________________________________

Nature of duties:_____________________________________________

---

(Please use additional sheet, if necessary.)

Please explain briefly why you would like to volunteer in the library.____________________

Seminole County is authorized to verify any or all of the information contained in this application. All statements are subject to investigation, and a criminal background check will be conducted. Your application may be subject to inspection in accordance with Florida Public Records Law, Chapter 119, Florida Statutes.

Please complete the following:

Legal Name: ______________ ______ ______________
(First) (MI) (Last)

Date of Birth: ______________ Social Security No.______________

Length of residence in the State of Florida: ______________

Other states of residence in the last five (5) years: ______________

---

*I agree to abide by and comply with all rules, regulations, policies and procedures of Seminole County and the Seminole County Public Library System.*

______________________________ ______________

Signature Date

Used by permission of the Seminole County (Fla.) Public Library System.

**Figure 4–4**
**Clearwater Public Library—Teen Volunteer Guidelines**

# Summer Teen Volunteer Guidelines - 2004

Treat your volunteer job as you would a paying job. The work you will be doing here is important to the community and to the library staff.

◎ Sign in for work at the start of your shift.

◎ Wear a volunteer badge whenever you are working your shift.

◎ Be on time for your shift. If you will be absent or unable to make it on time, please call in advance to let us know. Our number is 562-4970 x5236.

◎ Dress neatly. Tank tops, crop tops, short-shorts, very short skirts are NOT acceptable. Wear clothing that allows you to easily bend and stretch, so that it is easy to do your work.

◎ Clean up your work area before the end of your shift.

◎ Respect the library rules for behavior. Remember you will be representing the library when you are volunteering.

◎ Only go up to the other floors or in the back work areas if you have a project that demands you be in those areas.

◎ When you finish a project, report back to us (Jen, JoAnne, or David).

◎ If you are not working on a specific project your primary duty is to keep things straightened up in the Youth Area, sign up patrons for the reading program, and to help library patrons find different items.

# Thank you for volunteering. We appreciate your help!

At the end of the training, you may want to give the volunteers a quiz to assure the rest of the library staff that the teens have a basic level of knowledge about the library. This also will assure that the teen volunteers are able to provide accurate assistance to patrons whom they help.

If you are already accustomed to scheduling staff to cover public service desks, scheduling teen volunteers should not create too much of an additional burden. If you have not tried your hand at scheduling before, this will give you some much needed supervisory experience.

The length of time per day or per week that a volunteer works depends on several things. First thing to consider is the number of volunteers participating in your program. Your schedule has a finite number of slots. The more volunteers you have, the fewer hours you will be able to allow each teen to volunteer. Second, and more important, is the level of effort the staff is willing and able to provide this project. In other words, you need to know how much staff time you are willing and able to invest in supervising the volunteens. Do not schedule any one volunteer for too many hours, especially if this is the first summer that this person has volunteered. Two 2-hour or one 3- or 4-hour shift per volunteer will usually provide enough time slots for the teen volunteers to accomplish something substantial, thus having a positive work experience and not enough time for them to get bored with the job. Permitting one 15-minute break during a shift makes the volunteer experience more of an authentic work experience.

As with regular employees, the volunteers should notify their supervisor in advance if they are not going to be able to work their assigned shift. While calling a parent or guardian may not be the usual procedure for a regular employee, it may be advisable if a volunteer does not arrive within 15 minutes of scheduled time.

It is extremely important to the teens and to your library administration that you keep track of how many hours of service the teens donate during the summer. Use "Form 25—Individual Youth Participation Record" and "Form 26—Youth Participation Tally Sheet" from *Output Measures and More: Planning and Evaluating Public Library Services for Young Adults* to track when your volunteers work, how many hours they put in, and what jobs they perform.[14] Other ways to keep track of time donated is to keep a notebook of the applications with a time sheet on the back or have the teens sign in on a large wall calendar.

Other library staff and patrons need to recognize that these teens are performing a service—not just for the library but for the community as a whole. Provide name tags for each of your volunteers. Staff who do not work directly with the youth program can readily recognize volunteers who are in "staff only" areas of the library when they are wearing a name tag. The name tag also gives the volunteer a sense of belonging. The use of program-theme clip art, if available, strengthens the relationship of the volunteer program to the entire summer library program. If you, the teens themselves, or their parents or caregivers are concerned about safety, just use the teen's first name or have generic "Volunteer" tags made.

If you want to make your volunteer program an ongoing aspect of your annual summer library program, don't forget to reward and recognize the volunteers. A pizza party, a special excursion (with parental permission), or even an overnight stay in the library adds to the caché of the whole experience. A letter of recommendation that these teens can use when applying for other jobs is a tangible and significant reward. Don't forget to send press releases to the local media telling about the success of the program, the number of teens who participated, and the number of hours that they donated. Depending on the confidentiality laws in your state and the wishes of the parents or guardians of your volunteens, you may or may not be able to release individual names to the press.

Having teens volunteer is integral in youth involvement.

It builds on the idea that the voice of youth is important, it matters, and it should be allowed to be heard. Youth involvement allows teens to make a contribution to the library and thus to the community. Youth involvement benefits everyone involved: the library, which gains energy, ideas, enthusiasm, and extra sets of hands; the librarian, who gains value in watching young people learn and grow; the community, which finds youth actively involved and making a difference; and the young people themselves.[15]

And making a difference in the lives of the people the library serves is what outcome-based evaluation is all about.

In addition to the examples described above, numerous other examples of programs that are age- and developmentally-appropriate for teens are discussed in Chapter 7, "Exploring Programs and Service Types." In addition to booktalks and book-discussion programs, libraries that want special programs for teens might want to have teens participate in a video-production program. Poetry slams and open-mike programs can attract teens. Service-learning programs attract teens who want to contribute to the community while tie-ins with popular television shows are for teens who want to participate in activities that celebrate popular culture.

## Family and Multi-age Programs

Over the past several years, many local libraries have followed the lead of the King County Library System (KCLS). Headquartered in Seattle, Washington, King County Library System was one of the first libraries to institute a program that reaches out to all members of the community, regardless of age. A 75-page program book lists well over one thousand library programs and events for all ages. The programs that took place at all 39-branches of the KCLS during eight weeks of the summer of 1996 were all centered on the theme "Mysterious Summer." The mysteries are "whatever interests you, whatever sparks your curiosity."[16] In addition to providing a variety of programs for all ages, toddlers to retirees, the library and its partners have set a community-wide goal to read 1,000,000 hours during the summer. All members of the community are urged to

- read books or magazines, watch videos, listen to tapes and CDs;
- track time spent reading, viewing, and listening;
- turn in their tracking/entry form each week at the neighborhood branch library.

To entice people to turn in their tracking forms on an ongoing basis during the eight weeks that the program runs, KCLS held weekly prize drawings in three age categories: for children (0–11 years); young adults (12–18 years); and adults (over 18), with a grand prize drawing for each group at the end of the summer. Young children also received weekly stickers for participating in the program.

Working with corporate sponsors, "Families Reading for Families" is a special promotion that invites readers to contribute to the KCLS Foundation to support community literacy efforts such as the ones that are part of this unique summer program.[17]

Few people would dispute the fact that athletes discover how to run faster, jump further, or become more consistent when hitting a ball by being coached and practicing, sometimes for hours on end. With practice comes proficiency. With proficiency comes increased skill. With the success that increased skill brings, there is a proportional increase in the enjoyment of the activity. Success in reading encourages more reading and results in increased enjoyment. It is of little surprise then to find that reading researchers have concluded that all people learn to read by reading. Opportunities for children to listen to books and read for pleasure ingrain the book and reading habit. Without knowing it, children acquire almost all language skills that are required of adults. According to Stephen Krashen, professor of linguistics at the University of Southern California–Los Angeles, children will develop the ability to understand and use complex grammatical structures and develop a good writing style, though they will not necessarily become good spellers through voluntary free reading (as provided by summer library programs and other programs). Krashen also contends that people working to acquire a second language have the best chance of success through hearing books read aloud and reading themselves.[18]

## Serving Children with Disabilities

### *Americans with Disabilities Act of 1990*

Ever since the passage of the Americans with Disabilities Act of 1990 (ADA), public libraries have been working to provide equitable service to children with disabilities and to include them in their programs. Schools have been doing this since the passage of Public Law 94–142, the Education for All Handicapped Children Act of 1975. This landmark legislation provided that each child between the ages of 5 and 17 should receive an appropriate education in the least restrictive environment. The law states as its purpose:

> . . . to assure that all handicapped children have available to them . . . a free appropriate public education which emphasizes special education and related services designed to meet their unique needs, to assure that the rights of handicapped children and their parents or guardians are protected, to assist states and localities to provide for the education of all handicapped children and to assess and assure the effectiveness of efforts to educate handicapped children.[19]

Amendments to this law passed in 1983, as Public Law 98-199, the Education of the Handicapped Act Amendments of 1983, expanded Public Law 94-142 to include services to preschool children. States are required to institute early-intervention programs for children with developmental delays or those who have been diagnosed with a physical or mental condition that has a high probability of resulting in developmental delay. Children are eligible for these services from the time they are born. While these laws had little direct effect on public libraries, the ADA has meant that libraries must provide services to children with disabilities.

The Education for All Handicapped Children Act of 1975 (with all its amendments) has been replaced by the Individuals with Disabilities Act (IDEA), as amended in 1997.

> Today, early intervention programs and services are provided to almost 200,000 eligible infants and toddlers and their families, while nearly 6 million children and youth receive special education and related services to meet their individual needs. Other accomplishments directly attributable to IDEA include educating more children in their neighborhood schools, rather than in separate schools and institutions, and contributing to improvements in the rate of high school graduation, post-secondary school enrollment, and post-school employment for youth with disabilities who have benefited from IDEA.[20]

Because the majority of children with disabilities are now being educated in their neighborhood schools in regular classrooms with their nondisabled peers, summer library reading programs must adapt their programs to serve this underserved client group. Not only does IDEA address the instructional needs of the student, it mandates the development and implementation of "family-friendly practices to establish collaborative partnerships with parents and other caregivers, including those who do not speak English."[21] In addition to providing services to children with disabilities, libraries need to be providing services in languages other than English.

Well before the enactment of the ADA in 1990, public libraries were providing service to children with print handicaps through the network of the National Library Service for the Blind and Physically Handicapped (NLS). This program, administered by the Library of Congress, was established by the Pratt-Smoot Act of 1931. This act, which established the national free library service for blind adults, was amended in 1952 to include children as eligible Talking Book patrons. Participation in this program is open to anyone who cannot use print materials, because of either a visual or physical disability. Children with reading disabilities also qualify to use the program.

### *National Library Service for the Blind and Physically Handicapped (NLS)*

Many regional libraries in the NLS network that provide service to children with print disabilities furnish a summer library program for their young clients. Many times these summer programs run parallel to or are integrated into the statewide program sponsored by the state library agency or state library association. They provide reading lists of books on topics related to the theme of the statewide program. Children call their reading advisors, request that books be sent to them, and talk about the books they have completed. Many times, children who read a set number of books are rewarded with a certificate and some other incentive. Many libraries in the NLS network work with local libraries to connect them to children with disabilities who live in the local library's service area and encourage those children to become active participants in that library's programs. In addition, these NLS-network libraries work to increase awareness of the availability of the specialized resources they provide and the need to integrate these materials into local library programs.

Such was the case in 1989 when the Illinois State Library Talking Books and Braille Service, also known as the Illinois Regional Library, launched a program called "Lift Up Your Hearts . . . Open Your Doors." This Library Services and Construction Act (LSCA) grant–funded project had three major goals:

1. to expand public awareness of the needs of print handicapped children;
2. to enhance and enlarge the library collection; and
3. to lay the groundwork for a statewide summer reading program for print handicapped children.[22]

To run the program parallel with the statewide summer program sponsored by the Illinois Library Association, a staff member from the Illinois Regional Library met with the summer reading committee. Together they identified weaknesses in library collections and recommended specific titles in appropriate formats and media that would support the local public library summer reading programs for print-handicapped children. Rather than providing a children's book illustrator at programs as had originally been planned, the committee opted to use storytellers. This change was made to reinforce the oral traditions of children's services and because the majority of children using the Illinois NLS library were users of the talking-book service. Access to the world of print was actually through aural/oral means for these children; storytelling reinforces and adds credibility to this style of learning and communication. In addition, programs by Jean Little, a children's author who is blind, was also included as part of the grant. Both the storytelling and Little's programs provided a method to make communities aware of alternate forms of communication and reinforced the positive image and awareness that the grant hoped to foster.[23]

Even prior to Illinois' efforts, the Arizona Regional Library wanted children with visual disabilities to access the "same summer reading program as his peers and to encourage more extensive phone contact from our younger talking book patrons."[24] Designed to reach children whose families did not use the public library or who lived in rural areas, the program was conducted by mail and telephone using the same adventure theme and some of the same materials as the statewide program the public libraries were using. The Regional Library produced a cassette with booktalks and suggested bibliographies for each of the subthemes. Children aged 5 through 16 participated in the program; those who completed the program by reading five books, one from each of the subthemes, were sent a book bag and a certificate.[25]

## *Public Library Programs*

In addition to the regional libraries in the NLS network that provide service to patrons with print disabilities, public libraries, too, are devising programs to meet the needs of children with other types of disabilities. In 1982, in addition to mainstreaming children whose disabilities permit that, the Oceanside (N.Y.) Library started offering specialized, intimate programs for children who could not actively participate in the library's regular programs that were attended by a large number of children.

With the assistance of the local Special Education Parent Teacher Association (SEPTA), the library designed two types of programs. One program was for children who were accustomed to and required close supervision; parents or other caregivers attended the program with the child. The second one was for children who were ready for experiences independent of the parent or caregiver. Rather than holding these programs in the large meeting room, the library staff created a cozy, more contained area by moving a portable shelf unit and two free-standing bulletin boards. This private refuge could be erected and dismantled easily. To ensure that library staff knew what to expect of these special children, they spoke with their teachers prior to the first session. In addition to sharing useful information, a teacher volunteered to be present at the program. Parents who attended these library programs commented to the librarians that they enjoyed the opportunity to learn the finger and hand rhymes the librarian introduced and to sing with their children; as a result, new family traditions were born. Other families shared books introduced in storytimes with the children's teachers; some of the teachers commented that they did not know some of the titles prior to the library program.[26]

After completing a successful year of programs for the special needs children, the Oceanside Library applied for and was granted an LSCA mini-grant through the Nassau County (N.Y.) Library System. In an attempt to recruit exceptional children into the summer reading program, the library wanted to create a nurturing atmosphere where children with special needs would not feel overwhelmed or threatened by a summer reading club of 700 participants who reported the books they read to 60 teen volunteers. With funds from the mini-grant, a special kick-off party where the children's individual needs could be honored was planned. Again, with the cooperation of SEPTA, 18 families attended this program, many of them coming to the library for the first time.[27]

## Practical Applications [28]

Planning summer and year-round programs for children with disabilities depends not only on the resources available to the library, but the audience that you will be serving. As you can see from the examples above, there is a great deal of variance in the needs and abilities of exceptional children. You need to know if you will be working with children with low vision or children who have hearing impairments. Will the children attending your programs be developmentally disabled or will they be children with mobility impairments? Each of these disabilities needs special and distinct accommodations. In some cases, you may not know in advance who will be attending your programs, so you will need to adapt some techniques and add various methods of presentation to your repertoire that you can automatically include in your programs. You must remove as many barriers to access as possible so you can serve all children. Prior to initiating programs for children with disabilities, make certain that your library meets ADA accessibility standards. Shelving needs to be a minimum of 36 inches apart, with additional space for turning at the end of the aisles. Bathrooms have certain requirements, as do water fountains or bubblers. Lighting must be of a certain intensity. Signs also must meet certain requirements. Work with consumers in your community who are disabled to evaluate your facilities. Eliminating the physical barriers within the library is only the first step in providing service to diverse special populations.

Another important barrier to service that must be overcome is that of attitude. A child with a disability is, first and foremost, a child. Be sure that everyone who will be working with the children—pages, circulation staff, reference librarians, adult and teen volunteers—receives some specialized training. Invite a speaker to make a presentation or show a video during a staff meeting to sensitize everyone to the needs of children with disabilities. Rather than saying "a wheelchair-bound child" say "a child who uses a wheelchair." Practice this user-first language so that your description of the user's disability recognizes that he or she is, first and foremost, a person. If your conversation involves the child and the child is present, direct your speech and actions to the child, not to the parent or caregiver, just as you would with other children. For example, if a child who uses a wheelchair needs assistance in selecting a book, ask the child, not the parent, what types of books he or she would like to read. As you would when dealing with other children, try to bring your body in line with the child so that you can make eye contact.

## *Children with Visual Disabilities*

There are certain accommodations that public libraries can make that will allow a child or teen with limited vision to participate in summer library reading programs and activities. Make certain that the patron who is visually impaired is sitting close enough, or at an angle, in order to see the program more easily. This is especially important for parents who are visually disabled. We need to remember that while the primary audiences for most of our summer library reading programs (and other programs) are the children and teens, parents are also important program participants. We want to make certain that parents and caregivers can reinforce and expand library programs and these language and literacy experiences at home.

Accommodations in the collection must also be made. Most picture books and easy readers have large type. Permanent collections (as opposed to deposit collections on loan from the regional NLS library that every library should provide) should include some age-appropriate large-print materials. Many popular titles for elementary and middle school children are available in large print. If you are using handouts in your summer program, you can enlarge them on a photocopier so that the print size is equivalent to large print. Games and puzzles can be enlarged for children with limited sight or can be produced by a well-equipped print shop in a raised format for children whose sight is even more limited. Materials produced in house on a word processor can be formatted so that the font size and style is equivalent to large type. In addition to having sufficient kerning and leading (space) between individual letters, words, and lines, it is best to have a sharp contrast between the typeface and the background. In other words, as much as you like that hot pink, stick to the pastel pink paper. While designing Web pages for your summer program, make certain that all images are tagged, the size of the font is equivalent to large type even on the smallest monitor, and the backgrounds provide a clear contrast to the color of the type. People designing Web pages can use the free service of the Bobby Online Free Portal to test compliance with existing accessibility guidelines, such as Section 508 and the W3C's WCAG. Bobby Online can be accessed at http://bobby.watchfire.com/bobby.html/en/index.jsp.

Figure 4–5 shows the differences in type-point sizes. The minimum size for materials to be considered large print is 14 point. Notice that not only does the type size change but the kerning between the letters and the leading between the lines is adjusted proportionally.

Materials produced in house on a word processor can also be output to a special Braille printer. Contact local social service organizations that work with people with visual disabilities or your local NLS network library to locate a Braille printer that you can use to produce your materials in Braille.

When using picture books or adapting them for use in your programs, pay particular attention to the illustrations. Pictures should be large and clear and have good definition; avoid books that have busy backgrounds and lots of intricate detail. When creating flannel-board stories or box stories to share during your summer storytimes, you must also take these factors into consideration. Choose a solid color background instead of a print; use light-colored objects on a dark background. Use simple features for cutouts, and keep them uncluttered. Make your characters and figures as large as you can for your flannel board, and make certain that you describe the action as the figures move. Run through your story ahead of time with someone who is not looking at the visuals; make certain that person can understand your story. While this will take practice, the more you do it, the easier it will become.

This is especially important that children with visual impairments know where you are and what you are doing during a program. If you are walking about the room or preparing other materials, be certain to keep talking so the children can locate you and know what is happening at all times.

When setting out materials for an art activity, use the face of an analog clock as an example for children with visual impairments. Buttons are at twelve o'clock, the glue stick is at nine o'clock, and the yarn is at three o'clock. Place small items in shallow bowls; it makes it easier for the child with visual disabilities to locate and reach them. This also helps to contain small items, keeping them in one general area and thus making it easier for the child to locate and use them. This is a wonderful time to have a teen or senior-citizen volunteer around to assist.

**Figure 4–5**
**Comparison of Type Sizes**

As we have already read, summer library programs are the number one activity that not only entices children into becoming literate citizens, but are also the best predictor of academic success the following year.

Font size 12

As we have already read, summer library programs are the number one activity that not only entices children into becoming literate citizens, but are also the best predictor of academic success the following year.

Font size 14

As we have already read, summer library programs are the number one activity that not only entices children into becoming literate citizens, but are also the best predictor of academic success the following year.

Font size 16

As we have already read, summer library programs are the number one activity that not only entices children into becoming literate citizens, but are also the best predictor of academic success the following year.

Font size 18

As we have already read, summer library programs are the number one activity that not only entices children into becoming literate citizens, but are also the best predictor of academic success the following year.

Font size 22

### *Children with Hearing Impairments*

As with all types of disabilities, hearing impairments may range from mild hearing loss to total deafness. People with hearing impairments need varying forms of assistance—from assistive listening devices to sign-language interpreters or speech readers.

Libraries need to be prepared to provide sign-language interpreter services. The ideal situation would be if you or another staff member knows sign-language; short of that, you and other library staff should learn some basic signs so that you will be able to speak with patrons who use this method of communication. To be assured you have interpreters available when needed for programs, request that patrons notify the library ahead of time. Depending on the number of sign-language interpreters and how much demand there is for these professionals in your area, it is not unreasonable to ask that patrons inform you anywhere from 24 hours to two weeks in advance of a specific program. Make certain that you include a line in your budget for interpretive services so that you have funds to pay for this expensive, yet necessary, service for your patrons. You will want to include a statement in your promotional materials for your summer programs that this service is available. Also, let your patrons know that your library has a telecommunication device for the deaf (TDD); having this device will enable children who have access to a TDD at home or school to call the library. Providing a TDD at the library so hearing impaired patrons can reach you is equivalent to having telephone service for the rest of your patrons. This type of accommodation is exactly what the ADA requires.

Not all patrons will utilize the services of a sign-language interpreter. Many patrons with limited hearing loss will use assistive-listening devices. The newest ones are wireless and portable. The library should make them available so that patrons with hearing loss can communicate with staff and fully participate in programs. During programs, the presenter wears a lavalier or lapel microphone; the listener hears only the sounds from the person wearing the microphone. Any comments or questions from other children participating in the program will be lost unless you repeat these verbal exchanges for the children wearing the assistive-listening device. Also, make certain that the presenter turns the microphone off at the end of the program; any conversation carried on with the microphone switch open will be transmitted to the receiver. Assistive-listening devices should be available at all library service desks so patrons who need them for reference transactions and reader guidance will have easy access to them.

As any one who uses a hearing aid can tell you, extraneous noises can be very distracting and annoying; these noises can also reduce the ability of a child who has a hearing impairment to hear well and understand. Try to present your programs in an area that does not adjoin a high-traffic/high-noise area. Make sure the program area you use has sound-deadening baffles such as carpeting; this will help reduce the noise.

Sight is extremely important to children with hearing impairments. Make sure that children are seated so that they can see the entire area where your program will take place. You will need to keep everything in a compact area within the child's field of vision. If you are using a sign-language interpreter, make certain that the interpreter is right next to the program presenter; that way, the children will be able to see both the presenter and the interpreter at the same time. Make sure that there is light on the faces of both the presenter and interpreter and that neither are in the shadows. Whether telling a story or reading from a book, make sure the presenter faces the children at all times and speaks distinctly. Body language and facial expressions are important clues that help listeners interpret what you are saying. Even without formal training, many people have learned to lip read somewhat and can distinguish words if you speak slowly and clearly. There is no need to shout; speak at your normal voice level. Practice speaking in front of a mirror to make certain that you do not hide your mouth with your hands. Keep your eye on your audience. If you see that they are not understanding what you are saying, try saying it another way.

Rather than using a flannel board, which means you might have to have your face turned away from the audience, use a story apron instead. Commercially available story aprons are made from hook and loop fabric, or you can make one using felt. By using this prop, the children can see you speak, see the interpreter signing, and see the characters on your story apron all at the same time.

If you are using videos or DVDs in your programs, use captioned materials. Make certain that the reading level of the captions is appropriate for the audience.

A puppet-theater presentation should have an interpreter right alongside the stage. It may even be possible to incorporate the interpreter as the narrator for the puppet play.

People often assume that children who are deaf are also very quiet. On the contrary, quite the opposite is often true. Children with hearing impairments do not realize that they are noisy; they often bang on a table or make other loud sounds to get other people's attention. To gain the attention of children with hearing impairments, use some type of visual clue, such as flashing the lights in the room.

Many children who are deaf have low reading and written-language skills. They do not hear language so their language structure is different from that of people in the hearing world. Because of this, it is extremely important to have high-interest/low-reading-level materials in your collection. To assist children and their parents acquire sign-language skills, include picture books with sign-language descriptions; Gallaudet University Press publishes many such books. Including these materials in your library collection and featuring them during your summer library reading program helps the hearing community develop an awareness of these materials and this disability. These books also allow librarians to learn some stories in sign language. Learn a few stories in sign language and present them with signs, even to a hearing audience. This experience will help sensitize others to this type of disability.

Libraries needing additional assistance in providing services to children with hearing impairments should contact their local deaf-services center, local chapters of Self-Help for Hard of Hearing People (SHHH), and the regional NLS network library.

## Children with Mobility Impairments

It is very easy for unthinking people to make children or teens with physical disabilities the target of condescending attitudes. It is your responsibility to learn about each individual's abilities and needs and counter these attitudes. Find out if the child needs help getting to the rest room or using your electronic catalog. Online patron-access catalogs and Internet terminals should be equipped with large-print outputs and voice-activated inputs whenever possible. Allow extra time for a child who uses a walker or crutches to move from one area to another and to get settled; don't insist that all program participants sit on the floor for your programs if it makes it difficult for children or teens with mobility impairments to sit or get up from there. During storytimes, you may want to have the other children sit in chairs to bring them up to the same level as the child who uses a wheelchair. Offer assistance, but learn what the child can do independently. Follow each child's lead; what may look cumbersome and complicated to you may be of second nature to the child.

When providing reader guidance and reference services to a child or teen who uses a wheelchair, sit or bend down so that your upper body is at the same level as the patron; this is a good idea whenever you are talking with a patron of any age who uses a wheelchair. Most youth librarians do this automatically when working with young children, but other staff may need to be reminded of this. Remember, it is very hard on a person's neck always to be looking up. This superior/inferior position is one that can create a feeling of subservience on the part of the person in the wheelchair. By adopting a position of equality, we are reinforcing a positive self-image for the person who uses a wheelchair.

If you are including an art activity in your summer program, make sure that the wheelchair fits under the table or that the project can be placed on the wheelchair tray. Have special scissors and other implements that can be used by program participants who have poor muscle control. Make certain that all materials and equipment that the program participant may need to successfully complete the project are within easy reach; others may be able to move about trading glue, scissors, yarn, and glitter while the person with mobility impairments cannot do so easily.

To assist with the development of motor skills, don't be afraid to include some movement activities in your summer programs. Again, you need to be aware of each person's skills, abilities, and limitations. Your library may want to incorporate a toy-lending library into the collection as playing with and manipulating toys can also promote the development and improvement of motor skills. Toy-lending libraries are also beneficial to children and parents of children with developmental disabilities.

### *Children with Developmental Disabilities*

There are several levels of mental retardation: educable, trainable, severe, and profound. Children functioning at these different levels have differing needs. As with all children, they thrive on praise and positive reinforcement. Sometimes it is difficult for children with developmental disabilities to grasp a concept; they benefit greatly from a multisensory approach. This approach of incorporating as many senses and approaches as possible helps children without any disabilities as well. Since every person has different learning styles, using numerous methods and styles of presentation will help all children. Active participation through the use of songs, activities, and movement will help children with developmental disabilities understand and learn more.

When incorporating art activities into programs for children with developmental disabilities, keep the activities simple enough so that the children can do them with little assistance. If you have teen or senior volunteers assisting you and the program participants, make sure they allow children with developmental disabilities to do as much as they are able to do independently without the intervention of the volunteer; under no circumstances should the volunteer take over the project. It is not necessary, or even desirable, to have the child's finished product look like the librarian's sample. What matters is that the child not be frustrated while performing the task and have a sense of accomplishment when the activity is completed. When planning these summer activities, don't be afraid to ask for ideas and assistance from the children's parents, teachers, and caregivers; they can be a fountain of information regarding ability levels of their children and matching appropriate activities to each level.

One thing that is of the utmost importance to remember when working with children and teens of any age who have developmental disabilities: programs should be age appropriate and children and teens with developmental disabilities should receive whatever assistance they may require so that they can participate in activities appropriate to their chronological age.

## *Children with Multiple Disabilities*

Working with children and teens who have multiple disabilities means that libraries must be able to individualize their services even more. Again, parents, teachers, and caregivers of these special children can provide assistance in helping to establish what is appropriate for each individual child. Librarians should be alert to the possibility of bringing a new perspective to others who interact with the special child. Offer your services and provide materials to the parents, teachers, and caregivers of children with disabilities. Because of the varying nature of the disabilities, you will need to be patient, flexible, and always to be ready to learn.

## *Children with Learning and Reading Disabilities*

A learning disability is a disorder in the understanding or processing of language, thinking, talking, reading, or math. It is an umbrella term encompassing a variety of learning-dysfunctional symptoms, behaviors, and causes.[29] Dyslexia, processing disorders, and other learning disabilities are among the hidden disabilities that children already attending your summer programs may have. These learning disabilities keep children from using ordinary materials. Some children learn to work around their disabilities while others do not. Though it is not widely known, children who cannot read or manipulate traditional print materials because of their learning disabilities are eligible for services from the National Library Service. Assist them in enrolling in the NLS program. Rather than frustrating children with learning disabilities by asking them to read aloud from a reader's theater script, have them do the sound effects or just let them ad lib. Depending on the eye/hand coordination and other skills that the children have or have not developed, art activities may or may not be a problem. As with children with the other disabilities that have been discussed, you must learn from the child and find out what his or her abilities are and then focus your programs on enhancing those aptitudes.

Even before the ADA was enacted in 1990, public libraries were trying to meet the needs of students who were receiving an education in the least restrictive environment as provided for by the Education for All Handicapped Children Act of 1975, Public Law 94-142. In 1984, the Westchester (N.Y.) Library System received a grant from the Foundation for Children with Learning Disabilities to explore and develop ways in which librarians could become more responsive to the needs of children with learning disabilities, their families, and the professionals who work with them. One of the main aspects of the grant was an in-service training session for the children's librarians in the 38 public libraries in the system. The training included intensive "simulation education" to increase sensitivity to the needs of children with learning disabilities. Librarians also began examining and reviewing children's books with an awareness to the needs of these special children. Criteria used to critique materials addressed print, page design, general format, organization and clarity of the book, and use of language.[30]

As it was found that the physical act of writing, the act of putting pen to paper, was a skill that many children with learning disabilities lacked, creative writing using computers with word-processing programs was incorporated into the library program. Specially designed software to help the children with learning disabilities acquire basic typing skills was used. Typing proved to help the children with learning disabilities to improve their spelling and vocabulary skills. Without having to worry about handwriting or spelling, and knowing that the stories and essays they wrote were easily corrected without having to rewrite the entire paper, the creativity of these children was released and blossomed. The children's sense of accomplishment and success with a writing experience was, perhaps, one of the most important aspects of this program.[31]

For a more complete discussion of the developmental needs of children with disabilities and how libraries can respond, see Linda Lucas Walling and Marilyn H. Karrenbrock's *Disabilities, Children, and Libraries: Mainstreaming Services in Public Libraries and School Library Media Centers* (Englewood, Colo.: Libraries Unlimited, 1993).

## Vacation Time Equals Program Time

Traditionally, summer vacation was offered as a break from the classroom routine, thus providing the opportunity to digest and integrate learning that occurred during the past academic year. Summertime is commonly thought to be a time during which children are free from structured and rigid schedules that are imposed upon them and their families during the school year. More and more frequently, however, summer vacation is looked upon as a relic from a time when most people relied on agriculture for a living. With the rapid changes engendered by technology and automation and the competition for jobs in a worldwide market, people are finding that the summer break need not be a vacation from learning. Many people now think of summer vacation as a largely underutilized time that can be put to use to improve reading achievement and to highlight the enjoyment of discovery and self-generated learning.

To counter the educational losses that many children have after a ten-week summer vacation, many school districts are adapting their academic calendars to a year-round approach. There are numerous variations to the calendar. Sometimes all students are on the same track and attend classes for ten weeks then have a three-week vacation; this is repeated four times over the calendar year. All children are in school at the same time and are on vacation at the same time. Other school districts, faced with classroom shortages and a lack of funds to build new facilities (or a lag in building new facilities as the student population increases), have multiple tracks. With multiple tracks, one-third of the student body is on break at all times while the other two-thirds are in class. While this type of arrangement is harder on families because siblings may be on different tracks, it does allow for a greater use of school facilities. Many communities that have experimented with multiple tracks have either gone to the ten-three plan described above or returned to the traditional ten months of school with two months of vacation when their building program catches up with their school-age population. In some large school districts, all three types of calendars are in use. No matter which format of year-round schooling a school system adopts, the students still attend school the same number of days as they do with the traditional ten-month calendar. Rather than bunching vacation into just the summer months, it is spread throughout the year in clusters. When communities have any type of nontraditional school calendar, the public library must adapt its summer programs.

Starting in 1981, the County of Los Angeles Public Library was faced with year-round schools. Originally, the library system tried to deliver a program with a different theme every three months. This labor-intensive program was an attempt to give every child a different library experience with each and every program session during each of the four floating vacation periods. They soon found out that not every child participated in these vacation library programs during each of the school breaks. They also found that in trying to provide so many different programs annually, they were exhausting not only the themes that would attract children to the library, but they were exhausting the library staff. The library staff found that it was difficult to sustain the interest of children over several vacation periods and that the programs were becoming repetitive. It was eventually decided that rather than concentrating on the variety of programs, more attention would be paid to reading motivation. In an attempt to keep children reading over the various vacation times offered by the numerous schools served by this large library system, the children's librarians decided that program materials such as posters, bookmarks, and reading logs would be designed in such a way so that they could be used during any time during the program year, or even in other years. The only change in design was to eliminate two design elements: the year designation and the "summer library program" designation. This small change, combined with individual-reader guidance linked with programs that were repeated turned out to be a workable solution for the children and the library staff. The library now keeps track not only of how many children attend programs but also of how many children read and keep track of their reading on the reading logs.[32,33]

Staff burnout from overprogramming was a reason that the original attempt to adapt to year-round schools in Los Angeles almost failed. Staff burnout from running a summer library program for the entire ten-week summer vacation is also a possibility.

If schools in your community have a traditional ten-week summer vacation, start your summer programs as soon after the last day of school as possible and continue to offer programs for four to six or eight weeks. Depending on your staffing situation and the traditions in your community, you may want to take a break near the Fourth of July to permit yourself and other staff to attend the American Library Association annual conference, which occurs around then. If your audience is larger than you can handle in one six-week session, try splitting your programs and run two four-week sessions. Running successive sessions will allow you to reach more children without necessarily having to prepare eight sets of programs. This also allows children who visit out-of-town relatives to participate in one session without feeling as though they are missing out. It also allows children visiting your area the opportunity to participate by creating additional spaces in your program.

Not every child wants or needs to participate in every program. Don't make attendance at all sessions mandatory. Remember, you want to make this a pleasurable experience and forcing children to participate when they don't want to spoils the optional and self-regulated adventure of a summer or vacation program. Offering a variety of services and programs over the course of the summer and motivating children and teens to read will help prevent summer slide.

## Endnotes

1. Florida Library Youth Program Planning Committee. 2004. *Read around Florida. 2004 Florida Library Youth Program*. Tallahassee, Fla.: State Library and Archives of Florida, xv.
2. Barbara Heyns. 1978. *Summer Learning and the Effects of Schooling*. New York: Academic Press.
3. William H. Teale. 1995. "Public Libraries and Emergent Literacy: Helping Set the Foundation for School Success." In *Achieving School Readiness: Public Libraries and National Education Goal No. 1*, edited by Barbara Froling Immroth and Viki Ash-Geisler. Chicago: American Library Association.
4. Stephen Krashen. 1993. *The Power of Reading: Insights from the Research*. Englewood, Colo.: Libraries Unlimited, 39–40.
5. Young Adult Library Services Association. 1993. *Directions for Library Service to Young Adults*. Chicago: American Library Association.
6. National Center for Education Statistics. 1995. *Services and Resources for Children and Young Adults in Public Libraries*. Washington, D.C.: U.S. Department of Education, Office of Educational Research and Improvement.
7. Caroline A. Caywood, ed. 1995. *Youth Participation in School and Public Libraries: IT WORKS*. Chicago: Youth Participation Committee of the Young Adult Library Services Association, American Library Association.
8. Carnegie Council on Adolescent Development. 1992. *A Matter of Time: Risk and Opportunity in the Nonschool Hours*. New York: Carnegie Corporation of New York.
9. Carnegie Council on Adolescent Development.
10. Young Adult Library Services Association with Patrick Jones, Linda Waddle, ed. 2002. *New Directions for Library Service to Young Adults*. Chicago: American Library Association, 7.
11. Cathi Edgerton. 1986. "We Spent Our Summer Chasing Unicorns: A Young Adult Reading Game Update." *Top of the News* 42, no. 3 (Spring): 289–297.
12. Debbie Carton. 1992. "Cover to Cover at Berkeley PL." *School Library Journal* 38, no. 7 (July): 34.
13. Marsha McGrath and Jana Fine. 1996. "Teen Volunteers." In *Rhythm and Books—Feel the Beat! 1996 Florida Library Youth Program*, edited by Libby Rupert et al. Tallahassee, Fla.: Division of Library and Information Services, Florida Department of State, xix–xxix.

14. Virginia A. Walter. 1995. *Output Measures and More: Planning and Evaluating Public Library Services for Young Adults: Part of the Public Library Development Program.* Chicago: American Library Association.
15. Young Adult Library Services Association with Patrick Jones, Linda Waddle, ed, 2002, 20.
16. *Mysterious Summer.* 1996. Program Booklet. Seattle, Wash.: King County Library System.
17. *Mysterious Summer.*
18. Krashen, 84.
19. Education for All Handicapped Children Act of 1975, Public Law 94-142.
20. *History: Twenty-Five Years of Progress in Educating Children with Disabilities through IDEA.* N.d. Washington, D.C.: Office of Special Education Programs, Office of Special Education and Rehabilitative Services, United States Department of Education, 1.
21. *History*, 6.
22. James Pletz. 1990. "Lift Up Your Hearts . . . Open Your Doors—Summer Reading Program and Public Library Empathy Programming for Print Handicapped Children." *Illinois Libraries* 72, no. 4 (April): 360–364.
23. Eileen Sheppard. 1990. "Summer Reading BPH Style." *Illinois Libraries*, 72, no. 4 (April): 330–332.
24. Cynthia Holt and Betty Waznis. 1984. "Arizona Conducts Its First Summer Reading Program." *Dikta* 9, no. 3 (Fall): 100–103.
25. Holt and Waznis.
26. Judith Schimmel. 1993. "Programs That Open Doors: Programming for Children with Special Needs Lets Them Know That They Too Are Valued Library Patrons." *School Library Journal* 39, no. 11 (November): 36–38.
27. Schimmel.
28. Much of the information presented in this section is adapted from Mary Ann Sumner. 1992. "Library Services to Children with Disabilities: Practical Approaches." In *Into Books . . . And Out of This World: 1992 Florida Summer Library Program Manual,* Roberta Weber and Kathleen Matheny. Tallahassee, Fla.: Division of Library and Information Services, Florida Department of State, xiii–xix.
29. Education for All Handicapped Children Act of 1975, Public Law 94-142.
30. Judith Rovenger. 1987. "Learning Differences/Learning Directions: Library Service to Children with Learning Differences. *Library Trends*. 35, no. 3 (Winter): 427–435.
31. Rovenger.
32. Lois Phillips. 1978. "The Summer Reading Program—Touch Stone for a Year-Round Public Relations Program in Children's Services." *Public Libraries* 17, no. 1 (Spring): 12.
33. Penny Markey. Youth Services Coordinator, County of Los Angeles Public Library. Telephone interview, August 12, 1996.

## Recommended Reading

Baldwin, Liz. 1993. "A Summer Lesson in Service." *School Library Journal* 39, no. 5 (May): 40.

Carlin, Margaret F., Jeannine Lackey Laughlin, and Richard D. Saniga. 1991. *Understanding Abilities, Disabilities and Capabilities: A Guide to Children's Literature.* Englewood, Colo.: Libraries Unlimited.

Eisenhut, Lynn. 1990. "Teen Volunteers." In *The VOYA Reader,* edited by Dorothy M. Broderick. Metuchen, N.J.: Scarecrow, 91–98.

Eldridge, Leslie, comp. and ed. 1985. *R Is for Reading: Library Service to Blind and Physically Handicapped Children.* Washington, D.C.: National Library Service for the Blind and Physically Handicapped.

Foos, Donald D., and Nancy C. Pack, eds. 1992. *How Libraries Must Comply with the Americans with Disabilities Act (ADA).* Phoenix, Aza.: Oryx.

Gonen, Mubeccel Sara. 1992. "Picture Story Books and Children Who Are Hard of Hearing." *Bookbird* 30, no. 1 (March): 7–8.

Leach, Stacey. 1994. "Children with Physical Disabilities and Summer Reading Programs in Ohio Public Libraries." Master's research paper. Kent, Ohio: Kent State University.

McGrath, Marsha and Jana R. Fine. 1990. "Teen Volunteers in the Library." *Public Libraries.* 29; no. 1 (January/February): 24–28.

Medwid, Daria J., and Denise Chapman Weston. 1995. *Kid-Friendly Parenting with Deaf and Hard of Hearing Children: A Treasury of Fun Activities toward Better Behavior.* Washington, D.C.: Gallaudet University Press.

Palmer, Julie R. 1989. "Youth Workers: What's Right with the Picture." *VOYA* 11, no. 6 (February): 273–275.

Walling, Linda Lucas, and Marilyn H. Karrenbrock. 1993. *Disabilities, Children, and Libraries: Mainstreaming Services in Public Libraries and School Library Media Centers.* Englewood, Colo.: Libraries Unlimited.

# III

# Organizing and Promoting Your Program

# 5

# Beginning Your Program

Now that you have decided that you are going to provide a summer library reading program in your community, you have to start planning how you will actually implement this program. You should have already established your goals and objectives. You should also know what outcomes you hope to achieve through your program. Now you must develop an action plan that will let you accomplish all of this. If you are lucky enough to work in a state that offers a statewide program or participates in a regional cooperative program, some of your planning will be done for you. If you don't have access to a statewide or cooperative program, or if you decide not to take advantage of that service provided by your state library agency or association, you will have to do some additional work.

## Participating in a Statewide or Regional Program, including Multi-State Cooperative Programs

If you are involved in planning a statewide or regional program, you need to begin working on it approximately 18 to 24 months prior to implementation. This one-and-one-half- to two-year lead time is necessary to allow a statewide planning committee with wide representation from participating libraries to select a youth-oriented theme; provide direction for the development, production, and distribution of promotional materials; develop a program manual; and develop and present a staff development and training workshop that demonstrates ideas presented in the manual. All this must be done far enough in advance so that local participating libraries can adapt the statewide program and tailor it to meet the needs of their communities.

Most states that provide a statewide program have some type of planning committee. Usually, the committee is chaired by the youth services consultant from the state library; sometimes it is chaired by the head of the youth services section of the state library association. The number of people on the committee varies state by state, but each state that uses a committee ensures that they include representatives of libraries of varying size and geographic areas of the state. Most statewide planning committees also try to maintain a balance representing all users and potential users. Therefore, the committee usually includes someone from the regional NLS library or another representative of that user group. Other special populations should also be represented on the planning committee. If possible, representatives of the end users—the children and teens, their parents, teachers, and caregivers—should be on the committee. Even when this is not impossible, the needs of the users must be kept in mind during the entire planning process. In addition to selecting the theme, the summer library program planning committee usually assists with the production of the program manual, gives direction for the artist to use in interpreting the theme, and helps promote the program to all the libraries in the state.

Once the theme is selected, the state library, or whatever agency administers the project, has to develop order forms and solicit orders for the materials from participating local libraries. You must compile the orders as they are received; you must maintain accurate records. Once you have established how many and what types of promotional items you need, the materials are printed or manufactured and distributed. Materials design, production, and delivery can take anywhere from six to nine months. Of course, all of this is done with an eye on the budget. If grant funds are used to develop and provide these materials, the budget should have been established during the planning process. The larger the quantity of materials produced, the greater the economy of scale. Even when participating libraries purchase their materials, cost is a factor.

If you are not serving on the statewide planning committee, and are lucky enough to be able to participate in a statewide program, your planning starts about 11 months before your summer program actually begins—right after the end of last year's summer library reading program. During this phase of the planning, you need to think about how many individuals you will be serving and their ages. You need to be able to anticipate the ages you will serve and how many people you expect to participate so that you can order sufficient quantities of age- and developmentally-appropriate program materials. After you have decided to participate in the statewide program and have ordered the materials through your state library agency or library association, your tasks are similar to those who do not have the support of a statewide program.

Over the past 35 years, many states have used Library Services and Construction Act (LSCA) grant funds, and now are using Library Services and Technology Act (LSTA) grant funds, to provide materials at little or no cost to the public libraries in their jurisdictions. In addition to providing posters, bookmarks, reading logs, and other promotional materials, many state library agencies provide a program manual that includes program ideas, bibliographies, display ideas, and listings of audiovisual materials that enhance the theme. These manuals usually include public-relations suggestions that local libraries can use to promote their programs. Many states also sponsor a staff-development and training workshop that demonstrates ideas and methods presented in the program manual. Over the years, these program manuals have been added to many library collections both in the originating state and in other state libraries and are available on interlibrary loan. Appendix A provides a list of themes that state library agencies and some state library associations have implemented from 1990 through 2005. Have the interlibrary loan staff of your library check on the availability of manuals with themes you would like to investigate. These manuals provide a wealth of ideas for your own local programs—and not just for programs offered during the summer.

While statewide cooperative planning has relieved the staff in many local libraries from the burden of developing a program, the burden has shifted to state library agency staff. Over the past several years, several states have banded together to form multi-state cooperative programs. Appendices B and C provide theme lists for the two major collaborative/cooperative programs:

- *Collaborative Summer Library Program.* The 2004 Collaborative Summer Library Program participants were Alaska State Library, Arkansas State Library, Napa County (Calif.) Library System, Delaware Division of Libraries, Idaho State Library, State Library of Iowa, Kansas State Library, Maine State Library, Library of Michigan, Missouri State Library, Montana Library Association, Nebraska Library Association, Nevada State Library, New Jersey State Library, State Library of North Carolina, North Dakota Library Association, State Library of Ohio, Oregon Library Association, Commonwealth Libraries (Pa.), South Dakota State Library, Utah State Library Division, Washington State Library, and the Wisconsin Division of Libraries.
- *Southern States Summer Library Cooperative.* The 2004 Southern States Summer Library Cooperative participants were the Alabama Public Library Service, Georgia Public Library Services, Mississippi Library Commission, South Carolina Library Commission, South Carolina State Library, and the Library of Virginia.

Each entity that belongs to a cooperative has specific responsibilities to ensure the success of the overall program. For example, the following are the responsibilities that each state assumed for the 2004 Southern States Summer Library Cooperative Program:

- Alabama: Create a teen manual related to the theme that was selected for the children's program.
- Georgia: Develop the artwork used for the theme, produce a public-service announcement (PSA), provide contributions to the children's manual.

- Mississippi: Contribute materials to the YA and children's manuals. Share responsibility for editing of the manuals.
- South Carolina: Contribute materials to the YA and children's manuals. Share responsibility for editing of the manuals. Develop, mount, and maintain a Web site for the program.
- Virginia: Host a listserv for all children's staff in all participating states. Contribute materials to the YA and children's manuals. Share responsibility for editing of the manuals.

## Selecting a Theme

If you are not participating in a statewide or regional program, or if your state does not participate in one of the cooperative programs, you will need to determine a theme that will attract your target audience. You can either select from commercially developed programs or strike out on your own. Trying to create something unique and professional looking can be time consuming at the least and many times turns out to be frustrating; it can also turn out to be very expensive, in both time and money, if you and your staff must start from scratch. If you have the needed resources, such as a graphic artist, lots of ideas, a substantial printing budget, and the ability to process the necessary paperwork generated by such a project, and if you have specific needs that prepared programs just don't meet, then feel free to develop your own program and promotional materials. If you would rather use a commercially prepared theme, there are various options for you and your staff to investigate.

Whether it is a statewide planning committee that is developing the theme for statewide use or you are doing this independently for your own library, the theme selected should reflect the life of the children who will be participating. Themes that come out of pop culture or from titles of current movies are usually a good starting place. Care, however, should be taken when selecting a theme; make certain that it is not one that will be passé by the end of the summer.[1]

### Commercially Available Sources

One organization that has many years of experience in creating materials for libraries is the American Library Association (ALA). In the past, the Association for Library Service to Children (ALSC), a division of the ALA, sponsored the National Reading Program Committee. The purpose of this committee was to recommend to ALA Graphics themes and illustrators for the annual reading-promotion program. The committee also developed an annual program guide that enhanced the theme; it contained program ideas, promotional tools, and a bibliography of books and resources. While this committee no longer exists, ALA Graphics continues to create many programs to promote reading.

While it was in existence, the National Reading Program Committee created several programs. In 1992, an Olympic-inspired theme resulted in a partnership with *Sports Illustrated for Kids.* The materials created were of high quality; they also were somewhat expensive. The following year, McDonald's Family Restaurants approached ALA with an offer to sponsor the 1993 National Reading Program, which already had been developed. McDonald's underwrote the cost of production and distribution of "starter kits" to all public libraries in the United States. These starter kits consisted of the program guide, posters, and theme-related materials—bookmarks, reading logs, stickers, and certificates—for 100 participants. Libraries were also able to purchase program-related incentives, such as buttons, pencils, and theme-related trinkets. For many library outlets, this quantity was sufficient for their summer program; other libraries needed to purchase additional materials. This partnership with McDonald's continued through the summer of 1995.

In 1993, children's book illustrator James Stevenson designed the art for "Together Is Better," promoting intergenerational programs. "Reading Is a Magic Trip" provided the setting for a Magic School Bus program by Joanna Cole and Bruce Degan in 1994. Mystery fans were delighted with Edward Gorey's 1995 interpretation of "Solve Mysteries. Read!" From 1993 through 1995, these starter kits were distributed to 16,000 libraries annually.

National Reading Program materials provided through the grant from the corporate sponsor carried the sponsor's logo. Libraries with policies that prohibit using materials that have the logo of a corporate sponsor on them did not use the *free* materials provided by McDonald's, but were able to purchase materials that were identical in every way except that they had no corporate logo on them. Some libraries that participate in statewide programs used these free materials at other times of the year, such as Children's Book Week, National Library Week, and other school vacations.

In addition to assisting with the development of materials for the National Reading Program Committee, the ALSC administers the ALSC/Book Wholesalers Summer Reading Program grant. This grant is designed to encourage reading programs for children in a public library by providing financial assistance of $3,000 and, at the same time, recognizes ALSC members for outstanding program development. The applicant must plan and present an outline for a theme-based summer reading program in a public library. The committee encourages proposals with innovative ways to encourage involvement of children with physical or mental disabilities. A copy of the 2004 application is shown in Figure 5–1 as an example of the type of information that needs to be included. Current grant applications are available on the ALSC Web site at www.ala.org/alsc/awardsscholarships/profawards/bookwholesalers and are due annually on December 1.

Several commercial firms are also in the reading promotion business. They have a variety of materials from posters to bookmarks to reading incentives available for purchase. Several of these commercial vendors will either assist you in coming up with a theme or help you choose from prepackaged programs. For those of you whose programs are large enough for you to design your own program, the vendors will meet with the committee, hire the illustrator, design all the products, create order forms (hard copy and electronic), take and compile orders, produce products, and ship them to individual libraries. You may be able to contract with a vendor to provide all services or select from a menu of services that they offer. Outsourcing many of these activities frees library staff from doing parts of the project for which

**Figure 5–1**
**Grant Application**

Association for Library Service to Children

**ALSC/BWI Summer Reading Program Grant**
**for an Outstanding Public Library Summer Reading Program**
**for Children**

**Based on a Theme of Your Choice**

Administered by the Association for Library Service to Children (ALSC) of the American Library
Association
and sponsored by BWI.

This grant is designed to encourage outstanding summer reading programs by providing financial assistance, while recognizing ALSC members for outstanding program development. The applicant must plan and present an outline for a theme-based summer reading program in a public library. The program must be open to all children (birth -14 years). The committee also encourages innovative proposals involving children with physical or mental disabilities. The $3,000 grant, made possible by BWI, is to be used to support the program. Individual libraries within a larger system are welcome to apply. Applications are due December 1, 2004.

TO BE ELIGIBLE, YOU MUST BE ABLE
TO ANSWER "YES" TO THE FOLLOWING QUESTIONS:

Does your program have a theme?                          Yes _____   No _____

Is your program based in a public library?              Yes _____   No _____

Is your program open to all children in the Community?  Yes _____   No _____

Do you work directly with children?                    Yes _____   No _____

Are you a personal member of ALSC?                     Yes _____   No _____

Name  _____     ALA Membership Number  _____

Library  _____

Address  _____

Phone  _____

E-mail

Signature  _____

Director's Signature  _____
**APPLICATIONS WILL BE JUDGED ON RESPONSES TO THE FOLLOWING:**

---

**Figure 5–1**
*Continued*

---

Describe your community and target audience: _____

_____

_____

How will the program work? _____

_____

_____

How will the program be implemented? _____

_____

_____

What is creative about the program? _____

_____

_____

Why will children like the program? _____

_____

Why does your library need the $3,000; how will you use the $3,000 to enhance your program?  Please Include an itemized budget.

_____
_____
_____
_____
_____

Use additional sheets if necessary.  Return ten copies of the application, postmarked by *December 1, 2004,* to:

ALSC/BWI Summer Reading Grant Chair

---

they might not have the time or expertise and allows more time to provide direct service.

Many of the vendors that provide summer library reading products are happy to add you to their mailing list. The shaded box gives a list of some of these vendors:

- American Library Association, Graphic Department
  50 E. Huron St.
  Chicago, IL 60611
  1-800-545-2433
  Web site: www.alastore.ala.org
- Brodart, Co.
  P.O. Box 3037
  Williamsport, PA 17705
  1-888-820-4377
  Web site: www.shopbrodart.com/default.asp
- The Children's Book Council
  12 W. 37th St., 2nd Floor
  New York, NY 10018-7480
  212-966-1990.
  Web site: http://cbcbooks.org
- Demco, Inc.
  P.O. Box 7488
  Madison, WI 53707-7488
  1-800-962-4463
  Web site: www.demco.com
- Highsmith Co.,
  W5527 State Rd. 106
  P.O. Box 800
  Fort Atkinson, WI 53538-0800
  1-800-558-2110
  Web site: www.highsmith.com
- JanWay Co.
  11 Academy Rd.
  Cogan Station, PA 17728
  1-800-877-5242
  Web site: www.janway.com
- K-Read School and Library Promotions
  500 Capital of Texas Hwy N.
  Bldg. 1, Suite 125
  Austin, TX 78746
  512-330-0396
  Web site: www.kread.com
- Upstart: contact Highsmith Co.

## *Developing Your Own Theme*

If, rather than going with a ready-made program, you decide to design your own program, you will still need to make some decisions regarding the theme. It may seem that you don't necessarily want to do an entire series of programs based on one motif, but the children you are serving and the community at-large are better able to identify with your program if there is one unifying element. When selecting a theme, be sure to take care that it has appeal to the children and teens you are trying to attract. While the theme must attract children, it cannot appear to be "childish, didactic, or cutesy, but, rather, contemporary." [2] As you select your theme, you must keep in mind the current interests of the youth you want to attract. If they are interested in dinosaurs (and tell me what child does not go through a dinosaur stage at some time), then you might want to use that as the basis for your program. This does not mean that everything you do during the summer will be limited to dinosaurs; however, it does mean that it should somehow be related to dinosaurs.

For example, *Rhythm and Books—Feel the Beat!* was the theme selected for the 1996 Florida Library Youth Program. Many librarians were, at first, skeptical about having a program centered on music. Even though they knew that the target audience—from very young children all the way through to young adults and their parents, teachers, and caregivers—would be attracted to a music theme depending on how it was presented, some librarians thought they themselves would get bored having to work with what they considered a limited theme. Others were worried that they did not have any musical abilities and felt this would be a restricting factor. Both of these were extremely relevant comments; if the staff members implementing the summer program are not enjoying it, their boredom, frustration, or dislike of the theme is likely to come through and be picked up by the participants. These negative attitudes will chase participants away rather than attracting them. To counter that, the Florida Library Youth Program Planning Committee came up with ten subthemes that expanded and enhanced the central theme. Rather than featuring music in every aspect of the program, the planning committee incorporated various music-related subthemes.

- "Moving and Grooving" served as an introduction to basic movement activities.
- "Rhythm of the Road" focused on transportation and travel.
- Teens were especially attracted to the "Catch the Wave" segment; not only was surf music employed here, but this section of the program also allowed for programs related to sea life, things related to the beach, and activities that take place on the water. While there was much interest in this subtheme in Florida, it might not have the same appeal in Nebraska or Montana.
- For those librarians who really wanted to focus on the musical aspect of the theme, they provided programs and activities from the "Class Act" section. This subtheme focused on instruments, composers, and musical performance. Not only was classical music used, but garage bands featuring budding local teen musicians were part of the action and proved to be popular with teens.
- Square dancing and clogging were part of "Hand Clapping, Toe Tapping."

- To ensure that various cultures were included, the committee designed "Island Rhythms." This subtheme featured stories, music, and rhythms from Cuba, Haiti, Puerto Rico, and other Caribbean island nations as well as Hawaii, our island state. You could also include stories, music, and rhythms from Prince Edward Island, the British Isles, and Australia.
- The planning committee had long wanted to do an ecology/conservation theme but always stopped short of planning it for an entire summer; they did not want it to be overkill with such an important message. Neither did they want the program to be too didactic. After all, this is the summer library program and everyone wants it to be different from what the kids hear and are exposed to during the school year. Taking all this into consideration resulted in the inclusion of "Earth Beat." This subtheme focused on Mother Nature and the sounds of the earth, including animals, weather, the rain forest, and the Everglades.
- "Hummin' 'n' Strummin'" allowed libraries to feature country western music and the stories associated with the country, the South, and the West.
- Since humor and funny stories always appeal, "Whoop 'n' Holler" focused on songs and stories that tickle the funny bone.
- To highlight different cultures, "Different Beats for Different Feet" was offered. Not only was movement and dance featured, but other languages, foods, and folklore were offered as well.

These ten subthemes that the committee included in the manual provided enough material and program ideas so that librarians implementing the program had more than enough to choose from, not only for the four to ten weeks worth of programs they provide their communities during the summer and other school vacations, but also with numerous other program ideas for almost an entire year. Providing these variations on a theme allowed each individual library to create a program that was most appropriate for its clients and matched their collection.

The Southern Cooperative Program for 2004 used a similar theme. "Step to the Beat . . . READ!" and included more than just music. Using art work created for the program by children's book illustrator Peter Catalanotto, the program enticed children to explore music, the performing arts, and the visual arts. In addition to the program manual to assist library staff develop and deliver programs and services for preschool and school-age children, the program provided a separate manual with a related theme, "Rock 'n' Read," just for teens.

Having an overall theme that is enticing and exciting provides you with the opportunity to hook your community onto your library. Rather than trying to come up with new decorations each and every week, you can set up your area to reflect the theme and provide dramatic emphasis to reinforce the selected subject matter. Having an overall theme allows you to build your book and materials collection. Have displays of books, videos, and other materials that relate to your theme. Reading should not be limited to books nor viewing limited to videos that relate to your theme. Your theme and how you promote it, however, should have your community clamoring for theme-related materials.

If you do not have access to a theme-related program manual, you will need to start developing your own program ideas. Martha Seif Simpson compiled 50 theme-based library programs in her book *Summer Reading Clubs.* [3] Each of the 50 programs includes an introduction that can be used in news releases and other similar publicity materials. Simpson also includes a list of promotional items such as bookmarks that carry out the theme. In addition to a bibliography and videography, Simpson includes 15 activities that reinforce the theme. These activities, as she calls them, include bulletin board ideas, a reading-incentive game, an idea for a closing ceremony, and various individual and group projects. Themes that are covered include baseball, cars, earth sciences, farms, food, magic, pirates, summer camp, travel, theater, shopping, spies and detectives, toys and games, whales, the zoo, and lots more. While the ideas presented provide a good jumping off place, there is not enough in any one program to provide you with a summer full of ideas. You will need to expand on these suggestions if you wish to run a theme-based program for more than a week or two. You still will have to design your own posters or find ones that are commercially available to help promote your program.

Once you have established your theme, you will need to design the actual programs that you will present. Chapter 6 has suggestions for various types of programs. Use these suggestions, your favorite programming books, and suggestions from statewide program manuals to develop your theme. Books that will help you find related materials, develop programs, and adapt literature for your programs include those in the boxed list:

Arkansas Children's Services Advisory Committee. 1999. *Planning a Reading Program.* Little Rock, Ark.

Bauer, Caroline Feller. 1992. *Read for the Fun of It: Active Programming with Books for Children.* Bronx, N.Y.: H. W. Wilson.

———. 1993. *Caroline Feller Bauer's New Handbook for Storytellers: With Stories, Poems, Magic, and More.* Chicago: American Library Association.

———. 1996. *Leading Kids to Books through Magic,* Mighty Easy Motivators. Chicago: American Library Association.

———. 2000. *Leading Kids to Books through Crafts,* Mighty Easy Motivator Series. Chicago: American Library Association.

Bauer, Caroline Feller, and Edith Bingham. 1994. *The Poetry Break: An Annotated Anthology with Ideas for Introducing Children to Poetry.* Bronx: N.Y.: H. W. Wilson.

Benton, Gail, and Trisha Waichulaitis. 2003. *Ready-to-go Storytimes: Fingerplays, Scripts, Patterns, Music and More.* New York: Neal-Schuman.

Bromann, Jennifer. 2003. *Storytime Action: Ideas for Making 500 Picture Books Interactive.* New York: Neal-Schuman.

Canavan, Diane D., and LaVonne H. Sanborn. 1992. *Using Children's Books In Reading/Language Arts Programs: A How-To-Do-It Manual.* New York: Neal-Schuman.

Chupela, Dolores. 1994. *Ready, Set, Go!: Children's Programming for Bookmobiles and Other Small Spaces.* Fort Atkinson, Wis.: Alleyside Press.

Cook, Sybilla Avery, Frances Corcoran, Beverly Fonnesbeck, and Sybilla Cook. 2001. *Battle of the Books and More: Reading Activities for Middle School Students.* Fort Atkinson, Wisc.: Upstart.

DeSalvo, Nancy N. 1993. *Beginning with Books: Library Programming for Infants, Toddlers, and Preschoolers.* Hamden, Conn.: Library Professional Publications.

Elkin, Judith, Briony Train, and Debbie Denham. 2003. *Reading and Reader Development: The Pleasure of Reading.* London: Facet.

Fredericks, Anthony D. 1997. *The Librarian's Complete Guide to Involving Parents through Children's Literature: Grades K–6.* Englewood, Colo.: Libraries Unlimited.

Irving, Jan. 2004. *Stories Never Ending: A Program Guide for Schools and Libraries.* Peddler's Pack Series. Littleton, Colo.: Libraries Unlimited.

Irving, Jan, and Robin Currie. 1987. *Glad Rags: Stories and Activities Featuring Clothes for Children.* Littleton, Colo.: Libraries Unlimited.

———. 1986. *Mudluscious: Stories and Activities Featuring Food for Preschool Children.* Littleton, Colo.: Libraries Unlimited.

———. 1991. *Raising the Roof: Children's Stories and Activities on Houses.* Englewood, Colo.: Teacher Ideas Press.

Jay, M. Ellen, and Hilda L. Jay. 1998. *Ready-To-Go Reading Incentive Programs for Schools and Libraries.* New York: Neal-Schuman.

———. 1998. *250+ Activities and Ideas for Developing Literacy Skills.* New York: Neal-Schuman.

Johnson, Wayne L., and Yvette C. Johnson. 1999. *Summer Reading Program Fun: 10 Thrilling, Inspiring, Wacky Game Boards for Kids.* Chicago: American Library Association.

Kan, Katharine L., for the Young Adult Library Services Association. 1998. *Sizzling Summer Reading Programs for Young Adults.* Chicago: American Library Association.

Lima, Carolyn W., and John A. Lima. 2001. *A to Zoo: Subject Access to Children's Picture Books,* 6th ed. New York: R. R. Bowker.

Lipman, Doug. 1995. *Storytelling Games: Creative Activities for Language, Communication, and Composition Across the Curriculum.* Phoenix, Ariz.: Oryx.

Lund, Marcia. 1996. *Olympic Winner: Reading Activities for Schools and Libraries.* Fort Atkinson, Wis.: Alleyside Press, 1996.

MacDonald, Margaret Read. 1995. *Bookplay: 101 Creative Themes to Share with Young Children.* New Haven, Conn.: Library Professional Publication.

———. 2004. *Three-Minute Tales: Stories from around the World to Tell When Time Is Short.* Little Rock, Ark.: August House.

Nespeca, Sue McCleaf, and Joan B. Reeve. 2002. *Picture Books Plus: 100 Extension Activities in Art, Drama, Music, Math, and Science.* Chicago: American Library Association.

Polkinharn, Anne T., and Catherine Toohey. 1983. *Creative Encounters: Activities to Expand Children's Responses to Literature.* Littleton, Colo: Libraries Unlimited.

Polkinharns, Anne T., Catherine Toohey, and Lynn Welker. 1988. *More Creative Encounters: Activities to Expand Children's Responses to Literature.* Littleton, Colo.: Libraries Unlimited.

Reid, Rob. 2004. *Cool Story Programs for the School-age Crowd.* Chicago: American Library Association.

Simpson, Martha Seif. 1992. *Summer Reading Clubs: Complete Plans for 50 Theme-Based Library Programs.* Jefferson, N.C.: McFarland.

———. 1997. *Reading Programs for Young Adults: Complete Plans for 50 Theme-Related Units for Public, Middle School and High School Libraries.* Jefferson, N.C.: McFarland.

Thomas, James L., and Ruth M. Loring. 1983. *Motivating Children and Young Adults to Read: 2.* Phoenix, Ariz.: Oryx.

Vasquez, Vivian. 2003. *Getting beyond "I Like the Book": Creating Space for Critical Literacy in K–6 Classrooms.* Newark, Del.: International Reading Association.

Webber, Desiree, and Sandy Shropshire. 2001. *The Kids' Book Club: Lively Reading and Activities for Grades 1–3.* Littleton, Colo.: Libraries Unlimited.

Wisconsin Library Association, Children's and Young Adult Services Section, YA Task Force. 1991. *Young Adult Program Idea Booklet.* Stevens Point, Wis.: The Association.

Works, Robin. 1992. *Promoting Reading with Reading Programs: A How-To-Do-It Manual.* New York: Neal-Schuman.

## The Countdown Begins

### *Avoiding Scheduling Conflicts*

Approximately four to six months before your program actually begins, you will need to establish the exact dates your program will run. As previously discussed, start as soon after schools are dismissed for summer vacation as you can; get your participants involved early! Will you run a six-, eight-, or ten-week program, or two consecutive four-week sessions? Decide if you will have storytimes on Tuesday morning, Thursday afternoon, or even Saturday morning. Will your booknic program be once a week or once a month? (See Chapter 6, "Types of Programs, Book Discussion Groups" for a detailed description of this type of program.) Is your meeting room available all the times that you need it? Are there locations out in the community where you can hold some programs, thus making them more accessible to people who usually do not visit the library? Will you be providing programs at summer reading camps or summer schools? Make certain that sufficient staff will be available in all areas of the library when you are programming; adults and other siblings often come with the summer library program participants and use other library facilities while the program is being presented. You may find it convenient to create a calendar for scheduling all of your programs. While you are creating this tentative schedule, check with the other youth-serving organizations in your community to eliminate as many conflicts as possible. You do not want to spend lots of time and energy creating a program, inviting a guest presenter, and ordering special supplies only to find out that your program is scheduled opposite the event of the summer or another event too good to miss that is being presented elsewhere in the community. You don't want to force children and their families to miss out on either your special program or the other one that "everyone else" will be attending. Work together in partnership with these other agencies to eliminate as many conflicts as possible. Make coming to the library and participating in the summer library program a winning solution for all, not a compromise.

### *Scheduling Presenters*

It is during this part of the planning process that you can start investigating what people in the community have talents that are appropriate to be shared with your target audience during your summer programs. Staff and patrons may have special talents and interests that can be included. Make informal inquires now, and follow up later with confirmation letters.

Prepare a media release to solicit participation from other agencies. Send e-mails to your partners and to people and organizations who have been presenters for your library previously. Consult speakers' bureaus and find out who in your community is available to bring special programs to your library. Find out who the performers in your community are and contact them. Teens make wonderful presenters in programs for younger children. Teens make great role models, and giving them the opportunity to perform in the library shows that the community values them.

## *Plan Your Evaluation Now*

While you are still in the early stages of planning, it is also time to think of how you will evaluate your program. By now, you should know what your objectives are and the outcomes you want for program participants. Now is the time to decide how you will measure those outcomes and what data you need to collect along the way. Decide now if you will do surveys before and after the summer. Decide now what type of record keeping you will do. Are you going to count every book a child or young adult reads and reports to you, or are you going to have an honor system and let them fill in their reading logs independently? Do you want the participants to count number of books or pages read, or time spent reading? More details on how you can evaluate your summer library program and why you need to can be found in Chapter 8, "Evaluating Your Success."

## *Collection Development Activities*

As you are developing your program ideas, you should also start your collection development activities. Check to make sure you have sufficient duplicate copies of books that you will be booktalking at schools as you promote the program or that you will be sharing as reader's theater presentations. Order new materials to fill in gaps in the collection that you have discovered as you plan your programs. When necessary and appropriate, purchase multiple copies in paperback. Make certain that you have books and other materials in your collection that enhance your speakers' presentations. After all, one of the goals of the summer library program is to turn the youth of your community into lifelong readers and library users. If you run a program that is strictly entertainment and don't introduce participants to all the wonders that the library holds that are related to what the speakers and guests are sharing in their presentations, then you may never achieve your goal. Creating a demand for materials and not being able to satisfy that demand is almost worse than never creating the demand.

In addition to building your permanent collection, this is also the time to reserve videos or other media that you will need to borrow or rent for your programs. It is also the time to start exploring the Web and bookmarking age- and developmentally-appropriate Web sites that enhance your program.

## *Community Relations*

If you have decided that you will be offering prizes for contests, you need to start soliciting donations from local merchants. Stores that rely on the youth of the community to stay in business are appropriate sources. Prizes for YA programs can be solicited from places such as clothing stores, record shops, and cosmetic and beauty salons. Fast-food restaurant coupons are appropriate for all ages. Gift certificates at local bookstores are extremely appropriate and may seem very desirable to some children while others may prefer a full-day pass to a local amusement park or to a roller or skateboard rink. Be sure to mention your sponsors in your publicity.

Approximately two to three months before the program begins, your schedule should be complete. By this time, you should have in hand confirmations for your films, videos, and all your performers and guest speakers. If you have not tested your art activities on a group of children, now is the time to do so. Once you know that these activities work with your intended audience, it is time to order your craft materials and supplies. If you are planning on using some type of incentive materials, now is the time that you should order them as well.

Once all programs are confirmed, you should prepare calendars, program fliers, or other printed means of informing the community about the summer library program. You should include a sample of this information in the letter that you send to the schools in your area. This letter is also a request for you to visit the schools during the last month they are in session prior to vacation. Since many schools are involved in standardized testing in late spring, you need to make your request early so that you can be scheduled into as many classes as possible while disrupting the school schedule as little as possible. In addition to the public schools in your service area, you need to inform private and charter schools as well. Home schoolers use the library on a year-round basis; don't forget to include them in this part of your promotional scheme.

At the same time you are scheduling your school visits, you should also be arranging to speak with the leaders of community organizations that work with youth. Boys and Girls Clubs, scouting organizations, summer schools, camps, and child-care facilities are sure to be interested in knowing what programs you have to offer over the summer. As you have already contacted the managers of these organizations to make certain that your schedule has no major conflicts with theirs, you should encounter little resistance in introducing your program to the staff of these organizations.

Now is also the time to start planning how you will utilize teen and other volunteers. Know in advance how many people you can utilize and adequately supervise. Start preparing displays and bulletin board materials. If you are using a costume, this is the time to have it made. If you and other staff will be wearing theme-related T-shirts, order them now. The costume or T-shirt can be worn during your school visits next month as well as during programs throughout the summer. The purpose of wearing a costume or T-shirt that relates to the theme of the summer library reading program is to generate excitement and make your presentation memorable. For example, when libraries used the theme "Book Quest: Search for the Dragon's Treasure," librarians dressed as wizards (even before Harry Potter) and carried a dragon puppet or stuffed animal.

About six weeks before your program begins is when your initial news releases need to be sent out. As more and more people are trying to get information into the local paper or broadcast on radio and television, the necessary lead time is increasing. Know the requirements of your local media—for format, time, and content—and follow them. More information on marketing and promoting the summer library reading program can be found in Chapter 6.

Posters advertising the summer library programs should be placed in the library and prominently around the community about one month before the program officially begins. If you are trying to attract nonusers to the library, just putting the posters in the library will not attract those nonusers. Laundromats, the post office, grocery and convenience stores, the school media center, health care and well-baby clinics, community centers, and other places where children and their families gather are great places to put this type of publicity.

Don't rely only on printed posters. Place electronic announcements about your summer library reading program on the local community computing network. Provide information via the library's home page on the Web. Working with the technical services people in your library, or the computer class at your local high school or community college, you can design a home page that not only tells what programs you are offering and when, but can display your graphics as well. Provide your entire schedule on the home page. If people must preregister for your programs, include that information on the home page, too; if possible, allow them to register online. Investigate alternative methods of offering programs online so that more people can participate.

During that last month prior to summer, you will actually be making your school visits. If you have a large number of students to whom you are trying to deliver the message, you may want to present a large auditorium-style program. If you are not comfortable in that situation, or if the school cannot accommodate that type of a program, you may want to target specific grades. If, for example, you decide to target grades one, four, seven, and possibly ten, and you follow through and see the same grades each year, you will see the entire school population in three years. At the same time that you are doing your school visits and telling about the program, you can also be recruiting your teen volunteers.

About two to three weeks before your program officially begins, have a general staff meeting to make certain that everyone who works in the library knows about all aspects of the summer library reading program. Even though you have been working on this project for months now, not everyone will know the details until you tell them. Everyone, from the page up through the director needs to be informed about the program. Even custodians and guards should be informed about the program. You never know whom a patron will ask about your upcoming activities. Along with knowing when your program runs, they should know if children need to register, and if they must, how.

About two weeks before the summer programs begin, start decorating the youth areas. Your teen volunteers and the children involved in your program during the summer can complete the job. Decorating the area can be on ongoing process that does not have to be complete before you have your opening program.

Figure 5–2 is a summary time line that incorporates statewide and local activities and responsibilities for planning and presenting your summer library reading program.

## Registration—Including Online Registration

You need to decide if you will allow anyone to just show up for any or all of your programs or if you will require preregistration. There are pros and cons for both ways. If you are anticipating more people than you can accommodate in your space, then capping the number of people you allow to preregister will eliminate crowds of

| | Figure 5–2 Summer Reading Program Time Line | |
|---|---|---|
| **Time Frame** | **Statewide Program Responsibilities** | **Local Program Responsibilities** |
| 18–24 months in advance | • Planning committee meets to select theme | |
| 12–18 months in advance | • Work with artist on materials design (logo sheets, poster, bookmark, etc.) | • Establish goals for your program<br>• Decide which prepared program you will be using, Or<br>• Select theme and start materials preparation |
| 9–15 months in advance | • Develop program manual | • Refine objectives |
| 11 months in advance | • Solicit orders | • Order materials, Or<br>• If designing own materials, do so now |
| 10 months in advance | • Compile orders | |
| 9 months in advance | • Solicit bids for production of materials | • Solicit bids for production of materials |
| 3–7 months in advance | • Produce materials<br>• Pay bills as materials are received | • Hold planning meeting with other youth-serving agencies in your community<br>• Establish dates of local program |
| 4–6 months in advance | • Deliver program manual to local libraries | • Order books and other materials to enhance summer library reading program<br>• Block out schedule<br>• Reserve meeting room and other places where programs will be held<br>• Schedule presenters<br>• Book AV materials, such as videos and all necessary equipment |
| 2–3 months in advance | • Deliver program materials, such as posters, bookmarks, reproducible masters, incentives, to local libraries | • Send letters of confirmation to presenters<br>• Solicit prizes from community businesses<br>• Test art activities and order art materials<br>• Schedule school promotional visits<br>• Prepare costumes<br>• Prepare program fliers, calendar |

| | Figure 5–2 Continued | |
| --- | --- | --- |
| **Time Frame** | **Statewide Program Responsibilities** | **Local Program Responsibilities** |
| 1 month in advance | | • Send out media releases<br>• Start registration<br>• Start decorating program area, youth services area, and other areas of the library |

disappointed people on the day of the program. Unfortunately, some people who preregister may not honor their commitment to attend; this leaves you with empty seats and disappointed patrons who were turned away in advance. To remedy this, allow for a percentage of no shows in your preregistration numbers; over register by 10 to 15 percent, depending on your experience.

Will you be having programs that are for specific age groups? Having preregistration will ensure that only people in the target audience will be attending those specific programs. If you are preparing for a craft program, knowing how many people will be participating in that program will allow you to have just enough materials so that all may participate. In addition to registering patrons for specific programs, you need to decide if you will be registering program participants for the entire summer program. Many libraries choose to track program participants starting with the day they sign up. Libraries track what programs participants attend, books they report having read or having read to them, and the prizes they receive.

Manual record keeping is time consuming for staff. As many libraries count these items as part of their evaluation, automation has provided an alternative to time-consuming paper record keeping. "There are so many components to a summer reading program, and so many library staffers are involved, and so many participants registered, that the potential for miscues and miscommunication is very high."[4] Even a simple database will cut down on the number of times information has to be recorded or transferred from one form or document to another. Library staff or teen volunteers with computer skills can design a database that is able to record patron data information, including basics such as name, address, parent's or guardian's names, and phone number. Determine what information you need and will use before you design the database. Information can be collected on a paper form and entered into the database by volunteens—or patrons can enter the data directly.

Automated registration and tracking systems will save staff time and patrons frustration. Since the time frame for registration for the summer library reading program is usually short and the number of patrons to be registered is high, having an automated system will assist library staff in this effort. If you distribute reading logs for patrons on which they enter the titles of books read or literacy activities in which they have participated, there is always the possibility that those forms might be lost over the summer. If rewards are based on the number of books and activities that are recorded on these reading logs, then the program participants who lose their logs may be penalized. If patrons are allowed to record their entries into an automated system then that likelihood is diminished.

If you wish to be able to send e-mail reminders about programs, add the parent's or guardian's mail and e-mail addresses and, with permission of the parent, the child's e-mail address as fields in the database. If you usually contact schools in the fall to let them know how many of their students participated in the summer library reading program, you should add the names of the schools that patrons will be entering in the fall as well as their grade levels. Rather than manually sorting the information, using an electronic database will permit multiple ways of searching on different fields.

If your library is a branch of a system or a member of a cooperative, include information about which library outlet is the patron's primary library. You can add fields for each of the individual programs that are being offered as part of the summer library reading program and track program attendance. If there are specific requirements for participants to receive prizes, you can incorporate tracking and reporting of those efforts in the database as well.

If you provide certificates at the end of the summer, having collected all this information allows you to accurately customize those certificates. Exporting the information is a capability that these automated reading program–management databases have.

If there are criteria for customers to participate in certain programs, create a list of available programs and the criteria associated with each. This information needs to be stored in a table associated with the database. Because the patron-registration information contains data related to the criteria (age, grade), then the system, when properly programmed, will allow only those customers who meet the criteria to register for certain programs. And when the maximum number of participants is reached, the program will automatically stop accepting sign-ups for that specific program.

According to Deborah Dubois, children's outreach librarian at the Mansfield/Richland County (Ohio) Library, the effort needed to develop an electronic database is well worth the effort. Even with programs at several outlets, library staff collected the data on paper forms, and staff at a central location entered the data.

> I did the "programming." It is an Access Database and I learned as I went along. One of the things that motivated me was that at the end of the summer, I compiled the list of kids who completed the programs for the schools. . . . We have 9 locations and I had to take 9 lists and compile them into one for each school. We usually have around 2,000 kids finish the program. After creating the database, what used to take me three days [to compile] now takes about 2 hours. It took many hours to create the database first, but now we can reuse the format and just change the data.[5]

While having this type of a database on an individual workstation is an improvement over previous paper systems, this is not sufficient when there are multiple library outlets or large numbers of patrons who want to enter their information into the system. Rather than using a standalone electronic system, libraries are moving towards

Web-based reading program–management systems. These more sophisticated systems provide additional features that relieve staff and volunteers of data entry.

While some libraries or library systems have the capability of designing and maintaining Web-based databases, many libraries are outsourcing this function to commercial vendors. One such company is e-vanced Solutions (www.e-vancedsolutions.com). This Indiana-based company provides Web-based reading program–management systems that manage registration, allow patrons to log books they have read from any computer with Internet access, track when patrons have met requirements to receive prizes, and notify patrons of that. Library Insight (www.libraryinsighte.com/programs.asp) also provides a commercial summer reading program manager.

Information about using the Web to provide services will be discussed in Chapter 7.

## Endnotes

1. "An Interview with Two Hip Reading Educators on How Librarians and Others Can Put the Zing Back into Sleepy-Time Summer and Year-Round Reading Programs. 1973. *Wilson Library Bulletin* 47, no. 8 (April): 687–690.
2. Mary Somerville. 1981. "How to Knock the Stuffings out of Your Summer Reading Program." *Top of the News* 37, no. 3 (Spring): 266.
3. Martha Seif Simpson. 1992. *Summer Reading Clubs: Complete Plans of 50 Theme-Based Library Programs*. Jefferson, N.C.: McFarland.
4. Lynn Jurewicz and Todd Cutler. 2003. *High Tech, High Touch: Library Customer Service through Technology*. Chicago: American Library Association, 96–97.
5. E-mail message from Deborah Dubois to Carole Fiore. RE: SLP Programs. August 17, 2004.

## Recommended Reading

Association for Library Service to Children. 1982. *Programming for Summer*. Chicago: American Library Association.

Braun, Linda W. 2002. *Teens.library: Developing Internet Services for Young Adults*. Chicago: American Library Association.

Champelli, Lisa. 2002. *The Youth Cybrarian's Guide to Developing Instructional, Curriculum-Related, Summer Reading, and Recreational Programs*. New York: Neal-Schuman.

Miller, Betty Davis. 1988. *How to Do a Summer Library Program If You've Never Done One Before: Procedural Handbook for New Children's Librarians in Florida*. Tallahassee, Fla.: Division of Library and Information Services, Florida Department of State.

*Plant a Reading Seed: Summer Reading Program Librarians Manual, 1993*. 1993. Columbia, S.C.: South Carolina State Library.

Rhoads, Carol, Anitra Steele, and members of the Missouri Youth Library Program Committees, 198. 1995. *Planning for Summer Reading*. Jefferson City, Mo.: Missouri State Library.

# 6

# Promoting Your Summer Program

Whether you have chosen to go with a commercial vendor, your state's theme, or one you have designed independently, you will need to promote your program in a variety of ways. You may not choose to include all these elements, but a good public-relations program is multifaceted. Not only will good promotion attract a large audience, it will also increase community awareness of the library. The more effectively a library markets its summer reading program, the bigger the job for the library to support it. Publicity also benefits the community agencies that you have recruited to work with you and the corporate sponsors that are helping to underwrite your program. If you have not formed these private and public partnerships yet, your publicity will help you recruit them for a program to be presented at a later date.

## Marketing Magic

There really is nothing magical about marketing your summer library reading programs. Marketing is really about wants and needs of a consumer (members of the community) and the exchange of products and services with the supplier (the library). Successful marketers respond to needs of the consumer, influence their wants, and fulfill demands—deliver products and services. Marketing is also about changing the consumers perceptions and sometimes of the library staff as well. Everyone benefits

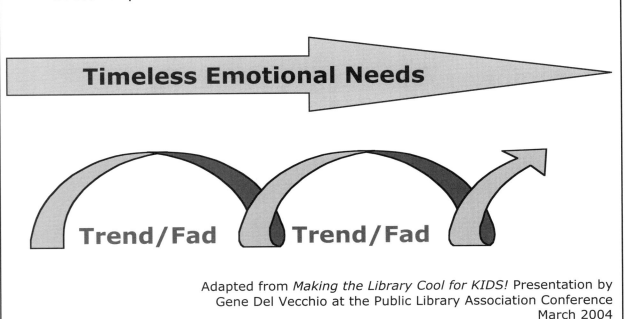

**Figure 6–1
A Successful Formula**

- Satisfy the timeless emotional needs of children and teens

- Dress it up in a current trend or fad

Timeless Emotional Needs

Trend/Fad     Trend/Fad

Adapted from *Making the Library Cool for KIDS!* Presentation by Gene Del Vecchio at the Public Library Association Conference March 2004

Used by permission of Gene Del Vecchio.

when we find out what users really want and when we let the community know what the library can offer.

The purpose of marketing is twofold—to inform and perform. First, you must tell customers and *possible* customers about products and services the library provides. Second, the library must provide the expertise and support to make those services work. As was discussed in the section on planning, no library can provide all services that could be provided. Libraries must make choices and be able to deliver what services and products they advertise.

Is there a difference between marketing and public relations (PR)? Yes, but they are closely related. Marketing focuses on the customer while PR views the organization in reaction to the external environment.

Marketing, as was said earlier, is to inform. Marketing is not just for new services; it must also reinforce the customer's positive opinion of existing services and improve those existing services. Marketing is an ongoing and dynamic process because the needs of the customer and the library products and services constantly change.

PR is one part of the process of selling your product and services to your public. Informing the community of users and nonusers is a service on its own. It includes press and media releases, bookmarks and brochures that are promotional items, fliers, newsletters, and public service announcements. These will be discussed later in this chapter.

Because libraries operate in a competitive environment and there may be other places for families to participate in summer recreation and learning activities, libraries need to be able to identify those other places where library patrons (and prospective patrons) can get their needs met. Marketing strategies can be used to reach both library users and nonusers.

Despite the best efforts libraries make at marketing their programs and services, there are still an alarming number of people in the community who do not know about the library, where it is located, how to get a library card, what services are offered, or how to avail themselves of the riches offered by the library. Marketing is the library's attempt to educate the community about the library.

## Developing a Marketing Program

Developing a marketing plan is similar to developing a long-range plan. There are a series of steps that need to be followed.

*Step 1* in developing a marketing plan is self-assessment. During this assessment, the staff needs to look at the current services the library offers, and what services it might potentially offer. It is also the time to look at the strengths and weakness as well as the opportunities that the library faces. If your library has recently gone through a planning process and has done a SWOT (*s*trengths, *w*eaknesses, *o*pportunities, *t*hreats) exercise, you will have this information.

*Step 2*, determine which audiences you will serve. Look at the demographics in your community, the services and programs that other agencies provide, and the skill and level of expertise and knowledge the staff and volunteers have. While you may have a large teen population, if you don't have staff with the experience and temperament to serve this demanding audience, you might not want to offer summer programs for teens. As much as we want to demonstrate the equality of the sexes and treat both girls and boys equally, there are differences. If you want to attract boys to your program, remember they will be attracted to power, grossness, bravery, and will want to succeed and show mastery of some skill. Girls, on the other hand, are attracted to beauty and glamour. They tend to want to participate in programs that foster their maternal instinct. While both boys and girls are attracted to silliness, the foolishness that attracts them is different. Boys like pratfalls and physical forms of silliness, while girls will laugh at social situations, such as watching parents kiss. All children want to exert a measure of control over their world. When children and teens are free to make choices and their own decisions, they call it fun. And if an activity is fun, it is more likely that the target audience will participate in your programs. Determine which audiences you will target before you proceed to the next step.

*Step 3*, now is the time to start product planning. Look at what services are *needed* and *desired* by the public.

*Step 4* is when you work on creating the product. As with commercial product development, you need to develop quality services and test them to make sure they work. Market research—asking your clients about the products and services before you complete product development and roll them out—is an integral part of this step.

During the planning process, you need to look at the 4Ps—*product*, *price*, *place*, and *promotion*. The products are the services that the library offers its customers. While the services public libraries provide do not have a visible price tag on them, there is still a cost to the consumers that is associated with availing themselves of the services, this is the time and effort people need to use the services. There also is cost to the library to produce and deliver the product, including staff time needed to deliver the services. Place refers to where and how the products and services are delivered. Services must be accessible. The fourth and final P in this formula is promotion—how libraries inform the community what products and services are available.

*Step 5* comes once you have test-marketed your services; now you need to start selling the product. Start your selling by informing the public and prospective customers and clients about the service. Then, once you have connected the public with the service, you need to deliver the service with quality and good customer service.

*Step 6* is the final step. You need to close the loop by evaluating the service. In addition to measuring the success of the program and service, you need to look at what worked and what did not. The reason to evaluate is not to prove, but to improve, and, in marketing terms, you need to repair the service. The final element to close the loop is to report and celebrate your success. More information about evaluation can be found in Chapter 8.

## Working with the Media

As you start to market your services and develop your public-relations campaign, you need to determine *what* you want to tell, *whom* you want to tell, *when* you want to tell them, *why* you want to inform them, and *what* you want them to do once they know. In other words, you need to determine the goal for these communications.

Media releases and public service announcements will help get your message out to more people than you can reach through literature distribution in the library and the community. If you limit your publicity to distributing materials in the library, you will only be reaching people who already are library users. If one of your goals is to increase the number of people using the library, than you need to look outside your committed base of users. Media releases and public service announcements that are picked up in the local media can attract people who are not already library users. Before sending your information to the media (newspapers, radio and television stations, etc.), establish a working relationship with the youth editor, family correspondent, or education consultant. Your media releases will get more attention if people in the media know you and expect to hear about your program in advance.

### *Media Releases*

Media releases can be one of the easiest methods to get your message out to a large number of people in the community. Use library letterhead or specially designed letterhead featuring the logo for your summer program. At the top of the media release, include the date the release is prepared, your name as the "Contact Person," a phone number, and the phrase "For Immediate Release." The body of the media release should be typed, double spaced, and single sided.

As with any news story, include the five Ws: *who, what, when, where, why;* don't forget to tell them how as well. Include as much information as possible in the first paragraph; if space is limited, "stories," as your media releases will become, are often cut from the bottom up. Use short, concise, active language. Even though you must try to limit your media release to one page, don't assume readers know about the library, your program, or how it will benefit the children and families who participate. Include all important and necessary information. If the media release runs longer than one page, type the word "more" at the bottom of the page. At the end of the last page, indicate that it is the end with a device such as "# # # # # # #." If your release is longer than one page, make sure that your library's name, the subject, the date, contact person's name, and the page number are included on *each* succeeding page.

When writing a media release, be as specific as you can. Include the day of the week as well as the date and the starting and ending times of specific programs. Don't assume everyone knows where the library is located; give the exact street address. Remember, you are trying to attract people who do not already use the library. Try to slip in a sentence that will cover the long-term benefit of sustaining reading interests over the summer as well as the immediate fun of the summer program.

Find out in advance who should receive your media releases. With a small town newspaper, there may only be one person on staff. In a larger operation, you want to make sure that the youth, education, or family editor gets your information by his or her deadline. Call and find out publication schedules and deadlines. Meet the appropriate staff. Include one of your fliers, the library calendar, or schedule of events with each release.

Before you send your media release out, reread it. Check your facts, your spelling, and your grammar. Give it to someone who is not directly involved with your program and see if that person can gain the information you wish to impart. Check the reading level of your media release. Since you may be trying to attract people who have not traditionally been library users, these people might not have high literacy levels; these potential users will not read a news story that is too long or too difficult.

Keep a file of your media releases and supporting information. If possible, keep a clippings file to show which of your media releases are picked up and published. These clippings can also be used as part of your evaluation. After your releases are published, call and thank the appropriate people. If they do not get into print, call to find out how you can improve your chances of getting published. Don't forget to write the publisher of the newspaper or the station manager of the television or radio station to thank him or her.

Figure 6–2 shows a media-release template that was used as part of the Georgia 2004 Vacation Read Club, part of the Southern Cooperative Program.

Sending a media release that is a general overview of your summer library program is just the start. Follow these with individual releases for specific programs or events.

**Figure 6–2**
**Media Release Template**

Media Contact:
*(Insert Name)*
*(Insert phone)*

FOR IMMEDIATE RELEASE                              KILL DATE
*(Insert Date)*                                     *(Insert Date)*

*(Insert Library Name)* **"Steps to the Beat"**
**for Vacation Reading Program 2004**

Kids of all ages are getting ready to "step to the beat" with the Vacation Reading Program 2004 at *(insert library name)*. The theme for this year's Vacation Reading Program is "Step to the Beat . . . READ!" *(Insert library name)* has many fun activities planned for children and teens that link music, dancing and reading.

*(Insert quote from library director or children's services librarian)*

The goal of the Vacation Reading Program is to encourage children to read for pleasure at times when they are not in school. *(Insert library name)* offers special programs and incentives to encourage children of all ages, from infants to teens, to read what they enjoy, and to read often. Parents, grandparents and other caregivers are also invited to participate and to help pre-literate children enjoy books and develop a love of reading.

This year, public libraries in Georgia, South Carolina, Alabama, Mississippi and Virginia will all sponsor vacation reading programs with the same up-tempo theme. This regional cooperation began with a partnership between Georgia and South Carolina for the Vacation Reading Program in 2002. Alabama and Mississippi joined the partnership in 2003, and Virginia joined this year.

MORE

---

**Figure 6–2**
*Continued*

---

The artwork reflecting the "Step to the Beat . . . READ!" theme was designed by children's book illustrator and author Peter Catalanotto. Catalanotto has illustrated many children's books and is the author of *Dad & Me, Matthew ABC, Daisy 123, Mr. Mumble, Dylan's Day Out* and many others. The "Step to the Beat . . . READ!" artwork features penguins stepping to various beats—forming a conga line, break dancing and even rocking with "The King."

The Vacation Reading Program is supported in part by the Institute for Museum and Library Services under the provisions of the Library Services and Technology Act as administered by the Georgia Public Library Service. Additional funding is provided by *(insert local funders if appropriate.)*

For more information about the Vacation Reading Program or children's reading programs at *(insert library name),* call *(insert phone)* or visit *(insert Web site.)* The library is located at *(insert address)* and is open *(insert hours of operation).*

#########

---

Used by permission of the Georgia Public Library Service.

We all know that a picture is worth a thousand words, and the media loves to publish photographs of children. When you know that you are having a program that will provide a photo opportunity, let the media know through a photo alert. See Figure 6-3.

The media, both print and television, like to highlight children in feature stories. Remember, however, that children and their families have the right to refuse to be included in these photo opportunities. Please respect your client's requests for confidentiality. Figure 6–4, Media Release Form, can be used to obtain permission from the parent or guardian of children and young adults prior to being photographed. It actually is a good idea to do this at the beginning of the summer so that you can take photographs of the programs for inclusion on the library's Web site, in annual reports, scrapbooks, and future promotional materials.

**Figure 6–3**
**Photo Opportunity Alert**

*(Use this template to invite newspapers and TV news to cover a Vacation Reading activity or event. Send out 3-4 days in advance.)*

**MEDIA ALERT**

***(Headline)***

**WHAT:** *(Name of Activity),* Vacation Reading Program 2004, "Step to the Beat…READ!"

*(3-4 sentence description of activity)*

**WHEN:** *(Day of the week), (Month) (Day), (Time) (AM/PM)*

**WHERE:** *(Name of library), (Address)*

**PHOTO/VIDEO OPPORTUNITIES:**

*(Bulleted list of visuals and potential interviews)*

*Examples*

- *Children dressed as their favorite storybook character*
- *Children wearing penguin hats and learning a line dance*
- *Interviews with children, parents and children's library staff*
- *Drummers from the high school marching band in uniform teaching younger children how to play the drums*

**ADDITIONAL INFORMATION:**

The goal of the Vacation Reading Program is to encourage children to read for pleasure at times when they are not in school. *(Insert library name)* offers special programs and incentives to encourage children of all ages, from infants to teens, to read what they enjoy, and to read often. Parents, grandparents and other caregivers are also invited to participate and to help pre-literate children enjoy books and develop a love of reading. The Vacation Reading Program is supported in part by the Institute for Museum and Library Services under the provisions of the Library Services and Technology Act as administered by the Georgia Public Library Service. Additional funding is provided by *(insert local funders if appropriate).*

**CONTACT:**

*(Name), (Phone number), (Email)*

Used by permission of the Georgia Public Library Service.

---

**Figure 6–4**
**Media Release Form**

MEDIA RELEASE FORM


I _____

*(name of parent or guardian)*

parent or guardian of _____ , age _____

*(name of child)*

grant permission for the _____Library to take photographs of this

child for use in promotional activities related to the Summer Library Program.  Photographs may

appear in newspapers or magazines or on television, or may be used in displays in the library or

in other promotions as the library deems appropriate.



Signed _____ Date _____

    Signature of Parent or Guardian

Name (printed) of Parent or Guardian _____

Address_____

Phone _____            E-mail_____

---

## *Public Service Announcements*

Though similar to releases for the print media, public service announcements, or PSAs, are shorter and intended to be read as word-for-word scripts. They are brief announcements that can be broadcast on the air, recorded or live, on either a radio or television station. They usually run 10, 20, 30, or 60 seconds. Short words and simple sentences make your program sound as exciting as possible. Many times, PSAs are recorded by radio station staff and played back several times; for that reason, make sure you include not only a start date but a "kill" or ending date. Include a one- or two-word description of the target audience for the PSA.

Format your PSAs to make them easy to read. Include basic information about the library, its location, and whom to contact for additional information. You should also include running time of the announcement. Running time is shown in seconds. A 10-second spot is noted ":10"; a one-minute announcement as ":60." Analyze the radio stations in your service area and send your PSAs only to those whose audience is similar to the target audience you are trying to attract. While you and your friends may listen to the local National Public Radio outlet, you might have a better chance of attracting YAs to your programs if your PSA ran on a rock- or rap-oriented station. If you want your message to be heard by the parents of elementary school–age children, send your PSAs to easy listening or oldies stations. Country Western stations attract a wide age range. Most stations have defined their target audience. Call and talk with the public service or program director to see if your PSA is appropriate for a specific station. Figure 6–5 a, b, and c are examples of various PSAs. When you send your PSAs out, each one should be on a separate page.

---

**Figure 6–5a**
**Public Service Announcement—30 Seconds**

For more information, please contact                    FOR IMMEDIATE RELEASE
Name/Title
Library Name                                            AUDIENCE:  CHILDREN AND
Phone number: (   )   -                                             FAMILIES
Fax: (   )   -
E-mail:
START: ------*insert date*---------          KILL:  ------*insert date*---------

**Step to the Beat . . . READ!**
© 2003 Georgia Public Library Service
**Vacation Reading Program 2004**


PUBLIC SERVICE ANNOUNCEMENT — :30

*Verse --*
All the way from the mountains down to the sea
There's a place that was made just for you and me
You'll find stories, books, song; so much to do and see
When you're stepping to the beat at the public library

*Chorus –*
We'll be stepping to the beat on the city streets
We'll be stepping to the beat in the suburban heat
We'll be stepping to the beat in the country so sweet
Step to the beat . . . READ!

*Coda –* The reading program at your public library

---

Used by permission of the Georgia Public Library Service.

---

**Figure 6–5b**
**Public Service Announcement—60 Seconds**

---

For more information, please contact                          FOR IMMEDIATE RELEASE
Name/Title
Library Name                                                 AUDIENCE:  CHILDREN AND
Phone number: (   )   -                                                FAMILIES
Fax: (   )   -
E-mail:
START: ------*insert date*---------                           KILL:  ------*insert date*---------

**Step to the Beat . . . READ!**
© 2003 Georgia Public Library Service
**Vacation Reading Program 2004**


PUBLIC SERVICE ANNOUNCEMENT — :60

*Verse 1 --*
All the way from the mountains down to the sea
There's a place that was made just for you and me
You'll find stories, books, song; so much to do and see
When you're stepping to the beat at the public library

*Chorus –*
We'll be stepping to the beat on the city streets
We'll be stepping to the beat in the suburban heat
We'll be stepping to the beat in the country so sweet
Step to the beat . . . READ!

*Verse 2 –*
You'll be as cool as a penguin in a conga line
Just follow the library sign
You can be all a girl or boy can be
Stayin' cool at the public library

*Chorus –*
We'll be stepping to the beat on the city streets
We'll be stepping to the beat in the suburban heat
We'll be stepping to the beat in the country so sweet
Step to the beat . . . READ!

*Coda –* The reading program at your public library

---

Used by permission of the Georgia Public Library Service.

---

**Figure 6–5c**
**Public Service Announcements**

---

# PUBLIC SERVICE ANNOUNCEMENTS
# FLORIDA LIBRARY YOUTH PROGRAM 2004

For additional information, please contact:

Name/Title: _____

Organization: _____

Phone Number: (____) _____ Fax Number: (_____)_____

E-Mail: _____

Audience: Children and Families

Start Date: _____ Kill Date:_____


## PUBLIC SERVICE ANNOUNCEMENT – 10

READ ALL ABOUT IT! FROM JACKSONVILLE TO KEY WEST, PENSACOLA TO

MIAMI AND EVERY PLACE IN BETWEEN, THE ___*(LIBRARY NAME)*___LIBRARY

WILL HELP YOU **READ AROUND FLORIDA** THIS SUMMER. FOR MORE

INFORMATION CONTACT THE LIBRARY AT *(PHONE NUMBER)* .


## PUBLIC SERVICE ANNOUNCEMENT - 20

WHAT FAMOUS SCIENTIST MADE HIS HOME IN FORT MYERS? HOW MANY

LIGHTHOUSES ARE THERE IN FLORIDA? WHAT SPORTS TEAMS MAKE THEIR

HOME IN THE SUNSHINE STATE? FIND OUT AS YOU **READ AROUND FLORIDA**

DURING THE FLORIDA LIBRARY YOUTH PROGRAM AT THE _____*(LIBRARY*

*NAME)*____LIBRARY. THE FUN AND EXCITEMENT BEGINS ON __*(DATE)*_____

AT THE __*(LIBRARY NAME)*___ LIBRARY. CALL __*(PHONE NUMBER)*_____

FOR MORE INFORMATION.

If you have recording facilities and can make a studio-quality tape, you may want to have children and young adults make their own PSAs. Allow the children and YAs to write their own scripts or tape them in impromptu sessions; do not give them scripts to read. The charm of this type of spot is the natural feel that the children bring to them. Before you invest time and raise expectations of the youth involved, check with the program director of the specific radio stations to determine whether the station will be able to use these PSAs.

## *Video Promotions*

Cable television providers are usually required to provide public service announcements as part of their franchise agreement with the local government. Because of this, you may be able to get them to create a short video that can be aired on the local channels.

An example of this is the video PSA that the Bright House Network, a cable provider in central Florida, did for the Seminole County Public Library. The market area that Bright House serves covers several counties in the Orlando area. Therefore, when the video was developed, no specific summer programs were promoted; the 30-second spot promoted the summer program in general. The children's manager at the Seminole County Public Library works with the cable company to bring this project to fruition. The library is in charge of recruiting children and teens who appear in the PSA, getting permission slips from parents allowing the children and teens to appear in the PSA, and preparing the storyboard. On the day of the shoot, the cable company provides the camera operator and sound person; the library has at least two staff to help set up the scenes and keep tabs on all the children and teens who become the real stars of the PSA. Group shots are done first, and this is followed by the close ups. The entire shoot takes about two hours. The raw footage is edited by the cable company to become the 30-second spot. The voice over is read by one of the children. The cable company provides multiple copies to the several library systems that are in the region. In addition to distributing it to the libraries, who in turn share it with local schools to air on their closed-circuit televisions, Bright House plays them on youth-oriented channels, such as Nickelodeon.

Because all of the public libraries in the geographic area served by this cable company participate in the statewide summer library program and, therefore, use the same theme and graphics, it benefits all libraries in the region. The purposes of informing prospective patrons about activities in all libraries and generating interest in children's summer programs were met with this commercial. And Bright House looks good in the community by providing this public service.

## *Billboards*

An area of promotion that libraries often overlook is billboard advertising. One of the reasons for this may be that the advertisement on the billboard needs to be in place for a longer time than most libraries are willing to commit to. The message needs to be of lasting value to the library and the community. While the impact of billboard advertising is difficult to assess, it is a powerful way to deliver a message to the community.

Most billboard companies have a design department that can assist with developing the layout and design of the billboard. Text on the billboard should be kept simple and to a minimum; the font should be clean and readable from a distance. The graphic should convey the message. When possible, enlarge and adapt some of the other print promotional materials (posters and bookmarks, both of which are discussed later in this chapter) to fit this format.

The location of the billboard in the community is important. It may be possible to place the advertisement in an area of the community where there are few library users but high numbers of your target audience. If the billboard you contract to use is located on a route that is used by commuters, you may promote the program to people who use other libraries. This presents an opportunity to partner with other libraries in your region.

Some billboard locations are not rented as frequently as others and, therefore, might not be as costly to use. You might be able to convince a billboard advertising company to provide a billboard on a pro bono basis or at a reduced cost.

## Products to Promote Your Program

### *Printed Promotional Materials*

Whether you are designing your own materials or purchasing them from a commercial vendor, common principles apply. Look at the layout and design of the posters, bookmarks, reproducible sheets, and reading logs. Has the artist consistently interpreted the theme on the various items? If there is a mascot character, is the character consistent throughout or does it look different in each pose? Is the message in the text clear? While an Old English-style font may appeal to you if you are doing a medieval theme, that type font may be difficult to read. A catch phrase that is too long may take up too much space on the poster. Will the artist's interpretation of the theme appeal to your target audience? One of the reasons that many libraries don't have success in attracting YAs to their summer programs is that they use the same art for all ages. What appeals to a 5-year-old does not hold the same attraction for a 15-year-old. Are the art and lettering on the poster bold enough to be seen clearly from a distance? Is the color combination or full-color art pleasing? Be careful about using red as a predominant color if your posters are going to be placed in store windows of neighborhood establishments; it tends to fade over time when exposed to sunlight.

Even if you are having your posters specially designed, you will want to be able to customize them for individual programs and events. Whether designing your own or purchasing them from a commercial vendor, look for an open space that has been worked into the design and layout where you can add information about your programs. At a minimum, you should be able to add the name and location of your library and the dates of your programs. If purchasing materials, make certain that you can buy posters and bookmarks untrimmed so that you can have a local printer overprint these items, adding your information. If you are not financially able to have a printer add your custom information, buy the items trimmed and use a lettering machine or press-on letters to customize the posters. By using a computer, you can print custom information onto clear labels and affix them onto the posters without interfering with the design. You may want to invest in a rubber stamp that is the same size as the bookmark. The rubber stamp should provide all the necessary information about your program. Have teen volunteers stamp the information on the back of the bookmarks before you distribute them.

When having materials designed for you and including a book character in your materials, make certain that you have all necessary copyright clearances. While most children's book illustrators will be flattered if you use their characters, children's books are covered by the copyright law and written permissions must be obtained. Just because you have purchased a rubber stamp from Kidstamps or another vendor, that does not mean that you have permission to enlarge that image to use as the basis of your posters and other promotional materials.

When you contract with a graphic or commercial artist or a children's book illustrator, you will need to specify exactly what pieces you want him or her to supply. Decide in advance how many sheets you will need in the reproducible masters pack. Let the artist know if there are limitations on the number of colors that can be used or if a specific color scheme is required. If possible, have the artist provide all of the art on a computer disc in the enhanced post script format (ESP) that printers use. If you are going to use the art on your Web site as well, then the files must also be provided in jpg format. The artist will also need to know the printing requirements, e.g., if the poster and the bookmarks require margins or if a "full bleed" is allowed. Full bleed is a technique in which posters are printed larger than the finished size so that the image and color extends to the edge of the finished product. This uses more paper and thus it may become more expensive than having a border. When you are having materials designed for you, decide in advance if you have exclusive rights to the images that the artist is developing for you and your program. Also decide who will hold the copyright on the materials. Many times other librarians who see your materials want to use them for their programs; you need to know if the other libraries requesting permission to use your logo and art work need to negotiate with the artist or whether your library controls the rights. Be certain that you negotiate these things with the artist right at the beginning. Take nothing for granted.

Many artists sell their originals after a project is done. If you want to develop a collection of original art used for your programs, make certain that ownership of the originals by the library is included in your contract with the artist.

Once you are satisfied with the design of the materials, you have to be concerned with reproduction. There are certain aspects of this process you need to be concerned with whether you are buying commercially produced materials or producing them yourself. The weight of the paper is extremely important, as is the texture and coating. Posters should be reproduced on 100-pound paper. A coating or varnish once the ink dries helps intensify the colors; it also acts as a preservative. This coating, however, makes it difficult for local printers to overprint the customized printing. Varnish can be applied to all but the area where the overprinting will go.

Bookmarks should be printed on heavier stock, such as 8-point chromecoat. Since you are encouraging children with visual disabilities to participate in your program, you need to supply bookmarks that they can read; you need paper that will be able to hold Braille impressions. Reproducible masters should be on glossy paper, thus producing a high-quality copy when reproduced locally.

Each program offers many types of materials. Knowing how they can be used will make your job of deciding which ones are necessary for your program a little easier.

### Posters

Posters are an inexpensive way to deliver your message visually throughout your community. Posters may come in a variety of sizes; costs to produce or purchase vary according to the size. Large posters (36 inches by 24 inches) are quite attractive and are easily visible. Their size, however, limits the places where they can be displayed. Smaller posters, ranging in size from 11 inches by 17 inches to 18 inches by 24 inches, are more likely to be accepted by local merchants for display in their windows. Large posters are usually not accepted in supermarkets for display on their community bulletin boards, but the smaller ones are.

Displaying posters in the library will help inform library users of your schedule of events for the summer. If you do not have sufficient space to add all of your local program information on the smaller poster, mount the poster on a larger sheet of poster board or foam core. Use the extra space to highlight specific programs and special events.

An imaginative alternative to posters are window clings. When working with the artist and production people on the posters, discuss how to take elements of the poster to create window clings that may be of more interest to local businesses than paper posters. Retailers have limited wall space; it is taken up with the products they are trying to sell. If you provide something they can affix to the windows and doors, they may be more likely to assist you in promoting the summer library program.

### Bookmarks

This inexpensive promotional item is an extremely effective form of publicity. Purchase them in sufficient quantities so that they can be distributed to every student during your spring visits to schools when you promote your summer program. You should also distribute them to other child-serving agencies in your service area; their clients should be informed of your programs and this is an easy way to remind them of your services. Bookmarks should also be available at all service points in the library from about one month before your program begins through the end of the summer.

In addition to purchasing printed bookmarks, some libraries may opt to use die-cut bookmarks. Letter press machines such as ones from Accu-Cut Systems and Ellison Educational Equipment, Inc., make easy work of creating these items. These die-cut items provide visual interest and the unusual shape is appropriate for use with children with visual disabilities.

As previously discussed, the library name and address and the dates of the program should be printed or stamped on whatever bookmarks you decide to distribute.

## *Reading Logs*

Reading logs are the traditional way for children to keep track of the books they read. Their format can vary from a bookmark to a folder to an activity booklet that includes the reading log. Traditionally, only readers were allowed to take part in this activity. In response to the growing number of prereaders who are participating in summer library programs, many libraries now have a "read to me" log in which the child and the adult reader can track books that have been shared.

Many libraries keep reading logs for program participants at a specially designated desk in the library staffed by teen volunteers and library staff. A child who wants to be able to record a book on his or her log must be able to tell about the book. Not only can this get to be very labor intensive, it can also discourage some children who find the reporting aspect a chore. This record keeping is necessary if awards and prizes are given when a certain number of books are read. This book counting does not really encourage children to read more books or to read more widely; rather, it may encourage some children to read as many short books as they can to get a prize they might not really care about.

Rather than counting number of books read, many libraries are now recording minutes read. Counting time spent reading or being read to rather than the number of books read or heard really puts the emphasis on the act of reading. It equalizes the amount of effort required by individuals with varying reading abilities. Counting time rewards slow, poor, or reluctant readers who must plod through a book with the same prize as the good reader, someone who already has discovered the pleasures of reading, someone who finds reading to be easy. All readers, regardless of ability, are rewarded equally for their efforts, regardless of how quickly they read or how many books or pages they complete.

However, since the goal of many summer library reading programs is to turn children and teens into lifelong readers, we need to design reading records that show how regularly children read or are read to. We want to establish the habit of reading every day. (See Chapters 2 and 3 for a more complete discussion of this.) While binge reading can be fun, we want children to become accustomed to reading something on a daily basis. Therefore, reading logs should include some type of calendar where readers can record if they read on a daily basis.

To encourage parental involvement and encourage them to read to their younger children, many libraries also provide read-to-me logs. Figure 6–7 is the master read-to-me log that the State Library and Archives of Florida provided to public libraries during the summer of 2004. Local libraries can customize both the reading log and the read-to-me log before they print them locally.

Many libraries have the participants of the summer library program track other library-related activities. Participants are encouraged to check off activities in which they engage. Library activities that may be included on this list include attending a program, watching a video that was borrowed from the library, reading aloud to someone, listening to a story that someone else reads, participating in an art activity at the library, writing a story, listening to a musical or spoken-word sound recording (cassette or CD) from the library, using the library's public-access computer, or similar

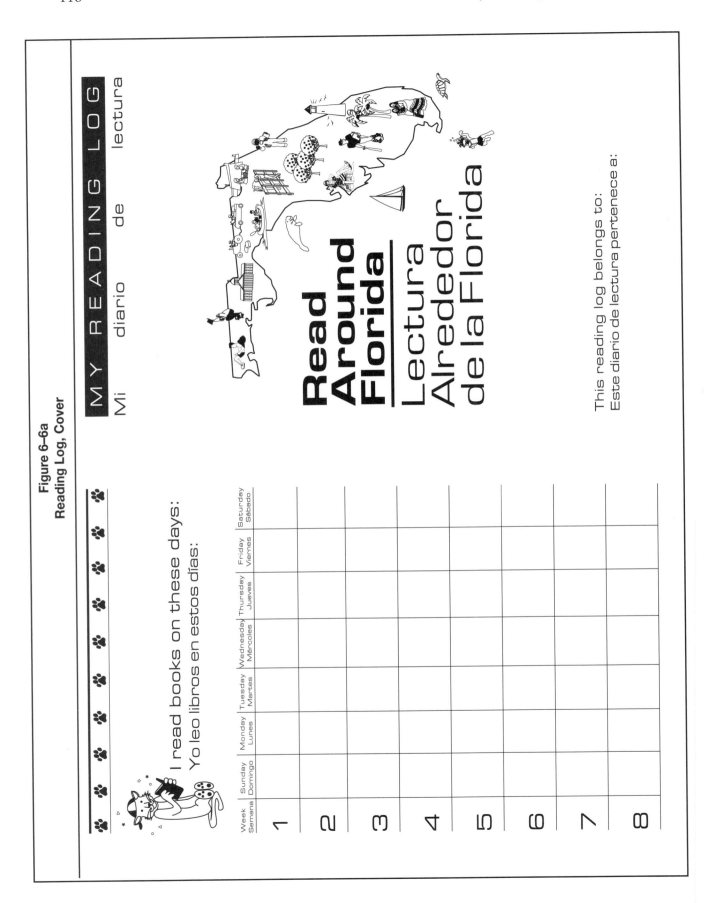

**Figure 6–6a
Reading Log, Cover**

MY READING LOG
Mi     diario     de     lectura

Read
Around
Florida
Lectura
Alrededor
de la Florida

This reading log belongs to:
Este diario de lectura pertenece a:

I read books on these days:
Yo leo libros en estos días:

| Week Semana | Sunday Domingo | Monday Lunes | Tuesday Martes | Wednesday Miércoles | Thursday Jueves | Friday Viernes | Saturday Sábado |
|---|---|---|---|---|---|---|---|
| 1 | | | | | | | |
| 2 | | | | | | | |
| 3 | | | | | | | |
| 4 | | | | | | | |
| 5 | | | | | | | |
| 6 | | | | | | | |
| 7 | | | | | | | |
| 8 | | | | | | | |

**Figure 6–6b**
**Reading Log, Inside Page**

Books I have read totally on my own:

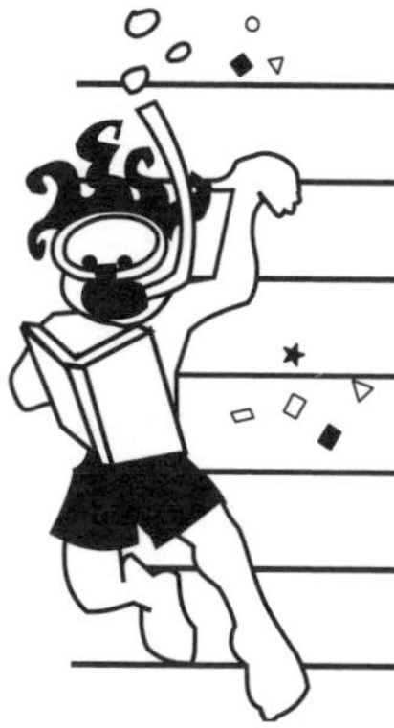

Libros que he leído completamente por mi cuenta:

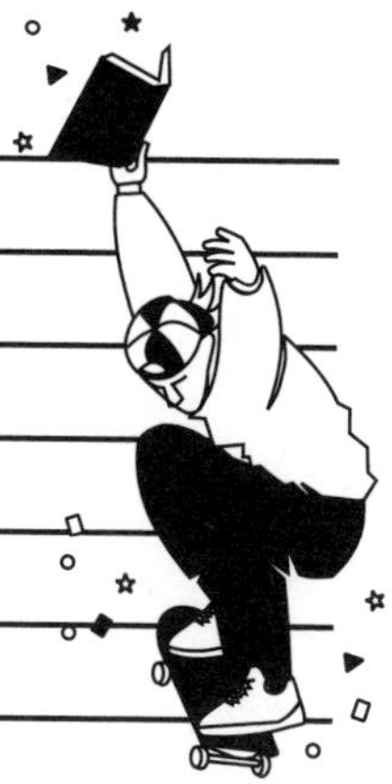

Used by permission of the State Library and Archives of Florida.

**Figure 6–7a**
**Read-to-Me Log, Cover**

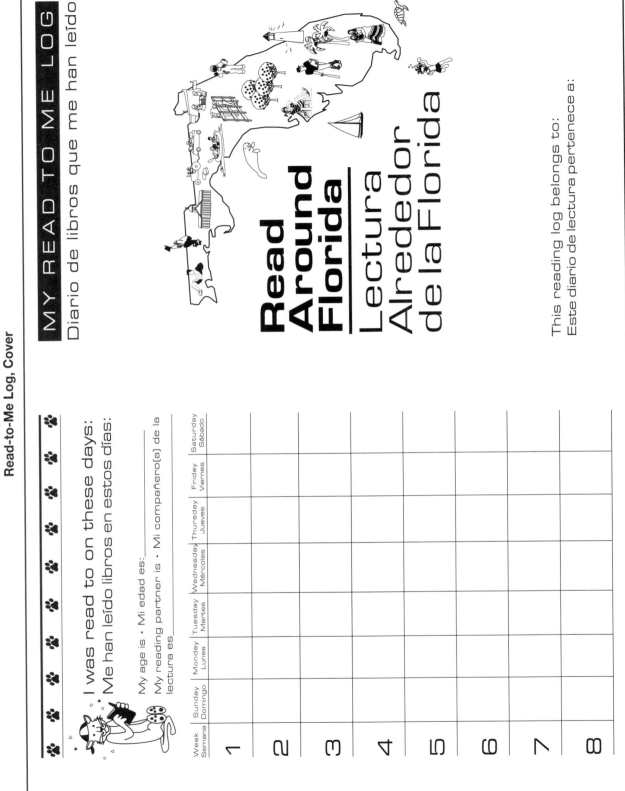

MY READ TO ME LOG
Diario de libros que me han leído

Read Around Florida
Lectura Alrededor de la Florida

I was read to on these days:
Me han leído libros en estos días:

My age is • Mi edad es:_____
My reading partner is • Mi compañero(a) de la lectura es _____

This reading log belongs to:
Este diario de lectura pertenece a:

| Week Semana | Sunday Domingo | Monday Lunes | Tuesday Martes | Wednesday Miércoles | Thursday Jueves | Friday Viernes | Saturday Sábado |
|---|---|---|---|---|---|---|---|
| 1 | | | | | | | |
| 2 | | | | | | | |
| 3 | | | | | | | |
| 4 | | | | | | | |
| 5 | | | | | | | |
| 6 | | | | | | | |
| 7 | | | | | | | |
| 8 | | | | | | | |

**Figure 6–7b**
**Read-to-Me Log, Inside Page**

Books I have read along with a friend.

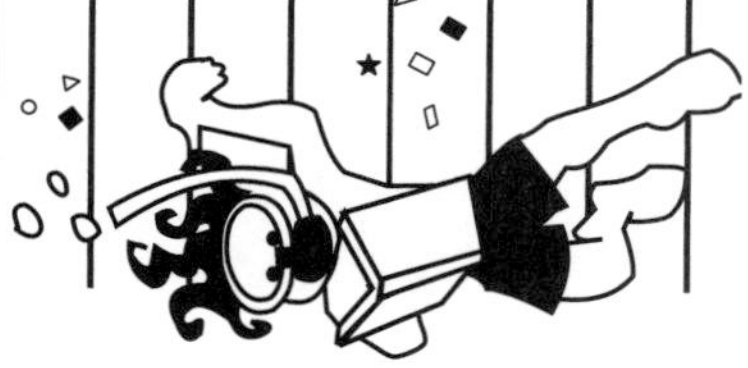

Libros que he leído con un[a] amigo[a].

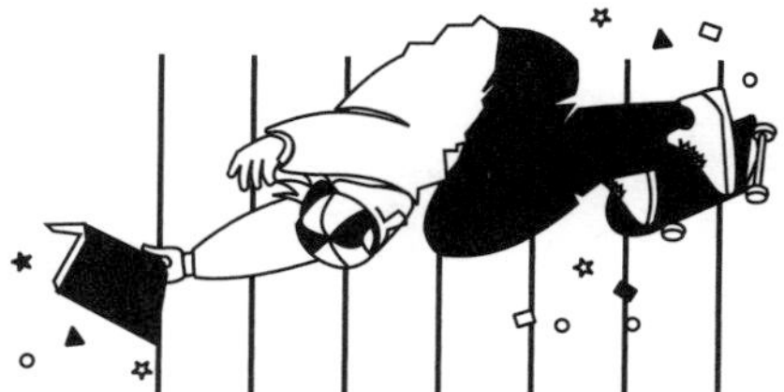

Used by permission of the State Library and Archives of Florida.

activities. By logging a variety of activities, those children who have a difficult time reading can still experience success during your summer library program. This success may lead them back to the library later, and eventually, they may become the lifelong readers and library users that we hope they will become.

In addition to having printed reading logs available for distribution, make sure there is a method for recording and tracking patron's reading is included in the registration database discussed in Chapter 5. Having patrons maintain their reading records in the database eliminates the need to keep patrons' reading records manually and eliminates the need to provide multiple copies of the reading log.

### *Reproducible Masters*

There are numerous items that libraries make available to the participants during the summer library programs. Not all of them need be commercially printed; many can be reproduced on the library copy machine or at a local copy shop. Producing these items locally allows libraries to customize them to the needs and interests of their local participants. Producing them locally also has another benefit; if you produce them as needed, you won't have to store them. Some of the items that may be included in the summer library program manual or in a separate reproducible pack include a logo sheet; activity sheets such as coloring sheets, follow-the-dot game sheets, mazes, word searches, crossword puzzles; and doorknob hangers. The best reproducible masters have high definition and are printed on high-gloss, white paper.

Logo sheets are an invaluable tool for designing locally produced promotional materials. A logo sheet provides the program character and slogan in several sizes and formats. Sometimes the slogan is provided in several font styles, such as bold, script, or outline. These logo sheets can be photocopied and enlarged or reduced as needed. They are used to create program announcements, invitations for guest speakers, thank-you notes, and letterhead that can be used for media releases. The point to having these logo sheets is to have a consistent visual image for your program. Copies of logo sheets should also accompany media releases and PSAs that you send to television stations and the print media.

Take-home coloring sheets and activity sheets, such as word-search or follow-the-dots puzzles, that are created specifically for your program help extend the activities from the library into the home. Under no circumstances should a library reproduce pages from a coloring book or a crossword-puzzle book without first obtaining written permission to do so from the copyright holder. This type of material is usually designed as a consumable supply, to be used once by a single user and then discarded. Occasionally, a publisher may grant permission to a library to make a specific and limited number of copies of one or two pages from a book that was designed to be consumed by one child. Don't assume that you can do so, however, without getting copyright clearance in writing. It is wise to allow a minimum of ten weeks to obtain copyright clearance in writing. Check the status of your request after four weeks and follow up with a reminder letter if necessary.

If the materials you purchase do not include activity sheets, you can create your own. Rather than trying to get permission to duplicate a crossword puzzle that has little or no relation to your program and its theme, construct your own using computer software. Many word-puzzle generating programs are available as commercial software packages or on the Internet. Creating word searches and crossword puzzles is as simple as inputting lists of words, authors, book titles, or words related to your theme. Use the clip art from the logo sheet to enhance the printout, then duplicate it for your patrons. By doing this, you can create puzzles as simple or as complicated as needed to meet the skills, interests, and reading levels of your participants.

## Newsletters

Newsletters are another method you can use to promote your summer library reading programs. Many libraries print a newsletter that is distributed on a regular basis—monthly, bimonthly, or quarterly. It is a great venue to promote these programs. A front-page article in the library newsletter is sure to be seen by those people who take the time to look at the newsletter. Unfortunately, these readers may already be library users, and if your goal is to generate new users, this might not generate the type of interest you want to develop. If you do special mailings to teachers, child-care providers, and people who work with other child-serving agencies, you may have more impact.

## Web Sites

Interactive Web sites are marketing tools in and of themselves and, when well designed, help reinforce the idea that summer library reading programs are fun as well as educational. Web sites make the summer program available even to those who are unable to visit the library in person as long as they have access to the Internet. Banners on Web sites should incorporate program graphics and color schemes. In addition to providing bibliographies and program schedules, Web sites can include an interactive way for participants to comment on books they have read as part of the summer program. Interactive games that expand and enhance the paper-and-pencil activity sheets that are distributed on site at the library will entice readers to use the site. A summer library program Web site should also include links to related Web sites. When designing Web sites, care needs to be taken to make certain that they are usable by patrons with disabilities. See chapter 4 for more information about making Web sites accessible to people with disabilities.

## Fliers

Another inexpensive way to promote your programs is to design fliers. Using the art work from your program, include information that targets a specific audience or provides a general introduction to your program. The New York State Library prepared a series of fliers with the statewide theme that local libraries could duplicate and distribute to specific audiences. Knowing that the library trustees are influential in the community, one of the fliers was targeted at them. Figure 6–8 is the trustee flier that libraries in New York State used during the summer of 2004.

Including the education community in your targeted promotion will help to build that necessary bridge between the public library and schools. Modifying the message

**Figure 6–8**
**Flier for Trustees**

© 2003 Ed Young

# *Trustees!*

## Help your young patrons with their reading skills...

**Encourage them to read all summer with**

## New York is Read, White and Blue!

### the New York State Library's summer reading program.

The **Statewide Summer Reading Program** will help kids maintain and improve reading levels over the summer while they have fun with books, enjoy reading-related activities, use computers and safely surf the Internet, create craft projects, and interact with their peers.

Studies show that **reading as a leisure activity** is one of the most powerful tools to **increase reading comprehension, speed and vocabulary**. For details, go to **www.nysl.nysed.gov/libdev/summer/research.htm**. **Unstructured reading for pleasure** of materials that children select themselves is **extremely effective in promoting literacy**, even when compared to direct reading instruction. Significant learning losses occur over the summer if children don't read, especially among children from lower income families.

Encourage the kids in your community to **sign up at their local public library, branch, or reading center**, and let them know that **participating kids will be eligible to win a collection of books from Scholastic Inc.**

For more information and resources, go to **www.summerreadingnys.org**
or contact Anne Simon at the New York State Library
via email at **asimon@mail.nysed.gov** or phone **(518) 486-2194**

to meet the educators' needs and couching it in their vocabulary will make a better impression. Figure 6–9 shows how the New York State Library took the same information that they provided to the trustees and modified it to create a flier targeted directly to educators.

## Reading Incentives

In chapter 1, we discussed the philosophy of rewarding children for reading. While some children respond to such incentives, don't make the incentive the be all and end all; rather, the incentive should be the means by which reluctant readers are hooked on the reading habit. Having contests where only the one child who reads the greatest number of books wins creates a situation in which only one participant wins and all the others lose. Prizes should be given in such a way that everyone has an equal chance of winning, and that there are many winners at various age, ability, and developmental levels.

Rather than incentives being considered as prizes, they should be thought of as another means of promoting your program. Incentives should be a low-cost way to remind people about the program. Incentives need to reflect the program theme and be developmentally appropriate for your target audience. The incentives themselves should be oriented to the age(s) of your target audience(s); those that please only the parent or caregiver are not appropriate. Care should be taken to make sure that whatever incentive is distributed is safe. For example, the 1996 Florida Library Youth Program theme, "Rhythm and Books—Feel the Beat," was especially suited to some type of musical instrument. The toy kazoos that were affordable and within the program budget had a removable ring that could be swallowed by young children; therefore, it was decided that this incentive would not be appropriate. Instead, the program took advantage of a fad and had temporary tattoos produced with our mascot character and our program slogan on them. While some parents objected to the tattoos, most of the children and teens thought they were "awesome!" Other libraries report success using imprinted water bottles, Frisbees, and CD cases as program incentives and rewards for their 'tweens and teens.

Incentives are one area in which you can really take advantage of fads and pop culture. A particularly successful incentive was the specially produced pogs that the State Library of Florida produced in 1995 to accompany the statewide program that introduced a new mascot character, a Florida panther named Flyp. Since the Florida Library Youth Program planning committee was trying especially hard to attract upper-elementary-age children, the use of this incentive was extremely suitable as pogs were of interest to that age group. We were very lucky that we hit the peak of the pog fad during the summer of 1995, when the local libraries were distributing these items. This is an example of satisfying a need (actually two—to be part of a group and to have fun) and wrapping it in a fad. Had we waited to produce and distribute pogs for the 1996 program, it would have been a disaster as it appeared that no one in Florida was collecting pogs at that time. The only thing worse than not having any incentives to distribute is to distribute one that is out-of-date.

**Figure 6–9**
**Flier to Educators**

© 2003 Ed Young

# *Educators!*

## Help your students raise their reading skills over the summer...

*Encourage them to read all summer with*

# New York is Read, White and Blue!

### the New York State Library's summer reading program.

Studies  show that **reading as a leisure activity** is one of the most powerful tools to **increase reading comprehension, speed and vocabulary. Unstructured reading for pleasure** of **materials that children select themselves** is **extremely effective in promoting literacy**, even when compared to direct reading instruction. Significant learning losses occur over the summer if children don't read, especially among children from lower income families.

The **free reading programs** at your local public library will help students **maintain and improve reading levels** over the summer while they have **fun** with books, reading-related fun, computers and the Internet, craft projects, and fun with their peers.

Encourage your students to **sign up at their local public library**, branch, or reading center, and let them know that participating kids will be **eligible to win a collection of books** from Scholastic Inc.

**Please share your ideas! Contact your local public library for other ways to promote summer reading.**

For more information and resources, go to **www.summerreadingnys.org**
or contact Anne Simon at the New York State Library
via email at **asimon@mail.nysed.gov; phone (518) 486-2194**

Whether you are having specially designed incentives prepared or are just purchasing in bulk, contact advertising specialty companies in your area; you'll find them in the yellow pages under "advertising specialties." These companies have access to numerous products with various price points. Prices vary not only by product but by the quantity needed. The more you need, the lower the cost per item. Here especially, combining orders from several libraries using the same theme can result in substantial savings. Having your pencils, plastic bags, water bottles, CD cases, or pogs imprinted with a special message and identification creates an image for your library. As your incentives travel through your community, even those who do not know about the program or your library are exposed to your message.

If yours is a smaller program and you either do not have the funds to do specially imprinted materials or do not want to create your own incentives but you still want to provide something, look at catalogs from toy and library-promotion companies. Often they have items that are appropriate for distribution to your participants. For example, if your program is centered on a theme such as "Weave a Story Web," you might want to distribute spider rings as they pick up on the spider web concept that is part of the theme. Or, if your program is centered on animals, there are numerous items that can enhance the theme. While plastic bags are always popular with adults, they are not as youth oriented as pencil toppers. Depending on the age of your participants, they might enjoy stickers. Pencils themselves are a utilitarian and necessary school supply and as such always welcome, but a rainbow-foil hologram pencil will have your participants clambering for more. Check with companies such as the JanWay Company, Rivershore Reading Store, and others for ideas. In addition to the suppliers listed in chapter 5, see a list of suppliers and vendors at the end of this chapter for additional suggestions.

## Setting the Stage

In many ways, the library becomes a stage for the summer, a stage upon which your program will enfold. Not only should your program area have decorations related to your theme, but the entire library should help carry out your program. This is especially true if you are having family programs with adults tracking their reading, too. You want visitors to the library to be drawn into your reading scheme from the moment they set foot inside.

While not all libraries will feel that it is appropriate to have decorations throughout the library, posters advertising the program should be prominently displayed near the library entrance and by the meeting and program rooms. Posters should also be displayed on the community bulletin board in the library. Bookmarks should be placed at every public service desk. Program fliers that announce and detail your programs should be available not only in the youth areas, but at the reference and circulation desks.

Decorating the youth areas can help library visitors imagine that they are on a pirate ship or preparing for an excursion to a foreign country. If your theme relates to life undersea, hang blue and green streamers representing the ocean from the ceiling of the youth department before the program begins. As one of your first program activities, you might want the participants to make fish, sea horses, jelly fish, and other sea creatures and add them to the display. Continue turning the youth area into an underwater world by transforming the service desk into a sunken ship.

During the summer of 2004, the Indianapolis-Marion County (Ind.) Public Library was fortunate to have the "NASA @ your library" Traveling Exhibit at their Glendale Branch Library. This interactive exhibit was developed by the National Aeronautics and Space Administration (NASA) and the Association for Library Service to Children (ALSC), a division of the ALA, with major funding provided by NASA and Apple. To coordinate with this exhibit, the library system selected "2004: A Space Odyssey" as the theme of the summer reading program. All promotional materials used this space theme, as did the decorations in the library. Stars abounded as did mission patches, space aliens, and space vehicles. Even though the NASA exhibit was housed at only one branch, all branches in the system were decorated to expand and enhance this space theme. Program incentives also centered on the space theme. Figure 6–10 shows some of the materials that the library produced and distributed.

Book displays help carry out your theme. Book displays, in addition to being attractive, are a passive way to provide reader and materials guidance. Don't forget to include appropriate audiovisual materials, including books on tape, videos, and DVDs.

"Decorating" the staff will also help people further identify the program. Whether you wear a costume or have T-shirts emblazoned with the program logo, you are sure to get positive comments. Costumes do not have to be elaborate or expensive; they just have to help expand your theme. For example, if your program is "Summer Yummers," a food-related program, you may want to wear something as simple as a chef's hat and apron. Star Trek–style shirts expand a space-related theme.

You may need to have some temporary props and decorations for specific programs. If you are having an open mike type of program where teens try their hands at being performers, you will need to be able to turn your meeting room into a nightclub. Borrow small tables and tablecloths from other members of the staff and the teens themselves. By providing the proper environment, the participants feel that they are, indeed, in a nightclub. The performers receive a better reception when the setting is right.

## Community Partnerships to Promote Visibility

The library is only one of the many social, educational, service, and cultural institutions in the community that is trying to influence and improve the lives of children, young adults, and their families. Each of these institutions has specific goals and objectives as well as programs and services that it offers. Many of these goals are compatible with the goals of the library. Since so many librarians are committed to improving the lives of children and the library and these other agencies have limited resources, libraries need to explore how they can work cooperatively with these other institutions to achieve common these goals and work towards the shared vision.

**Figure 6–10**
**Promotional Pieces from Indianapolis, Indiana**

A

B

C

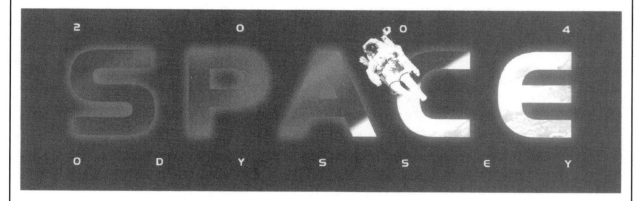

D

The Indianapolis-Marion County Public Library incorporated the NASA @ your library exhibit into their 2004 summer program. Materials were produced in full color. Above are several of the items the library used. A and C are the double sided pogs featuring astronauts from Indiana. There was a series of pogs that readers could collect and insert onto a pog board. B is the logo for the summer program. D is part of one of the posters used to promote the program.

A: Janice Voss - Front
B: Official 2004 SRP Logo on Black contrast
C: Janice Voss - Back
D: Space Logo with text

Partnerships and collaborations, though closely related, are not exactly the same. According to the *American Heritage Dictionary of the English Language,* to collaborate means "to work together, especially in a joint intellectual effort." Collaborative efforts allow youth-serving librarians to work in concert with others who have similar goals and interests. Once these similar goals are identified, those working in collaboration can provide support towards the shared vision.

A partnership is an association that involves a greater commitment on the part of all those working towards that shared vision. A partnership usually involves a more formal commitment. Often, there is a contract or letter of agreement in which all parties agree how responsibilities—monetary, staffing, space, etc.—are shared. Many times, one agency will provide staff, another will provide office space, and a third materials, all of which will be used to successfully implement a project for which all the agencies share beliefs and a philosophy.

Library staff and the staff of other youth-serving agencies are not the only ones who work in partnership and collaboration. Animals work naturally together, knowing that combined efforts are much more economical than individual and repetitive efforts. Figure 6–11, "Geese Have This All Figured Out," tells how geese work together and how we can apply the same principles demonstrated by their actions.

Examples of how libraries are involved in different types of partnerships are found throughout the remainder of this book.

### *Partnerships and Collaborative Efforts with the Education Community*

One of the simplest ways to get the word out to the children and young adults you are trying to reach with your summer library program is to visit as many schools as you can during the late spring. Schools know the value of your program, and many are willing and able to assist you in scheduling your visits.

As soon as you know your theme, have completed your schedule, and know the details of your summer program, contact the school district administration office and secure permission to distribute literature about your program as well as to visit the schools. Figure 6–12 is a sample letter that you can use to send to the district superintendent. In many school districts, you will need to obtain permission from the superintendent before you approach the local schools.

Sometimes the school superintendent will agree to send letters home with each pupil; sometimes this can be accomplished as a cooperative effort with the parent-teacher or home and school association. Figure 6–13 is a sample letter to parents that you may want to provide for that purpose. Adapt this and the other letters with your program theme, dates, and objectives. All letters should be written on library letterhead.

Once you have obtained permission to visit the schools, you will want to communicate with the principals at each of your area schools. Provide as much information about your program as you can. Be clear as to what information you want the schools to provide to you before you make your in-person promotion to your target audience. Figure 6–14 provides you with a guide on how to approach that aspect of your promotion. Adapt this letter to tell child-care center operators

**Figure 6–11**
**Geese Have This All Figured Out**

# GEESE *Have This All Figured Out*

*A*s each goose flaps its wings, it creates an "uplift" for the bird following. By following in a V formation, the whole flock adds 71 percent more flying range than if each bird flew alone.

*Lesson*: People who share a common direction and sense of community can get where they are going quicker and easier because they are traveling on the thrust of one another.

*W*henever a goose flies out of formation, it suddenly feels the drag and resistance of trying to fly alone and quickly gets back into formation to take advantage of the lifting power of the birds immediately in front.

*Lesson*: If we have as much sense as a goose, we will join in formation with those who are heading where we want to go.

*W*hen the lead goose gets tired, it rotates back into the formation and another goose flies at the point position.

*Lesson*: It pays to take turns doing the hard tasks and sharing leadership with people, as well as with geese, interdependent with one another.

*T*he geese in formation honk from behind to encourage those up front to keep up their speed.

*Lesson*: We need to make sure our honking from behind is encouraging—not something less helpful.

*W*hen a goose gets sick or wounded or shot down, two geese drop out of formation and follow their fellow member down to help and provide protection. They stay with this member of the flock until he or she either is able to fly again or dies. Then they launch out on their own, with another formation, or to catch up with their own flock.

*Lesson*: If we have as much sense as the geese, we'll stand by one another as they do.

— **Author Unknown**

---

**Figure 6–12**
**Sample Letter to the School District Superintendent**

---

(Type on Library Letterhead)

(Date)

(Inside Address)


Dear _____(*Name*):

The _____ Library is finalizing plans for our summer reading program. The goals of our program are to encourage children to keep reading during the summer and to introduce them to the public library as a place for lifelong learning. We appreciate your school district's help in getting the word out about summer reading and helping us to make these goals a reality. We would like your permission to contact your principals to arrange for visits during _____(*month[s]*).

We are excited about this year's summer reading theme, "Read Around the World." Children who participate will maintain or improve their reading skills while learning about multicultural experiences, world travel, and geography in a fun-filled series of programs and activities.

Enclosed is a copy of the letter that I would like to send to your principals. If you have any questions or concerns, please contact me within the next week or so (*or your time period*). We would like to send the letter out to them so that it arrives at the school by _____ (*date*).

I'm sure we agree that the ability to read and to enjoy reading are important factors in the future success of today's children. We look forward to working with you to encourage reading and increasing our children's ability to fulfill their dreams.

Sincerely,



(Your name)
(Title)

---

Used by permission of the Idaho State Library.

and their staff how the summer library reading program offered by your library can enhance their program. Be sure to tell what services you can offer their type of agency and how they can contact you.

In a study conducted in 1995, it was found that 47% of the parents who signed their children up for the summer program with the County of Los Angeles Public Library (COLAPL) were regular library users; only 21 percent of parents had heard about the summer library program from the school their children attended. While initial plans to inform parents through a special promotional program fell through because of a lack of funds, an adaptation of the original idea came to fruition in 2001. The nearby Torrance Public Library got permission to place stickers on report card envelops. The effort was a success; registration for the summer program expanded

---

**Figure 6–13**
**Sample Letter to Parents**

(Type on Library Letterhead)

(Date)

Dear Parent:

The _____Library invites your family to visit the library and to participate in the 1995 summer reading program.  Our theme is "Read Around the World" and a series of activities, books, and special events is planned for children ages (or grades) _____to _____.

Kids who read succeed.  Reading is important because students who read well and enjoy reading attain a higher success rate during their school years.  Reading skills also improve dramatically when students discover reading is fun.

Your child can register for the program _____(*first registration period*).  The summer reading program will begin _____ and run through _____.
Weekly programs will include _____ (list several planned activities).

All children who participate will receive _____ (*list program materials that you will use*).  (*Explain how you will keep track of books read and what and how incentives will be used. Include information about your preschool Read Aloud program if it is a part of summer reading.*) Children of all reading abilities are welcome.

Contact the library at _____(*address and phone number*) for a complete schedule of events.  Library hours are _____ (*list*).

We look forward to helping your child maintain or improve his or her reading skills while learning about multicultural experiences, world travel and geography in a fun-filled series of programs and activities.

Sincerely,

(Your Name)
(Title)

Used by permission of the Idaho State Library.

from 1,800 to 2,300. In addition to providing information to parents about the summer library program and promoting a better relationship with the schools, the library maintained a spreadsheet that listed every program participant as well as each participant's school and grade. At the end of the summer, the library sent letters to the principal of each school.[1]

Visiting each classroom can be a very time-consuming undertaking. In large schools and communities where there are large student populations, you may not be able to visit every classroom. Rather than making a series of 15-minute presentations in each

---

**Figure 6–14**
**Sample Letter to School Principals**

---

(Type on Library Letterhead)

(Date)

(Inside Address)

Dear _____(Name):

The _____ Library is excited about this year's summer reading program and we are getting ready to let the children and parents in _____ (*your city, county, or district*) know about our plans. We hope that you will help us in promoting the program. In _____month(s), our staff would like to visit your school and tell your students and faculty about our summer of reading and programs.

We are excited about this year's summer reading theme, "Read Around the World." Children who participate will maintain or improve their reading skills while learning about multicultural experiences, world travel, and geography in a fun-filled series of programs and activities.

To publicize our summer reading program, we would like to speak briefly with the children in _____ (*list grades*). Our presentation lasts _____ minutes and can accommodate _____(*size of group*) at a time. We hope that it will not be too difficult to fit us into your busy year-end schedule.

Please let us know if you would like to arrange a visit from us. If so, we will need the following information:
    Total number of students
    Number of classes in each grade level
    Number of students in each class
    Location of our visit – library, gym, classroom
    Suggested date and time of our visit.

I have enclosed a copy of a flyer that we would like to distribute during our school visit. Because many children do not arrive home with the flyers, we would appreciate it if you could include the information in your final school flyer or newsletter as a reminder to parents.

If you would like to schedule a visit, please contact _____ (*name*) at the _____ (*library*) at _____ (*telephone number*). We look forward to hearing from you and visiting your school this spring.

Sincerely,
(Your name)
(Title)

classroom, you may want to take advantage of the closed circuit television systems that many schools have. Many schools broadcast important messages via closed circuit TV every morning; students may even produce this morning news show. Have students who were participants in last year's summer program tell, in their own words, why they are going to join in the activities again.

Another way to promote your summer library program is to enter into a partnership with the high schools and community colleges in your area. Many secondary schools, and some elementary and middle schools, have video-production facilities. Approach the media specialist and the technology teachers and arrange to have their students create a video promotional piece to be aired on the school district's closed circuit television system. If you do not have the funds to hire a professional artist to design your posters and bookmarks, work with the art teachers in your area schools to hold a contest and have the youth of the community design your promotional materials. Recruit local businesses to provide prizes for this activity. Working in partnership with area schools should be an ongoing aspect of your overall program, not relegated only to the time just prior to your summer library program.

To respond to the *No Child Left Behind* Act, many state library agencies are partnering with state-level departments of education. In Connecticut, the governor has created a program "The Governor's Summer Reading Challenge." In an effort to communicate effectively with the single message that participating in summer library reading programs supports the governor's program and to enhance children's learning over the summer, the Connecticut State Library and the Connecticut State Department of Education have developed several items. "Linking the Governor's 'Summer Reading Challenge' with Your Public Library Summer Reading Program" provides suggestions for ways local schools and libraries can work together. (See Figure 6–15) They have also created a two-page flier that communicates this important message to parents.

Many schools provide suggested or required reading lists for their students. Many people feel that by requiring that classics and curriculum-related materials be read over the summer, schools are destroying children's interest in reading for life.

> By requiring students to read classics, we squelch motivation for reading— a necessary component to increase reading skill. . . . Though teachers and parents want their children to be exposed to the best that cultures and literature have to offer, early pressure to read books that are too difficult often destroys students' interest in reading and the possibility they will ever read the classics.[2]

Creating bibliographies that promote reading is another way that schools and public libraries can work in partnership to make students successful. The Connecticut State Library has prepared two brochures that provide suggestions for schools as they work on developing those reading lists. Figure 6–16 is the version for elementary and middle schools. A version for high schools is also available. See http://ct.webjundtion.org/do/DisplayContent?id=6087 for the parent flier, the suggestions for creating high school reading lists, and other additional materials that have been developed by the Connecticut State Library.

## *Partnerships with the After-School Community*

Over the past several years, there has been much interest in after-school programs. While many in the library community might not see a summer library reading program as part of after school, many in the after-school arena do. All programs that serve

**Figure 6–15**
**Governor's "Summer Reading Challenge" and the Library**

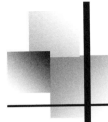

Linking the Governor's
*Summer Reading Challenge*
with Your Public Library Summer Reading Program

Student reading skills continue to be a major focus of media attention, school district resources and parent concern. Children who read during the summer vacation are more likely than non-readers to retain or improve their reading skills. **It is essential that schools and public libraries work together** to maximize each other's summer reading programs and remove any barriers to reading motivation. An effective way to ensure that this happens is to **put in place a permanent summer reading committee** that includes membership from the school and the public library. Such a committee could:

➤ Share summer reading goals and plans. Ask how programs can work together to benefit students and families.

➤ Use the same reading record for all programs, or make it very clear that the reading records for the school and public library are interchangeable (can be used for all programs).

➤ Explore developing a single summer reading effort for the town.

➤ Develop summer reading lists that engage and empower student readers. Consider town-wide reading lists developed jointly by the public library and the schools.

➤ Make sure the public library owns the books on the list and can adequately supply them to students.

➤ Consider loaning school copies of summer reading titles to the public library during the summer.

➤ Make sure the public library understands the school's summer reading goals and assignments.

➤ Plan a joint publicity campaign alerting the community to the importance of summer reading. Make sure parents know that books and reading motivation programs are available for their children throughout the summer.

➤ Plan a joint celebration recognizing your children's success. Invite your public librarian, mayor and other dignitaries.

A coordinated effort between the schools and the public library will strengthen the message to students and parents about the importance of summer reading.

Connecticut State Library
Connecticut State Department of Education
March 2004

Used by permission of the Connecticut State Library.

**Figure 6–16**
**"Creating Summer Reading Lists" Brochure**

*Creating Summer Reading Lists*

Ideas from the
Connecticut State Library

For Elementary and Middle Schools

*Does the summer reading list...*

- *Have clearly stated goals for summer reading?*

- *Include classics, award books, all genres, "just for fun" reading such as favorite series, comic books, graphic novels, a range of reading and interest levels and some free choice?*

- *Include annotations to help students choose what to read?*

*Have you...*

- *Invited a librarian to be a part of the planning process?*

- *Proofread the list?*

- *Made sure that the public library staff understands summer reading goals so they can support them when the school is closed for the summer?*

- *Shared high-demand titles with the public library?*

- *Included library programs for children on the summer reading handout?*

This flyer was written and prepared by Linda Williams and Susan Cormier, Children's Services Consultants at the Connecticut State Library. For additional resources to assist in planning for summer reading, please go to our website (www.cslib.org/sumread.htm).

**Connecticut State Library**

231 Capitol Avenue, Hartford, Connecticut 06106

March 2004

**Figure 6–16**
*Continued*

Encourage your students to read this summer by using these tips from the Connecticut State Library as you create your summer reading lists. Form a partnership with your public library to make summer reading an exciting, enjoyable activity for your students and their families.

## Summer reading goals

- *Clearly state the goals for summer reading*

  Is the goal to acquaint students with particular titles, to encourage reading enjoyment, or something else?

- *Be sure that the public library staff understands summer reading goals so that they can support them*

  The summer reading list becomes solely the charge of the public library (unless the school's media center is open and staffed in the summer) when doors close on the last day of school. Empower the library to assist your students during the summer months.

## The list – Titles and arrangement

- *Classics?*

  If the goal is to acquaint students with particular classic titles, has the selection of titles been explained (e.g., why *The Secret Garden* rather than *Winnie-the-Pooh*)? Are the chosen books still in-print and readily available (preferably in paperback)?

- *Series books, comic books, graphic novels, all genres, nonfiction books, range of reading and interest levels?*

  If the goal of summer reading is to encourage the enjoyment of reading, will all the titles students are asked to read support that goal? Because a major focus of the public library's work with children is reading motivation, contact the public librarian for recommendations of new titles that kids have enjoyed.

- *Award books?*

  If the goal is to encourage reading quality books, be aware of the awards given yearly by the American Library Association for children (www.ala.org/ala/alsc/awardsscholarships). Be sure to include books from Connecticut's own *Nutmeg Children's Book Award* Nomination List for students in grades four through six (www.biblio.org/nutmegaward).

- *Free choice?*

  Is a list necessary? If the goal is to encourage the reading habit, suggest a wide range of authors, genres and series rather than specific titles. Encourage children to read books about their favorite hobbies and pastimes. Connect students with the *What Do I Read Next?* database at iCONN (www.iconn.org) to select titles for summer reading.

- *Annotation and arrangement?*

  Annotating recommendations and arranging by genre help kids to come to the library knowing what listed titles they would like to borrow. Arranging fiction by author (as they are on library shelves) will help them to find titles more quickly in the library.

- *Proofread! Have more than one person check the list!*

  Has the list been proofread for correct authors, titles, and spellings? Most library catalogs are computerized, and computers require exact spelling to produce correct information. If Steinbeck's book for instance, is listed as *Of Men and Mice*, students will not find it in a library catalog. They may assume the title is not in the library, unless they ask a librarian.

- *Make your list attractive!*

  Children today are graphically sophisticated. Why not ask the art department to design the summer reading handout? Summer reading is a valuable activity; the physical appearance of your reading list should reflect that value.

## Involve the public library!

- *Collaborate with public librarians*

  Be sure to involve a librarian so that you know how the public library can and cannot help with summer reading. Are the books on the list still in print? Does the library own them? Does the library own enough to meet the demand the list will create? Librarians can suggest new titles that they know children enjoy. Teachers and librarians together can assure success for all students.

- *Share*

  If large numbers of students are required to read a select few books, consider sharing school copies with the public library over the summer. It will help students to get access to the titles they are expected to read more easily.

- *Include library programs for children on your summer reading handout*

  Work with the public library to develop a single summer reading program with unified goals and requirements so that children don't feel forced to choose between reading for school or reading for the library. Be sure your students know what library events and reading motivation programs will take place at their public library over the summer.

children and their families when school is not in session—before school, after school, evenings, weekends, and summers—are part of after school time. More correctly, it should be referred to as "out of school" time. Since summer library reading programs occur during the summer, they are already part of the after school network of services. Summer camps are also part of the after school network and should be considered possible partners in library programs.

Adapting an idea that was found in the 2004 "Southern Collaborative Summer Reading Program Manual," programs at the Birmingham (Ala.) Public Library reached approximately 300 campers who might not have been able to participate were it not for the creativity of Grace Slaughter and her colleagues. Since many children are enrolled in summer camps and child-care programs and cannot participate in summer library reading programs on an individual basis, the camps and centers register as a group. The groups sign up and have group, rather than individual, reading logs. When the groups come to storytimes at the library, those books are added to the reading logs. In addition, books that staff at the camps and child-care centers share with the children in their care are added to the logs. In the face of declining participation, this group-participation method of tracking reading and participation has enhanced the library's visibility in the community and has proved beneficial to the participating programs. One of several youth librarians in the library system who have implemented this program, Slaughter states:

> When your child care center/camps learn how easy it is for the group to participate, it'll be a snap to capture those statistics. It makes the child care center/camps look good to parents for their participation, the students feel good about earning a certificate, and the library has documented Summer Reading participation. . . . It's a little more work (which we'll assign to our Teen Summer Volunteers) but worth it in terms of boosting our young readers' reading self-esteem, child care center/camp cooperation, and our statistics.[3]

This is exactly what a partnership is all about—a win-win situation for all involved.

## Partnerships with the Local Business Community

Area business can be a valuable asset to your program. If you are offering prizes, local businesses may be able to provide them. Passes to the local roller skating arena can be a coveted reward for attending a special program. Food coupons for fast-food restaurants will attract teens as well as younger children. A gift certificate to an art supply store is an appropriate prize if you are sponsoring a contest to have the YAs design your promotional materials. Posters from video and music stores are an attraction that many children and teens will appreciate. These donations cost local merchants little but add much to your program. In addition to contacting local retailers, libraries should approach other cultural institutions in the community. These mutually beneficial marketing techniques provide visibility for all involved.

To obtain these items as well as financial support, you need to invest time and effort. Contact potential sponsors and donors in person. Make an appointment rather than just dropping in unexpectedly; small business operators are busy people and you want to make a good impression and have their attention while you make your presentation. Trying to talk with the manager of a restaurant during lunch hour would not be appropriate. Be prepared to discuss your program and share past successes with them. You need to be able to tell these potential donors why the summer library program is important to the community and beneficial to their businesses. If you have your promotional materials for the summer available, take samples with you and be prepared to leave them. If your materials for the current program are not yet ready, take samples from previous years. Know in advance how you will publicly acknowledge your donor's actions. Most important, be able to tell how their participation in your summer library program will benefit their business and enhance their company's image in the community.

Don't expect your prospective donors to give you a definite answer during your visit. They may need to think about your request, weigh the benefits that their businesses will accrue through participation in your program, or discuss it with other people in their organizations. Be prepared to send a thank-you immediately when you return to the library. Thank-you notes are in order even if you don't get a positive answer; they have listened to your request and given their time already. Courtesy this year, even with a negative response, may lay the groundwork for a positive one in the future.

### Partnerships with the Media

Establishing an ongoing working relationship with the media in your local area is of prime importance. In addition to sending press kits and media releases to the local media, work with the education coordinator at the paper by providing bibliographies related to feature stories throughout the year, not just during the summer. Once this relationship is established it can be mutually productive.

A nationwide program that can be beneficial to local summer library programs is the Newspapers in Education (NIE) program. The goal of this program is to encourage the use of newspapers in classrooms and other educational settings. Encouraging youth to read newspapers results in the creation of a new generation of newspaper readers; this is similar to the goal of most summer library programs—to create a new generation of library users. The overall goal of both types of programs is to establish lifelong readers, so NIE newspapers and libraries can be effective partners. There are more than 700 local newspapers in this network nationally; most of the major newspaper chains, including Gannett, Knight-Ridder, Media General, New York Times, Scripps, Tribune, Times Mirror, and others have at least one local paper that participates in the Newspapers in Education program. Many NIE papers have a weekly "Kids Page" that includes activities relating to what appears in the local paper. Most also have an NIE coordinator who works not only with local schools but also with the business community to generate sponsors to fund and support local NIE activities.

NIE papers and the local coordinators are remarkably responsive to public libraries' need to promote their summer programs and other literacy activities. Over the past few years, several NIE newspapers in Florida have worked in partnership with their local libraries to create special tabloid sections for the summer library program. The libraries provide copies of the statewide poster and other print promotional materials that are incorporated into full-color tabloids. Library staff also develop annotated bibliographies (based on the program manual provided through the State Library and Archives of Florida) for specific programs that the local library will be presenting and that reflect local library collections. In addition to including a reading log, the tabloids also contain the locations of branch libraries and schedules for the summer programs. The NIE coordinator recruits local corporate sponsors to underwrite the cost of producing the tabloid and writes additional copy for the tabloid that incorporates newspaper usage into the summer library program. The NIE coordinator assists in having the special summer library program tabloid section distributed to the local schools and other child-serving agencies. Additional copies are provided by the newspaper directly to the library for distribution on site.

## Partnerships with Individuals in the Community and Community Organizations

Many communities have service organizations that are looking for projects through which their energies can be put to good use and will be appreciated. Do not wait until late spring to approach these groups. Many of these groups establish their priorities at the beginning of the academic or calendar year for an entire year and design their service programs accordingly. Find out when these local service organizations make decisions about volunteer opportunities for their members as well as when they establish their budget. The money raised through their fund-raising activities in the fall may have already been committed to another group who made their presentation the previous spring.

Your Friends of the Library may be able to help you underwrite special parts of your program, such as an author appearance, or lobby your funding agency to get permanent funding for the summer library program. It is important that they be informed early of how they might be able to assist not only financially but also by providing services and materials. Your Friends group can also help you establish a Junior Friends of the Library group.

Whether your library is in a retirement community, has lots of working parents, has a high unemployment rate, or is made up of many single people, there are many individuals who would be happy to present a program if only they were asked. Many people have hobbies that they would love to share with others; people want to pass their interests on to others and a library program is the perfect way to do so. More than likely, no matter where your library is located, there are individuals who have spent their lives developing collections of all manner of things. Through your Friends of the Library newsletter or a media release to the local media, let your community know that you have space available to display their collections. If your summer program theme is travel related, ask people to share their souvenirs from their excursions. Many people may have created travelogues with slides or videos that they shot on vacation. Preview these presentations to ensure that they are appropriate to the interests of your target audience. People who are unemployed may want to hone their computer skills; provide them with the opportunity to design and format bibliographies after you have selected the books to be included. Skills practiced while donating services at the library may be useful in establishing gainful employment.

Whether your partners are area schools and their teachers, the business community, local newspapers, service organizations, teens, parents, grandparents, or other individuals, all should be recognized for their contributions to your summer library program.

## *Partnerships with State, Regional, and National Professional Organizations*

Many professional organizations initiate various campaigns that promote libraries and reading. Many of these campaigns can provide the impetus for a summer program. As a result of the care that is taken to develop these promotions and the resources that are brought to bear on these efforts, local libraries can piggy back on these statewide, regional, and national efforts.

For the past several years, the ALA has spearheaded the "@ your library®" campaign. This national campaign helps libraries of all types promote their services and programs in their local communities as well as create higher visibility for libraries. The campaign has several different aspects and focuses.

One of the facets of the "@ your library" clearly has a summer focus. "Join the Major Leagues @ your library®" is a 21st-century literacy initiative developed by ALA, major league baseball (MLB), and the Major League Baseball Players Association. The goal of this program is to help children, teens, and adults build their literacy skills. These skills include learning how to read; learning how to use computers and other media; and learning how to find, use, and evaluate information to communicate effectively.

The core element in this program, which was initiated in 2002, is an online baseball-trivia contest that tests information-literacy skills. It also encourages participants to use library resources—including librarians—to find the answers to the trivia questions. The questions are developed by the staff of the library of the National Baseball Hall of Fame and are organized by age group. In addition to age grouping (10 and under, 11–13, 14–17, and 18 and older) questions are organized by level of difficulty within each age group. In addition to a grand-prize winner, who receives two tickets to a designated game of the World Series, there are other prizes for each age group.

ALA and MLB developed an all-Spanish version of the program Web site. A Spanish-language baseball bibliography was developed and mounted on the Web site. A toolkit of publicity materials is also available in both English and Spanish to help librarians implement the program. The program Web site can be found at www.ala.org/@yourlibrary/jointhemajorleagues.

ALA and MLB are planning a new campaign that will be initiated in spring 2005 and run through mid-September. The library staff at the National Baseball Hall of Fame will develop new questions in several categories: Major League Baseball, Hispanics in Baseball, African Americans in Baseball, and Women in Baseball. The 2005 campaign will be promoted in English and Spanish and will also include a new poster. Support for the 2005 campaign is provided by REFORMA and the Hispanic Heritage Baseball Museum. The museum, based in San Francisco, has agreed to help promote the program via its Web site.

Local libraries can incorporate this promotional campaign based on America's favorite pastime into their summer programs and help people of all ages improve their reading and information literacy skills.

## Suppliers

In addition to the vendors and suppliers listed in chapter 5, here are some other suppliers of promotional materials and reading incentives and prizes. You can also check the Toy Industry Association Web site at www.toy-tia.org and in your local Yellow Pages or on the net for advertising specialties companies.

| | |
|---|---|
| Accu-Cut Systems<br>1035 E. Dodge St.<br>Fremont, NE 68025<br>1-800-288-1670<br>Web site: www.accucut.com | Oriental Trading Company, Inc.<br>P.O. Box 2308<br>Omaha, NE 68103–2308<br>1-800-228-2269<br>Web site: www.orientaltrading.com |
| Ellison Educational Equipment, Inc.<br>25862 Commercentre Dr.<br>Lake Forest, CA 92630–8804<br>1-800-253-2238<br>Web site: www.ellison.com | Rhode Island Novelty<br>19 Industrial Ln.<br>Johnston, RI 02919<br>1-800-528-5599<br>Web site: www.rinovelty.com/ |
| Hambley Studios, Inc.<br>941 George St.<br>Santa Clara, CA 95054<br>408-496-1100<br>Web site: www.hamblystudios.com | Rivershore Reading Store<br>2005 32nd St.<br>Rock Island, IL 61201<br>309-788-7717 (Phone or Fax)<br>Web site: www.libraryfun.com/about.html |
| Kidstamps<br>P.O. Box 18699<br>Cleveland Heights, OH 44118<br>1-800-727-5437<br>Web site: www.kidstamps.com | Sherman Specialty Company, Inc.<br>P.O. Box 401<br>Merrick, NY 11556–0401<br>1-800-645-6513<br>Web site: www.shermanspecialty.com/ |
| Kipp Brothers<br>P. O. Box 781080<br>Indianapolis, IN 46278<br>1-800-428-1153<br>Web site: www.kipbro.com | SmileMakers–US<br>P.O. Box 2543<br>Spartanburg, SC 29304<br>1-800-825-8085<br>Web site: www.smilemakers.com |
| Lakeshore Learning Materials<br>2695 E. Dominguez St.<br>Carson, CA 90810<br>1-800-421-5354<br>Web site: www.lakeshorelearning.com | U.S. Toy Company<br>Constructive Playthings<br>13201 Arrington Rd.<br>Grandview, MO 64030<br>1-800-832-0224<br>Web site: www.ustoy.com/ |

## Endnotes

1. Walter Minkel. 2003. "Making a Splash with Summer Reading: Seven Ways Public Librarians Can Team Up with Schools." *School Library Journal* 49, no. 1 (January): 54–56.
2. "Summer Reading Belongs in the Hands of Students: Celebrating Choice in School Reading Lists." 2003. *Voice of Youth Advocates* 26, no. 5 (December): 368–371.
3. E-mails from Grace Slaughter to PUBYAC listserv, November 10, 2004, and to Carole Fiore, November 12, 2004.

## Recomended Reading

Champelli, Lisa. 2002. *The Youth Cybrarian's Guide to Developing Instructional, Curriculum-Related, Summer Reading and Recreational Programs.* New York: Neal-Schuman, 2002.

DelVecchio, Gene. 1998. *Creating Ever-Cool: A Marketer's Guide to a Kid's Heart.* Gretna, La.: Pelican.

Field, Selma G., and Edwin M. Field. 1993. *Publicity Manual for Libraries: A Comprehensive Professional Guide to Communications . . . A Book That No Library Should Be Without.* Monticello, N.Y.: Knowledge Network Press.

Flowers, Helen F. 1998. *Public Relations for School Library Media Programs: 500 Ways to Influence People and Win Friends for Your School Library Media Center.* New York: Neal-Schuman.

Geisler, Viki Ash. 1993. *Marketing the Texas Reading Club: A Guide for Youth Specialists.* Austin, Tex.: Tex. State Library.

Hill, Ann, and Julieta Dias Fisher. 2002 *Tooting Your Own Horn: Web-Based Public Relations for the 21st Century Librarian.* Worthington, Ohio: Linworth.

Jurewicz, Lynn, and Todd Cutler. 2003. *High Tech, High Touch: Library Customer Service through Technology.* Chicago: American Library Association.

Karp, Rashelle S., ed. 1995. *Part-Time Public Relations with Full-Time Results: A PR Primer for Libraries.* Chicago: American Library Association.

———. 2002. *Powerful Public Relations: How-To Guide for Librarians.* Chicago: American Librarian Association.

Kies, Cosette N. 2003. *Marketing and Public Relations for Libraries.* Lanham, Md.: Scarecrow.

Lawrence, Natalie J. 2004. "There's No 'I' In Partnership (Oh, Wait . . . )." *Public Libraries* 42, no. 3 (May/June): 147–148.

*Library Marketing for Public Libraries, Web-Based Training.* Also available: www.olc.org/marketing. 2003–2004. Columbus, Ohio: Ohio Library Foundation.

Schor, Juliet. 2004. *Born to Buy: Marketing and the Transformation of Childhood and Culture.* New York: Scribner.

Sutherland, Anne, and Beth Thompson. 2003. *Kidfluence: The Marketer's Guide to Understanding and Reaching Generation Y—Kids, Tweens and Teens. New York:* McGraw-Hill Trade.

Walters, Suzanne. 2003. *Library Marketing That Works.* New York: Neal-Schuman.

Weingand, Darlene E. 1999. *Marketing/Planning Library and Information Services, 2nd Ed.* Englewood, Colo.: Libraries Unlimited.

Wolfe, Lisa A. 2004. *Library Public Relations, Promotions, and Communications: A How-to-Do-It Manual, 2nd ed.* New York: Neal-Schuman.

# IV

# Designing and Evaluating Your Program

# 7

# Exploring the A to Z of Summer Reading Programs

You and your library's administration have made the decision to invest staff time and energy in planning and presenting a series of summer programs. You have gone through the planning process, including establishing goals and objectives for the summer library reading program. You have made some of the decisions about how your program will be organized. Now is the time to actually start planning individual programs. Since goals of most summer library reading programs include promoting library use and turning children, teens, their families, and others in the community into readers, it is vital that you have multifaceted collections that attract people of all ages in your community and makes them want to read. You have already selected a theme that has broad community appeal—especially for the youth. Now you must make sure that your collection and the activities you offer during the summer will attract your target audience. All successful summer library programs include various types of activities; this chapter has a sampling of some of the types that you can offer. It may not be feasible, nor is it necessary, for every library to offer all types of programs and services in one summer. These are suggestions that you will want to consider as you reach out to your community.

As you develop your theme into specific programs, you will be able to feature various aspects of your library collection. Good programs integrate materials from both the fiction and nonfiction areas. Also, various formats are needed to address the needs, abilities, and interests of the youth in your community. You should make considerable efforts to involve parents and other primary caregivers—such as grandparents—and other family members in many of your activities. This is especially important when designing programs and services for young children.

Summer library programs are a great time to introduce members of your community to cultures with which they are not familiar or with which they might not ordinarily associate. A theme such as *Read around the World* allows you to integrate factual information about geography, map skills, countries of the world as well as the cultural aspects of these countries into your programs. The addition of folklore, music, food, language, and dress from various countries and cultures into programs expands the experience of reading a book and provides for variations on a central theme. Inviting people from the community to share their cultural heritage with program participants provides a fulfilling experience for all.

Make sure that the materials you select are accurate and unbiased representations of other cultures. Resources that can help you as you add appropriate materials to your collection are in the shaded box:

*The Black Experience in Children's Books.* 1994. New York: New York Public Library.

Cooperative Children's Book Center, University of Wisconsin–Madison. www.soemadison.wisc.edu/ccbc

Day, Frances Ann. 1997. *Latina and Latino Voices in Literature for Children and Teenagers.* Portsmouth, N.H.: Heinemann.

"Guidelines for Selecting Bias-Free Textbooks and Storybooks." 1989. *Anti-Bias Curriculum: Tools for Empowering Young Children*, edited by Louise Derman-Sparks. Washington, D.C.: National Association for the Education of Young Children.

Hansen-Krening, Elaine M. Aoki, and Donald T. Mizokawa. 2003. *Kaleidoscope: A Multicultural Booklist for Grades K–8, 4th ed.* Urbana, Ill.: National Council of Teachers of English.

Kruse, Ginny Moore and Kathleen T. Horning, with Merri V. Lindgren and Katherine Odahowski. 1991. *Multicultural Literature for Children and Young Adults: A Selected Listing of Books, 1980–1990, by and about People of Color.* Madison, Wis.: Wisconsin Department of Public Instruction.

Kruse, Ginny Moore, Kathleen T. Horning, and Megan Schliesman. 1997. *Multicultural Literature for Children and Young Adults, Vol. 2, 1991–1996.* Madison, Wis.: Wisconsin Department of Public Instruction.

Lindgren, Merri V., ed. 1991. *The Multicolored Mirror: Cultural Substance in Literature for Children and Young Adults.* Fort Atkinson, Wis.: Highsmith Press.

Manna, Anthony L., and Carolyn S. Brodie, eds. 1992. *Many Faces, Many Voices: Multicultural Literary Experiences for Youth: The Virginia Hamilton Conference.* Fort Atkinson, Wis.: Highsmith Press.

Miller-Lachman, Lyn. 1992. *Our Family, Our Friends, Our World: An Annotated Guide to Significant Multicultural Books for Children and Teenagers.* New Providence, N.J.: R. R. Bowker.

Rand, Donna, Toni Trent Parker, and Sheila Foster. 1998. *Black Books Galore! Guide to Great African American Children's Books.* New York: Wiley.

_____. 2000. *Black Books Galore! Guide to Great African American Children's Books about Boys.* New York: Wiley.

_____. 2000. *Black Books Galore! Guide to Great African American Children's Books about Girls.* New York: Wiley.

_____. 2001. *Black Books Galore! Guide to More Great African American Children's Books.* New York: Wiley.

Schon, Isabel. 2003. *The Best of Latino Heritage 1996–2002: A Guide to the Best Juvenile Books about Latino People and Cultures.* Lanham, Md.: Scarecrow.

_____. 2004. *Recommended Books in Spanish for Children and Young Adults: 2000 through 2004.* Recommended Books in Spanish for Children and Young Adults. Scarecrow.

Slapin, Beverly, and Doris Seals, eds. 1998. *Through Indian Eyes: The Native Experience in Books for Children.* Los Angeles, Calif.: American Indian Studies Center, University of California.

Totten, Herman L., and Risa W. Brown. 1994. *Culturally Diverse Library Collections for Children.* New York: Neal-Schuman.

Totten, Herman L., Carolyn Garner, and Risa W. Brown. 1996. *Culturally Diverse Library Collections for Youth.* New York: Neal-Schuman.

Toussaint, Pamela. 1999. *Great Books for African American Children.* New York: Plume Books.

White-Parks, Annette, ed. 1994. *A Gathering of Voices of the Asian American Experience.* Fort Atkinson, Wis.: Highsmith Press.

Wood, Irene, ed. 1999. *Culturally Diverse Videos and CD-ROMs for Children and Young Adults.* New York: Neal-Schuman.

Since one of the goals of your summer library program is to entice children and young adults in your community into reading and using books and other library materials, you are, of course, going to want to use as many books in as many formats as possible. All children, including children without disabilities, have various learning styles. Some people learn visually, while others do better when information is presented orally. Still others learn better from tactile involvement or kinesthetic experiences. For this reason, it is best to be able to use various presentation styles in every program so at least one portion of every program directly reaches and involves every participant in some way.

One way to do this is to vary your presentation style. Don't just read aloud every book you have selected. Sometimes, tell the story without ever showing the pictures; allow those children that enjoy imagining the setting and characters to draw the pictures that the words paint in their mind's eye. For those children who do not have a vivid imagination, show the pictures if they are large enough, or use a big-book version when one is available. Whether working with large groups or small, you need to ensure that all who attend the programs can see the illustrations when you show them. Allow children who need movement to act out a story either through creative dramatics, reader's theater, or in a puppet presentation. Children who need tactile stimulation may perform better during an art activity than those who like to read independently. Vary your presentations and program offerings so that all participants have at least one segment of the summer library reading program in which they can fully partake.

## Before You Begin

### *Copyright Considerations in Program Planning*

You will need to present books in other than the traditional read-aloud format, especially when presenting programs to large groups. Take care when you are adapting books for your storytime presentations. The current copyright law, Public Law

94-553, was enacted in 1976 and went into effect in 1978. While there have been recent revisions directed to life in the electronic age, legislation related to books and adapting materials for storytime have not changed. The copyright law gives certain rights to the owner or creator of a work. Among the rights given to authors and illustrators is the sole right to have their work reproduced, the sole right to have a derivative work prepared that is based on the copyrighted work, and the sole right to have their works performed publicly. Types of works protected under the copyright law include, but are not limited to, books, poems, music, lyrics, videos, pantomimes, blueprints, plays, and works of art.[1]

While copyright does not protect ideas, it does protect the format in which an idea is expressed. For example, if in writing a reader's theater script, you are taking an *idea* from a work and using it to create another work, that is not considered a copyright violation. If, however, you are making an adaptation of another person's copyrighted work and are using a significant portion of the copyrighted work in the creation, this would be considered a derivative work. This spin-off work based on the author's original work is not legal because creating derivative works is a right reserved solely for the author. Thus, if you are using the same characters and setting as contained in a novel but creating more dialogue for the characters, you have actually created a spin-off from the original, not a totally new creation.[2]

Unfortunately, under the Copyright Act of 1976 and its various amendments (and clarifications) through 2002, creating this type of derivative work is not permitted. What seems to cause confusion in both the education and library communities is that there does not appear to be any case law relating to a school media center, public library, or staff from such agencies being sued for violating copyright for by creating derivative works or for related activities, such as creating puppet shows, box stories, slide shows, flannel boards, or similar adaptations. This situation tends to lead one to believe that since the law is not being enforced that the activity of creating various adaptations is legal.[3]

However, just because you are not making a profit from the adaptation you create, you do not automatically have the right to change the format. Nor is there tacit permission given for you to create an adaptation or change the format if such adaptations are not currently available. For example, years ago, librarians wishing to share small books with large groups started making what many call board stories. Library staff enlarged the illustrations from books onto poster board, often placing the text on the back of these cards; the illustrations were then large enough to share with large groups. Librarians or other reading partners read the text aloud and showed the illustrations to the group. As publishers found out about this practice, they began producing big books. Just because your library does not own the big-book version of the small book you want to share with a large group or there is no big-book version available, that does not mean that you can go ahead and make one on your own.

On the other hand, it does not mean that you must drop your project either. While the copyright holder is given a series of rights, they also have the ability to give those rights away or lease them for a fee should they choose to do so. When you want to create a puppet show based on a book, mount a bulletin board display using characters enlarged from a children's picture book, or have children tape the dialogue in a book and circulate that tape with the book, you do have a course of action that you can follow. Rather than giving up on the project, ask for permission.[4]

To obtain permission to make any adaptation, you need to put your request in writing and submit it to the rights and permissions department of the publisher of the book. Be as specific as possible in explaining how you intend to use the material and what format you will be using. Tell how many times you will be using the material—one time this summer, once a week for eight weeks this summer, or every summer for the next five years—and how many people you anticipate will be exposed to your presentation. If you are going to create a mural using characters from children's books, you may be asked to submit a sketch of what the entire mural will look like when it is completed. If you wish to present programs that will be broadcast on the local cable television station or over closed circuit television in the local schools, include information about why your program is being broadcast and if there is a commercial sponsor for the show. Be up front and open about whether or not you have funds available to purchase permissions. Give a specific date by which you need a reply. Be realistic in your requests and allow publishers, authors, and illustrators sufficient time to make a decision. Many authors, illustrators, and publishers are willing to grant permission—as long as they know in advance exactly how you are going to use their material.

Start early when seeking permissions, and be prepared to be patient. Many times the publisher does have authority to make those decisions: sometimes, however, you will be referred to a literary agent, lawyer, or the author or illustrator him- or herself. Be prepared to make multiple contacts to get the permission you need for a specific book. With the mergers of many publishing houses, it may take time to locate the person who actually controls such decisions.

Figure 7–1 is a sample letter requesting copyright permission. Adapt this to include information about your own library and how you intend to use the material in question. Figure 7–2 is the Permission Release Form. Complete as much of this form as possible before sending it to the publisher in duplicate as an enclosure with your letter requesting permission. To make it even easier for the publisher to reply, enclose a self-addressed, stamped envelope. Keep complete records of every request you make and the disposition of each. The more you do this, the easier it becomes. You will quickly learn how to work with the publishing community and find out which publishers are prompt in their replies. Have alternatives in mind should you not get the copyright clearance that you desire. Don't expect to be able to obtain copyright permissions for every book, short story, poem, song, or illustration that you have requested; you can, however, expect a positive response approximately 75 percent of the time if your requests are not unreasonable.

While you may be tempted to do your permissions requests via e-mail, you must remember that the permissions are legal documents and should be in hard copy with original signatures. If you must do your requests via e-mail and receive permission

**Figure 7–1**
**Permission Request for Use of Copyrighted Materials**

Rights and Permissions Department
Publisher Name
Address

To Whom It May Concern:

The _____ Library is currently planning for our 2006 summer library program.
We have selected _____ as our theme.  We will be presenting programs at the
library and at various outreach locations such as parks and recreation centers, child day cares, and
summer schools within our community.  We hope to reach a total of 5,000 children during our
six-week series of programs.

As part of this program, we would like to present a puppet show based on the book
_____ written by _____ and illustrated by
_____.  This book was published by your company in _____.
If granted permission to adapt this book into a puppet show, we intend to present it at 20
programs this summer.  Since writing puppet scripts, preparing scenery based on the
illustrations, and creating the puppets is such time-consuming work, we would like to retain the
puppet show for use again in approximately 3 years when we have another group of children
who would not have participated in this year's programs.

I would appreciate it if you would complete and sign one copy of the enclosed release form.  For
your convenience, I have enclosed two copies.  Please retain one for your files and return a
completed one to me by _____.  If you do not control the necessary rights to
grant such permission, would you please let me know who does. Please be advised that the
Library has a policy that does not permit any fee be paid for use of copyrighted material.

Thank you in advance for your consideration and prompt reply.

Sincerely,


Name
Title

Enclosure

---

**Figure 7–2**
**Permission-Release Form**

---

I hereby grant permission to _____ Library to use the
following material as specified:

_____ , written by _____

and illustrated by _____ .

Permission is granted permission to adapt this book into a puppet show, to be presented at 20
library-sponsored programs during the summer of 2006.

Permission is also granted for the Library to use this puppet show through 2009.

We require that you print the following credit line in promotional materials announcing this
program:

_____

_____

_____

I am authorized to grant this permission:

Permission granted by:

_____
Signature

_____
Print name

_____
Title

_____
Date

via e-mail, make certain you maintain printouts of all this correspondence. The printouts should include the entire e-mail header and all of the information requested on the permission to reprint form.

After the program is over, don't forget to send thank-you notes to the publisher's representatives with whom you have dealt. Photographs showing how you have used the materials and letters from children are sure to be appreciated by people in the publishing house as well as the author and illustrator of the books that you adapted. Common courtesy in this area goes a long way in establishing a long-lasting working relationship that can cut the time needed to gain permissions in the future.

### *Variety and Diversity in Programs*

While storytimes for preschoolers and early readers may form the bulk of your summer programs offerings, there are numerous other ways of enticing your community to become part of a nation of readers and lifelong library users. This rest of this chapter offers suggestions for different types of programs and services that can be offered. They range from small segments or parts of presentations to an entire series of programs. While many are literature based, this is not a necessity. After all, your goal is not only to get your community excited about reading and books, but also to understand that the library can open new worlds to them. Specific program plans are not given as you need to develop your programs in relation to the theme you have selected for your summer library reading program, your community and users, and your library collection. Many of these programs are appropriate at any time of the year, not just as part of your summer program. You can use some of these program ideas with individuals and small groups as well as with large groups. The physical setting in which you work and the number of children and teens participating in your program will help you determine what is appropriate for your setting.

Not all programs need be presented in the library. Consider taking your programs on the road and out into the community to reach people who are transportationally disadvantaged, or who, because of past experiences or cultural differences, may not be comfortable in public (government) buildings. Especially during the summer, outreach locations such as parks and recreation centers provide you with an audience that may not want to go to the library on a regular basis, if at all.

It is hoped that the program ideas included here will spark your imagination as you reach out to all segments of your community. Programs are listed alphabetically to aid in ease of location. Additional ideas can be found in the books listed in the list of recommended readings at the end of this chapter.

## Programs from A to Z

### *Adults as Readers*

While most of your summer library reading program activities will be focused on children and teens, providing an adult component allows the youth of the community to see that adults value reading and reading-related activities. Modeling literacy behaviors is an important reason for including adults in your program.

Many libraries are now including adult activities in their summer library programs. For example, the Grace A. Dow Library in Midland, Michigan, included an adult reading component in their summer library program for the past several years. For a two-month period that corresponds to the time the youth department holds their summer library program, the reference department coordinates the adult summer reading program. For every adult book an adult read and "reported" on, adults are rewarded a "free-hold" coupon—redeemable for a free reserve, a service that the library usually charges for—and are entered into weekly drawings. Five slips are drawn each week for weekly prizes, including gift certificates to local bookstores, movie theaters, or restaurants. Slips that aren't selected in the weekly drawing are then entered into the grand prize drawing at the end of the summer. Grand prizes are donated by local businesses and range from a $100 gift certificate to a weekend package at a local hotel. Figure 7–3 shows the type of information that is included on the entry form. Don't forget to include some youth summer program graphics on these forms to show the relationship between these two programs.

---

**Figure 7–3**
**Adult Summer Reading Program**

**Adult Summer Reading Program**

Title: _____

Author: _____

Your Name: _____

Phone number: __( ____ )_____

Email: _____

How would you rate this book?  (Use other side of the entry form if you have any comments.)

☆              ☆☆              ☆☆☆              ☆☆☆☆              ☆☆☆☆☆

The Normal (Ill.) Public Library has another variant on adult summer programs. Adults Reading Kids Stuff (ARKS) has adults reading children's books. The adults read in a variety of categories, including Caldecott and Newbery books, series books, Dr. Seuss, as well as listening to books on tape. One of the benefits of this program is that parents and caregivers can recommend books to their children. As with many of the adult reading programs, adults are rewarded with prizes such as coupons for books from the next Friends of the Library book sale, passes to a local comedy club, a basket full of gourmet coffee and a coffee mug, or tote bags.

During the summer of 2004, the Prince George's County (Md.) Memorial Library System offered "Escape to Reading: Summer Reading Programs for Adults." This program was for those over 18 years of age. A separate personal reading log for adults was prepared; there were spaces for 12 books. When adult readers completed four books (either a book they read or listened to), they were eligible for their first gift; at six books, they could get their second gift and enter the drawing for the final prize. A "Kick-Off Reading" and a "Midsummer Reading" program were offered, as was a grand finale concert. The outdoor concert on the lawn of one of the branch libraries was when the "Escape" grand prizes were drawn. Prizes included gift certificates for dinner at local restaurants; the grand prize was a weekend escape at a resort hotel that had been donated.

Adult programs provide a win-win situation. Involving parents in a reading program that corresponds with what their children are involved in promotes the concept of family and individual reading. Children and teens see their parents and other adults in the community participating in reading-related activities and learn that people read for their own enjoyment. In addition to promoting lifelong reading and library use, adult reading programs strengthen and build support for children's and teen programs. They also build community awareness of the larger library program.[5]

### *Back to School*

In the initial weeks of summer vacation, neither the children and teens in your community nor the parents and teachers will really want to think about the end of summer. However, towards the end of your summer program, you may want to feature several back to school programs for different ages.

"Count Down to Kindergarten" will help parents and their young children get ready for the first day of school. Even for those children who have been in Head Start or preschool, the first day of kindergarten is exciting and can be traumatic. With so many working parents, having this program over the weekend or in the evening may promote better attendance. Work with the kindergarten teachers at your neighborhood schools. Let them help you promote this program during registration for class. Include lists of school supplies that are needed, and make certain that one of the supplies every child receives is a library card.

Moving from elementary to middle school can be almost as traumatic for both students and parents as the first day of elementary school. Again, work with the teachers and administration at the local schools to promote this program. Invite the school principal and counselor to attend. Have several of the homeroom teachers in attendance. By planning this program in the spring while school is still in session, you can contact several current middle school students and have them assist with this orientation to middle school. Students new to this experience need to know about moving from class to class, and school policies about backpacks, use of lockers, when and where you enter the building, among other things. By including students who have survived this first year of middle school on your program you show that you value teens.

### *Book Bucks*

In an attempt to keep participants reading over the entire summer and returning to the library, several libraries have instituted "Book Bucks" or "Library Loot" programs. As readers complete their reading logs and report back to the library, they are rewarded with book bucks. The book bucks are redeemable for prizes and incentives that are in the "library store." The incentives include food coupons, donated books, and, according to Pat Vasilik of the Clifton (N.J.) Public Library, "lots and lots of donated toys. . . . Families have been generous with donations—I think some parents are grateful to get rid of some stuff! And the kids love to shop. Our 'prices' range from 1 point for stickers to bigger items for 30 points."[6] The Newport Branch of the Campbell County Library in Newport, Kentucky, called their store the Trading Post to go along with the Lewis and Clark theme they used. Libraries from all around the country are adding this type of reward program for readers of all ages.

### *Book Discussions: Booknic, Book Award Programs, and PRIME TIME Family Reading Time*®

Book discussion programs have long been a mainstay of library programming for adults. This type of program is readily adapted for many ages. While book discussions usually attracts people who already are readers, it does broaden their reading horizons and expose participants to authors, illustrators, titles, and genres that they might not otherwise select. "Just as reading can be a lifetime pleasure, so can discussing books provide a continuing source of satisfaction."[7]

A good discussion leader is the key to the success and vitality of book discussion programs. It is vital that the facilitator not be judgmental and respect all points of views. Elizabeth Poe states of her experiences working with youth in various situations, "The juvenile delinquents I worked with in group homes and detention centers helped me see the necessity of respecting all points of view. The low-ability language arts students I taught led me to see the value of choice in reading materials. The gifted students in my after-school book club showed me what can happen when we develop our student's intellectual and neglect their emotional capacities."[8] Creating a positive atmosphere is imperative no matter what format your book discussion takes. You must create an atmosphere in which readers and discussion participants feel comfortable expressing their thoughts on the books. Trust and respect for the participants is an essential ingredient for the program, and a skilled discussion leader should help members develop mutual trust for one another.

To keep discussions moving, groups should be limited to no more than 20 people.

To promote continued attendance, the discussion group sessions should be held at the same time every week. Participants can help select the books to be discussed at the first meeting of the group. With adult discussion groups, you need enough copies of the same books so that everyone will be able to read and discuss one title. While this usually works well with adults, it is sometimes difficult to obtain enough copies of a children's book to ensure this. It may also be difficult to structure this voluntary reading activity for youth so that everyone reads the same book. For children and young adults, you may opt to have everyone in the group read a book of the same genre. The discussions may not be as rich as when everyone reads the same book, but it does provide practice in discussion techniques and sets the stage for future involvement in adult book discussion groups.

Ruhama Kordatzky, youth services librarian at the Burlington (Wis.) Public Library has two book discussion groups. The Youth Book Group (YBG) is specifically for 9- to 12-year-olds. This group meets once a month for about a half hour. The library purchases multiple copies of the discussion book in paperback so everyone has access to it at the same time. This program extends past the summer and runs all year, involving school librarians and teachers as well. The Teen Book Club is similar to the YBG but for students in 7th through 12th grades.

For detailed information on how to organize adult discussion groups, see *Programming for Introducing Adults to Children's Literature.*[9]

## BOOKNIC[10]

A book discussion program that attracts children who already are readers is one called booknic. The gimmick of this program lies in the "nic" of booknic—from picnic. Yes, the children are allowed to eat in the library—as long as they clean up at the end of the program. Sometimes libraries have these picnics outside under a tree or in the library meeting room, which has been decorated to resemble a park. During the summer library reading program, participants are invited to bring their lunch to the library along with the books they want to discuss. The library usually supplies a drink and something for dessert. For this type of program, it is best to group students by age and interest level. If possible, have one group for upper elementary-age students and another for middle school–age students. Students in high school may find that they want an adult-styled book discussion group or would rather have a coffee house–style discussion group.

Booknic was originally designed by Susan Oliver of the Tampa-Hillsborough County (Fla.) Public Library System. Oliver had so much success with booknic during the summer that she continued it (upon the request of the readers) during the school year as an after-school program with participants bringing an after-school snack. Depending on the reading habits and schedules of your patrons, special booknic sessions can also be arranged during the short vacation breaks that are interspersed in the school calendar.

Oliver breaks the 90-minute booknic program into thirds. During the first third of the booknic program, participants eat while the librarian booktalks. The first of only two rules comes into play here; participants must clean up after themselves when they finish eating. Booktalks range from new books, to theme-related books, to nonfiction, to even video talks about videos in the library collection. (For more information on booktalking, see "Booktalks" below.)

The second third of the program belongs to the participants. The second and only other rule comes into play during this part of the program. As each participant talks about any book he or she has read and wants to recommend to others in the group, the rest of the members of the group must listen; respect for each other's choices and opinions is vital to the success of the program, especially when participants are sharing feelings and personal tastes. During this portion of the program, participants listen to others as they speak. They may not interrupt, laugh, or make comments when someone else is talking about the books read. Oliver reports that children's reading habits are varied; one child talked about one book for the entire summer while another wanted to share three or four books weekly. Participants learned from the librarian's booktalks and from each other's reports how not to tell the whole story or give too much of the plot away, yet still make the presentation interesting and exciting. As the librarian sets up for the third and final segment of the program, participants look at the books that have been presented by their peers and the librarian and make selections for the following week.

The final segment of the program consists of book-related games such as Book *Jeopardy*, *Wheel of Fortune* (where authors, titles, and book characters are the phrases), and Name That Book. Over the years, Oliver has added Booknic Baseball and book-oriented versions of *Win, Lose, or Draw*. Game boards from home versions of *Jeopardy* and *Wheel of Fortune* can be used or you and the group can make larger ones. The librarian and participants make up questions based on the books in the collection. Name That Book questions are also based on the reading habits of the participants and the library collection. Oliver suggests playing these games with teams rather than pitting individual against individual, thus promoting cooperation rather than competition. She also recommends that the librarian choose the teams so as to avoid cliques and to balance the teams. Prizes such as posters, paperback books, and coupons from local fast-food restaurants are given as prizes to everyone who participates.

The benefits of this low-cost program are numerous. Booknic is a success because program participants who already are excited about reading become more so because of the opportunity to share their favorite books with their peers. By listening to their peers, children and young adults are encouraged to try books they might otherwise not have picked up. Oliver reports that participants' library skills improve as a result of having to locate additional copies of a book that someone else has spoken about. As participants talk about the program with their peers, their excitement about the games, the prizes, and the books is transferred to others who then want to join in the next booknic.

Materials and time needed to make this program a success are minimal. Aside from the initial game-board construction (or time needed to find them in your community) and the continuous gathering of prizes, little time is needed for booknic's continuing appeal and success. The librarian must, however, constantly read and prepare additional booktalks and gather and review questions. This really is not much considering the response and the great results. Discussion and sharing activities really do help develop habitual readers.

A variation of this program would be Lunch with the Librarian or Listen While You Lunch. During these programs, the librarian reads aloud a short chapter book, such as a book in the *Junie B. Jones* or *Cam Jansen* series. Reading aloud to children is so important that the Commission on Reading called it "the single most important activity for building the knowledge required for eventual success in reading."[11] Folk tales and short stories would also work well. The Burlington (Wis.) Public Library shares picture books, pop-up books, and big books that fit the overall summer program theme. Participants bring their own lunches and the library supplies a drink and dessert. Again, as with Booknic, weather permitting, the picnic is held outside.

### BOOK AWARD PROGRAMS

A program that can be used for participants of various ages, from young readers through adult, is a book award program. Many states have a young readers award program that is sponsored by the state library agency, state library association, state department of education, state reading association, state association of media educators (school librarians), or a combination of these groups. *Children's Books Awards and Prizes*[12] or the Awards and Prizes Web site maintained by the Children's Book Council (http://awardsandprizes.cbcbooks.org) contains lists of these local awards and numerous others along with the criteria for them. Public libraries should have the books that are nominated for their local awards in the library collection. Booktalking the books on the master nomination list will encourage readers to read these books independently. Reading these books aloud so that nonreaders or children who have difficulty reading are exposed to them is another way for public libraries to participate in these book award programs. Libraries can also hold book discussion programs based on the books nominated for these statewide awards. Parents and primary caregivers as well as their school-age children who are participating in the voting can participate in these discussions.

Along with sponsoring book discussions based on these statewide awards, libraries can work with local teachers who may be participating in the International Reading Association (IRA) sponsored Children's Choices, Young Adult Choices, or the Teacher's Choices projects. Teachers in various locations across the nation share recently published books with their classes to select an annual list of quality books that children and young adults actually read. The results of the discussion process are annotated lists that are published in the IRA journals *Journal of Adolescent and Adult Literacy* and *The Reading Teacher*. Children's Choices are books chosen by children aged 5 through 13 as their favorites; Young Adult Choices are selected by students in grades 7 through 12 as their favorites. Teachers' Choices are books selected by teachers and librarians and include books that children might not discover or fully appreciate without the help of a teacher, parent, or other adult. If your budget permits, you may be able to supply additional copies of books so that more people may participate. Librarians can also assist by providing expertise on how to evaluate books. For more information on these three Choices projects, to find out if there is a local program in your area, or to order reprints of current and back Choices lists, contact the IRA at 1-800-336-READ or visit their Web site at www.reading.org/.

Awards that most librarians, teachers, and parents know about are the John Newbery and Randolph Caldecott Medals. These awards are presented annually by the Association for Library Service to Children (ALSC), a division of the American Library Association (ALA), for "the most significant contribution to American literature for children" and the "most distinguished American picture book for children" respectively. To encourage children, parents, caregivers, and teachers to understand the process of how books are selected to win these prestigious awards, libraries can sponsor Newbery and Caldecott mock elections. This type of book discussion program works well at any time of year, but is especially good for the winter vacation period immediately preceding the actual deliberations of the two committees. A mock-election kit available from ALSC provides detailed procedures for choosing books for evaluation and tips on publicizing the event. The kit also contains certificates of participation and bookmarks for participants. Refill kits with additional certificates and bookmarks are also available.[13] Terms and criteria for the ALSC awards are available online at www.ala.org/alsc.

Another successful model for book discussions is the Junior Great Books program. A library in Colorado reports success with hosting a Breakfast Club discussion group. The young adult group meets in the library once every other week over the summer prior to the library's opening to the public in the morning.[14]

## PRIME TIME FAMILY READING TIME®

PRIME TIME Family Reading Time® is a unique intergenerational literacy program. This family-based model features award-winning children's books to stimulate discussion about themes and problems encountered in daily life. PRIME TIME is a program that runs either six or eight weeks, so it fits easily into most summer library reading program schedules. These programs feature reading, discussion, and storytelling. The programs are led by a humanities scholar and a storyteller who share the role of discussion leader. This turnkey program, using a curriculum developed by the Louisiana Endowment for the Humanities, introduces families with children 6 though 10 years of age (and older) to award-winning children's books. The program:

> reinforces the role of the family as a major social and economic unit; it trains parents and children to bond together around the act of reading and learning together to improve skill and achievements; it teaches parents and children to read and discuss humanities topics (history, literature, and ethical issues, such as fairness, greed, honor, and deceit) as a way of fostering high academic expectations and achievements in low-literacy, low-income families; it encourages low-literacy, low-income parents to enter or continue their own educational programs, whether GED or other training, and enter the workforce; it helps parents and children learn how to select books and become active library users.[15]

This book discussion program began in Louisiana and is expanding with additional support from the National Endowment for the Humanities and assistance from the ALA Public Programs Office. In 2004, the program was expanded to include five sites in each of four states: California, Kentucky, Pennsylvania, and Florida.

### Booktalks

One of the best ways to get children and adults excited about books is to tell them something, but not too much, about them. Being able to craft and deliver booktalks is a skill that all librarians need to develop and use frequently. A booktalk is a short presentation, usually from 30 seconds to no more than five minutes. Its sole purpose is to entice the people listening to the booktalk to read the book. Teachers as well as librarians use this technique to entice their students to read. Rachel Fishbaugh states, "The main purpose of a book talk is to grab the audience's interest and make them want to read the book."[16] Mary K. Chelton writes that "the booktalk falls into place between storytelling and book reviewing, partakes of both, and is unlike either."[17] Booktalks can be formal presentations to groups or informal presentations to individuals. A group of booktalks can become a program by itself, or individual booktalks can be interspersed when talking with patrons. Booktalks can become one of your primary methods of providing reader guidance.

When selecting books to booktalk, choose only those books that you have read and are enthusiastic about. Not only should you like the books you booktalk, but they should appeal to your audience. Books that are fast moving, have credible plots and settings, and whose characters are authentic and involve intriguing situations are excellent candidates for booktalking. Be honest about the books you booktalk. If one has a slow start and is hard to get into, include that fact in your booktalk. While every book may be suitable for someone to booktalk, not all are suitable for you; you need to fit your booktalks to your style.

Develop your booktalks as soon after you finish reading the book as possible. You want to capture your immediate personal reactions to the book; analysis is fine for a research paper but not when you are trying to sell a book. While many people want to write out their booktalks in their entirety, you may feel just as comfortable writing only an outline that includes the important names, dates, and settings in the book. Be sure to include an exciting scene in your booktalk; lead up to it but do not reveal the resolution. Leave the characters at a point where they make a critical decision or choice. Never, ever tell the ending. You want to leave your listeners wanting more and the only way they can find out is to read the book. Even so, never say, "Read the book and find out."

Questions that you may want to answer or issues that you may want to discuss in your booktalk include, but are not limited to, the following:

- What genre is the book?
- Why did you choose a specific segment of the book to share?
- If illustrations are central to the book, what is the style of illustration and why are they important?

Booktalking works exceptionally well with middle and high school students but can be used with younger children as well as with adults.

## Computers and Online Activities

With the growth of the Internet, summer library reading programs should be taking advantage of the technology available to them. In addition to having registration and tracking available online, as previously discussed, some other aspects of the program can be placed online to take the library and its programs beyond the walls of the library. Recommended reading lists can be posted on library Web sites. When linked to the library catalog and the reserve system, patrons will have easier access to materials. Rather than coming to the library for a specific book and being disappointed by finding it is not on the shelf, library patrons can check availability in advance.

Libraries can include activities that relate to and enhance the summer program by placing them on the Web. People who do not have the ability to get to programs at the library may be able to participate in online activities. Mazes, word search, and crossword puzzles can be mounted on the library Web site to drive traffic not only to the site but eventually to the library.

## Contests

While contests where there is only one winner and many losers should be discouraged, opportunities for children and young adults to showcase their interests and abilities are appropriate. Before announcing any type of contest, decide the rules governing the contest in advance. Decide the number of participants you will allow and if you will have different age categories. Each type of contest requires different standards by which the entries will be judged. Determine these standards and distribute this information along with any other rules you have established in advance of the event. Whenever possible, display all contest entries so that everyone feels like a winner. If you are awarding prizes, determine what they will be, and how they will be awarded. Prizes should not be so extravagant that participants lose sight of the activity and concentrate only on the reward. Have experts act as judges; you may also want to have children and young adults serve on the jury as well. Contests offer unique opportunities for promoting library collections and services in the community and creating partnerships with individuals and organizations that might not otherwise be part of the library family.

One type of contest that everyone enjoys is a cook-off. A cook-off where children, teens, and even adults (in separate categories) bring a favorite food that they have prepared along with the recipe creates an opportunity for everyone, even those who have not brought any food to share, to become a winner. Recipes collected from participants can be compiled into a cookbook that can be added to the library collection, given to all participants as a prize for participating, and sold to others in the community. Children and teens who might not otherwise be recognized can be rewarded in this program. Judges for this type of program can include high school and community college food- and restaurant-service instructors, representatives from the local office of the Food and Consumers Services Section or Extension Services of the U.S. Department of Agriculture, and chefs from local restaurants.

Another contest that is in reality an educational opportunity is a pet show. This type of activity can include displays from local pet shops; the humane society; animal clubs, such as reptile and birds clubs; and clubs that specialize in distinctive breeds of dogs and cats. One requirement for this type of program is that all animals be on a leash or in a cage. Owners of all animals participating in either the educational displays or the contest should be required to show proof that all necessary shots (rabies, distemper, etc.) are current and that all animals are properly licensed. If holding the pet show outside, provide a place under the trees or have a tent or canopy erected so that the animal and human participants can be sheltered from the summer sun. Human participants are judged not only on the appearance of their animals, but on their knowledge about that breed of animal and how to take care of it. Your program can also include stories featuring animals as pets. Prepare displays and bibliographies of fiction and nonfiction books and other library materials related to the topic of pets and pet care.

Another type of contest that can be related to your summer library program is actually held prior to the summer: a contest to design the poster or bookmark for the program. Children and teens who are not normally attracted to the library may wish to participate in this activity; they may come to the library to get a better idea of what to include in their design. Afterwards, the contestants may return to the library, especially if all entries are displayed for the entire community to see. Expensive prizes are not necessary for this activity. As all participants in this activity are interested in art, gift certificates for art supplies or tickets to a special exhibit at a nearby museum are appropriate awards. The best reward for these budding young artists will be seeing their work on display; they will be even more excited to see their designs reproduced on bookmarks and posters that are distributed and displayed throughout the community.

Participants must know in advance the size of the entry and the colors allowed. If a specific theme is to be portrayed or slogan included, make sure that participants are aware of these requirements. Don't permit full-color entries if you do not have the capability to reproduce the bookmarks in full color. Be consistent in what identifying information you want contestants to provide: name, age, home address, school, grade, etc. Provide an entry blank for this information that can be placed on the back of the entry. This will allow judges to review the work impartially without revealing who the artist is. Judges for this activity can include local art teachers, hobbyists, artists, and gallery owners.

## *Crafts and Art Activities*

Art activities have long been part of library programming. Art activities should be included to permit participants to have an esthetic and creative experience as well as the chance to develop eye-hand coordination. Even if you have little or no artistic ability, that should not deter you from including art activities in your library programs. It is not necessary, or even desirable, for children to copy from a sample the librarian provides. The finished product is not as important as the creative act and the satisfaction the child gets from the experience.

Activities can be as simple or as complex as you and the participants desire. Provide a variety of media so that children can experience what it takes to be creative, using crayons, papier-mâché, collage, charcoal, pastels, and other media.

To ensure that the art activity has a relationship to books and literature, encourage children to illustrate their favorite scene from a book or make a collage illustrating a verse from a poem or song. Children should not be limited to two-dimensional art activities. Opportunities should also be provided for participants to create various types of three-dimensional constructions, models, and puppets. Young children can make paper plate stick puppets portraying faces of characters from books; older children can construct mitt puppets, while participants of high school age can construct more elaborate puppets, such as full-size Bunraku–style puppets. A mural created by a group of children based on the setting in a book can become the backdrop for a puppet show and encourages group participation and accomplishment rather than competition between individuals. Teen volunteers can assist in decorating the library and the youth areas for the summer library program by creating props and other backdrops that relate to your theme. Discuss the various techniques used by illustrators of picture books to interest participants in exploring new techniques. Incorporate simple techniques, such as crayon resists, for younger children and a more advanced one, such as scratch-board activities for older children and YAs into the techniques that children have the opportunity to try. Discussions should show how these methods are similar to those used by picture book artists.

Make certain that the art projects in your programs are developmentally appropriate for the participants. While finger painting may be messy, it is one of the activities that is appropriate for young children. Soap carving, on the other hand, would not be appropriate even for primary-grade students; it is more suited to middle school students, and even older. While many children enjoy the mess and squishy feel of papier-mâché, asking young children to make small detailed objects in this medium is not developmentally appropriate, but it would be for children in upper grades. Primary-grade children can create masks that do not need a great deal of detail from this media, and children even younger can make simple masks out of grocery bags. Program participants should be encouraged to try media that are unfamiliar to them. Needle crafts, such as embroidery, crocheting, and knitting, for example, provide a challenge to many middle grade students and adults as well.

Sewing is a life skill that all participants, regardless of age, need to experience. Start with simple running stitches with large-eyed plastic needles. Progress to smaller needles and more detailed stitching. Stitching puppets together or making stuffed animals is an enjoyable experience that teaches a necessary skill.

Children of the 60s who are now parents will relate to a tie-dye party. Children and teens who want to participate in this somewhat messy program are instructed to bring a plain, prewashed, white T-shirt to the program. Arrange to hold the program either on the library patio, on the grass outside the library, or in a roped-off area of the parking lot. Have rubber bands, plastic gloves, self-seal plastic bags, and the prepared cold-water liquid dye in squirt bottles—and lots of teen volunteers to assist. According to Katie Klopp, children's services manager at the Johnson County Public Library in Franklin, Indiana, this program generated lots of interest in the summer program. "We had 123 people attend, 22 of those were adults. We had 4 staff members and 2 teen volunteers running the program. We provided [supplies . . . and] instructions for each participant. . . . It was really fun to see the families wearing their t-shirts later on during the summer."[18]

Photography programs, while somewhat expensive, provide another esthetic experience for participants. Check with the local arts council to see if they have a grant to pay for disposable cameras and processing. Digital and Polaroid cameras provide immediate feedback. While elementary school children can participate in this activity, this is a program that teens find attractive. Have a professional photographer come in to discuss composition, use of light, and other techniques that will enhance their photographs. If using disposable cameras, send them home with instructions to return them in one week filled with photos they have taken. To relate this experience to the library program, have the photographers take pictures related to the theme of the summer program or have them capture people in literacy-related activities. After having the photographs developed, have each participant select his or her favorite and have it enlarged. Create a display in the library and on the library Web site featuring these photos.

Graphic novels are popular with many teens and comic books have always held a soft spot in the hearts of some. Many communities have comic book stores and swap shops. In addition to having a comic-book swap at the library, invite someone in to discuss and demonstrate how comics and graphic novels are created. Provide story boards and markers and allow participants to create their own strips. This could be part of a "Guys Read" program. For additional details on "Guys Read," see that section below.

Another craft activity that will allow program participations to soar to new heights is a paper airplane–construction workshop and contest. Many aeronautical engineers first tried their wings and designs by flying paper airplanes. Don't forget to display all the airplane, flying, and paper airplane–construction books and videos at the program.

For those of you who don't want to include craft activates in your programs, there is an alterative. If you have the space, set up a self-serve craft activity table or area. Change the activity weekly to encourage children (and parents) to return on a regular basis. Make certain that there are enough supplies and sufficient space for several children to participate in the activity simultaneously. If there is not sufficient space for this type of a learning center in the library, provide a handout with a suggested activity that can be made with found materials. Make and take allows families to continue the library experience at home. The families you serve may not have glitter and silver markers, but most have crayons and access to some basic supplies. If time and funds permit, construct take-home craft activity bags.

Lack of supplies may be a deterrent in some libraries; don't let it be. Solicit donations from art organizations and craft stores. Many times, merchants are willing to donate materials; they may also be willing to furnish someone from their own store or refer you to someone who can provide a demonstration using the materials that they have so generously donated. Community colleges with theater and art departments may also be able to provide the needed expertise and materials for your programs.

## *Deposit Collections*

Taking the library beyond the walls is a challenge, but doing so not only enhances the visibility of the library in the community, it also improves the community's access to books. Provide small collections of books in locations that children and teens frequent during the summer and throughout the year. Public health centers welcome small collections that are refreshed on a regular (semiannual) basis. Partner with camps, parks and recreation centers to have materials for them.

## *Dramatic, Musical, and Performance Activities*

There is no reason why part of your summer library program cannot be an entertaining event for the community. Children and young adults welcome the opportunity to showcase their talents and abilities. Having a talent show allows those with a bent for the dramatic or who have some type of musical ability the chance to perform for their peers. Since this type of program tends to take a great deal of time to organize, this may be an appropriate activity to celebrate the end or your summer program.

Establish ground rules for the talent show and publicize them in advance. Determine how many acts you will have in the show and how long each performer will be allotted. Announce if you are going to have auditions, nominations and recommendations, or if your show will be on a first-to-register-gets-to-perform basis. Rather than making these decisions yourself, you may wish to delegate the responsibility for this program to your teen volunteers. Work with the teens to set up an appropriate stage area. Have the teens consult with the local little theater for assistance in creating props and lighting. Teens can also create the *Playbill* for the performance in addition to acting as ushers and master of ceremonies for the program. A talent show at a community branch library can become an event that attracts a wide audience. Promote joke books from the library collection for your future comedians; magic books for the magicians, and books on ventriloquism, costume design, and other related arts.

In addition to doing an entire play or a selection from one, these talent shows can include music (from rap and reggae to rock to classical), dance (tap, jazz, modern, ballet, ballroom), magic, mime, poetry and prose readings, monologues, and skits. The talents of the participants should be the only limiting factor.

One aspect of drama and theater that can be its own separate program or incorporated into other programs is face painting. Not the exclusive territory of clowns, makeup is an important part of any theatrical performance. Invite someone from the theater arts program of the community college or the community theater group to come in to show how it is done. Allow teens the opportunity to participate by applying theater makeup or designing a clown face.

### Extended Loan Programs

If people in your community leave for the summer and vacation elsewhere, you may want to institute an extended loan period. Allowing families to borrow more books than normal and extending the loan period will allow your readers to continue reading over the summer. Make your program flexible enough so that if you are tracking hours, number of books, or pages that patrons read, they can be included in the count when they return from vacation.

School libraries, too, can be involved in summer library programs. The most popular young adult books from the West Liberty (Iowa) Junior–Senior High School are lent to the town's public library to be circulated over the summer. According to Virginia Miehe, school librarian, it is logical to share books with public library patrons when the school library collection would otherwise just be sitting unused. "YA circulation over the summer months has grown every year (an increase of 1000 percent over three summers), and a book has never been lost or damaged through this program."[19]

### Film and Video Programs

Much as we hate to admit it, not everyone wants to read or enjoys reading. Many children, 'tweens and teens today are visual learners, and library programming, especially during the summer, needs to include programs that attract visually oriented patrons. Film festivals are one possibility. Try, however, to tie the films and videos you select to their original written sources. Someone wrote the script, and it was probably based on a book. You can have exhibits, book displays, and bibliographies featuring the original story resources.

When designing a film festival, you must decide if this will be a single program, a series of programs over several days (similar to a real film festival), or a series of programs spread out over the summer. Depending on the age and interests of your patrons, you may want to have all the films relate to the theme of your summer library program. Young adults, on the other hand, may find a series of teen flicks from the 1950s through the 1970s camp; the *Beach Blanket* movies, *Godzilla*, super heroes such as *Superman*, or *I Was a Teenage Werewolf* may be just the ticket to combat the summer doldrums. Movies from the *Star Trek* series will bring out Treckies of all ages, many in costume. Adults who find themselves with little time or money to travel may flock to a travel-film series. Films and videos can take viewers places that they are unable to go themselves, whether into the future or the past, or to worlds too distant or too small for us to see. A film festival that explores film and video as an art form may encourage some young film makers in your service area to try their hand at producing a short. Work with the middle and high schools in your area to cosponsor such a project by providing the festival where all student entries can be viewed.

You will have to use care in selecting the movies and videos you will be showing during your programs. With so many films available at neighborhood video-rental stores and in your library's own video collection, you do not want to schedule movies that program participants have seen previously.

Film and video programs need to be special, not only in content, but in format. Children and YAs are used to seeing films on a television screen, but this is not the way most were intended to be viewed. Large-screen video projection units permit large groups of viewers to see the video as it was intended to be viewed—on a big screen. Darkening the room and setting your meeting room up cabaret style adds to the ambiance. Teens especially like this setting, and all ages enjoy having popcorn at these video shows.

A special word of caution when planning your film and video programs: make sure that the videos you select have public performance rights. In the past, most 16mm films were purchased with public performance rights. Most videos available today are covered by the Copyright Act of 1976; showing them at a library or at library outreach locations, such as camps, city parks or recreation centers, or child-care centers, constitutes a public performance and would be a violation of that law if you have not purchased public performance rights for them. It is extremely important that you negotiate these public performance rights at the time you purchase videos to add to your library's collection. Most videos that are rented from neighborhood video stores are for "home use only" and cannot be used in a public library or in a classroom, even for educational use. Make certain that the videos that you use in your programs are for public performance. If you are renting films and videos from a commercial distributor, make certain that public performance rights are included in the rental agreement.

In addition to having a special film and video program, you can add individual short videos to storytime programs. They can also serve as a jumping-off places for an art activity.

While showing films and videos is one aspect of programming, having older children and teens create their own films and videos adds another dimension to your program. When the new Fort Braden Branch Library was opened by the LeRoy Collins Leon County Library (Tallahassee, Fla.) in late 2003, Beverly Bass, the branch librarian, wanted to design a program for the summer of 2004 that would attract members of the rural community to the library. What resulted was the Summer Film Project. The library partnered with Unique Video Creations, a local video production company, the Tallahassee Film Society, and a popular radio station. Each of the partners provided unique contributions to the project.

The program was advertised throughout the community in the spring and a core group of youth 7 through 13 years of age signed up for the series of programs. For three hours every Monday afternoon, the group learned about film making from a professional videographer. Members of the Tallahassee Film Society shared films and videos from their collection and led discussions about the quality of the production and techniques that were used. Workshop participants were given weekly assignments to make note of the different techniques they observed while they watched television during the week.

Each weekly session consisted of lecture (learning about camera equipment, techniques, and tricks); discussion of sample clips, practice with equipment, and critiquing that practice, and finally, script development and rehearsal for the final projects.

Several storyboards were developed by the group. Each person had the opportunity to work behind the camera and, if they desired, to become part of the action. In the end, four shorts were developed.

The final public screening was treated as an awards ceremony. It was held at the community center, and the children and teens arrived dressed to the nines. They walked down the red carpet to cheers from their friends and families. The event was hosted by a local radio personality.

What were the outcomes of this series of programs? For the library, circulation in all areas of the library was up. Since this library is located in a rural area and there is little public transportation available, other members of the family would usually accompany the participants to the weekly program. While there, all parts of the library were active. This "cool" program attracted more teens to the library than just showing movies. The participants, as parents and library staff noted, had an improved self-image. They learned that making a movie was not easy, but they were able to do it. The kids learned that the library was a fun place to be. At the awards program, one teen who was attending the final program asked another teen who had been part of the film-making project when and where they made the videos that they were showing. The teen who had participated in the project replied that it was a summer library program activity and that there had been fliers out about it last spring. The first teen replied that he had seen them but didn't think it would have been this cool. He signed up to participate in the next film series.

### Feed Them, They Will Come

In addition to the Lunch with the Librarian and Booknic programs already discussed, any time you add food to a program, it will entice people who do not regularly attend library programs to make the effort to get to the library. If you are doing programs featuring Dr. Seuss books and characters, whip up a batch of green eggs and ham. Use a pasteurized egg substitute, some green food coloring, and bacon bits for an enticing treat. Or make homemade ice cream, either in an electric or hand-crank ice cream maker or use the rolling coffee can method. Have a pot of vegetable soup ready to serve after you "cook" up a batch of Stone Soup.

### Games and Tournaments

People of all ages enjoy games. Adapting television game shows and board games for the library is sure to attract positive attention. Hold Monopoly® or Scrabble® tournaments for competitors in various age groupings. Incorporate cooperative games for younger children into your storytime programs.

Young adults especially are attracted to games. Since most games offered in library settings are designed and constructed in such a way that there are many winners and usually no losers, teens feel a sense of security when participating in these activities. Library games can assist teens in their quest for independence and provide them with a way to manage the excitement (changes) in their lives. By providing games that can be individualized, the library helps teens in their search for their identities. When properly designed, these games will be accepted by the teen community as a whole;

therefore, those teens who participate will find approval from their peers as well as from many of the significant adults in their lives.

One library held a Scrabble® Tournament for middle school–age students. Participants drew numbers to see which table they would play at. They played for 30 minutes, and then drew again for a second round. After the two 30-minute games, scores were totaled and prizes awarded.

Family game nights provide another opportunity for involvement. Some of the most popular games in library settings include Twister®, Jenga®, Uno®, chess and checkers, and Candy Land®. Library scavenger hunts can help develop an awareness of the many sections of the library and the services that the library offers.

Several libraries have based their entire summer library program for young adults around games. One program was initiated by the Brentwood Library in Springfield, Missouri, in 1985. Rather than having YAs keep track of individual titles, teens were encouraged to read titles of various genres by using a game board. Teens were encouraged to read as few as four books during the course of the summer library program using the "Chart Your Own Course" maze that featured a pirate ship at the start and a treasure chest at the finish. The maze included no dead ends, so the reader could "win" no matter which path was chosen. Scattered along the path were the names of different genres. Before proceeding past that spot, the participant had to read a book from that category. Since the paths intersected, participants could sidestep or reverse directions to avoid a genre they did not want, or to read something from a category that they really wanted. The original game board was designed so that less popular areas of the collection—biography and poetry—stood between popular types such as mystery, science fiction, and fantasy.[20]

One of the most successful game programs originated at the Enoch Pratt Free Library in Baltimore, Maryland. "Bookjack" is a program that provides incentive for young adults to read during the summer. As with summer programs of a century ago, as staff from the Enoch Pratt Free Library moved to other locations, they took the programs they had been using with them and adapted them for use in other libraries with other library patrons. Such is the case with "Bookjack."

The first "Bookjack" program was created in 1982 when Cathi Dunn MacRae and Gail Gormley incorporated the card game of blackjack with reading and a picture-puzzle element. When "Bookjack" traveled from Maryland to North Carolina, the element of chance in the card game hooked players into returning to the game and the library again and again, thus increasing the reading of the teens who participated in the game. Since no money or even prizes were related to the card playing, this deviation from blackjack was not considered gambling. When MacRae moved to Boulder, Colorado, she introduced librarians in that state to this teen-oriented reading game. In 1991, the Colorado Department of Education produced "Bookjack" as the statewide summer reading program for young adults. The philosophy behind this program is based on MacRae's observation that personal contacts between the librarian and the young adult are the key to positive library experiences for the teens. "Any young adult reading game must incorporate such caring contacts as a basic element, as young adult players value the game in direct relation to its fulfillment of their needs for recognition and self-esteem."[21]

To earn any of the 21 pieces of the picture puzzle, teens read or participate in library activities. Teens earn each of the 7 pieces in Column A by reading a book of their choice; from Column B by watching a video or movie based on a book, reading a short story or a magazine article, or reading a Blue Spruce winner or nominee (Blue Spruce is a state author award); and from Column C, by writing a book review, reading a story to a child, or volunteering in the library. Participants are also able to earn picture-puzzle pieces by playing the "Bookjack" card game.[22] "Bookjack" manuals are available from program originator, Cathi MacRae. Contact her at *Voice of Youth Advocates,* 4720 Boston Way, Lanham, MD, 20706, phone 301-459-3366, ext. 5700, or by e-mail at cmacrae@voya.com.

A game that involves many age groups is "Family Bingo." Initiated by the Thomas Crane Public Library in Quincy, Massachusetts, this game has a format that is familiar to most patrons and is easy enough to explain to patrons who have limited English-speaking skills. It also is not a staff-intensive program. There are game sheets for various ages, from infant and toddlers through adult. The squares have things such as read a book (of various genres), visit the library Web site, participate in a program or do an art project or science experiment at home. Since the center square is a visit to the library, when they pick up their game cards at the library they already have one square filled and are on their way to completing a bingo. Each member of the family gets his or her own bingo card. When each member of the family scores bingo, five vertically, horizontally, or diagonally, the sheets are returned and a prize and certificate is awarded.

### *Guest Speaker and Other Community Resources*

Summer library programs are an excellent time to expose patrons of all ages to the resources that can be found in your community. As discussed in Chapter 3, there are many individuals and organizations within each community who would be delighted to share their professional expertise and hobbies with others. A job fair for teens is greatly enhanced if people with diverse jobs are part of it. Guests such as a beautician from a local salon can talk about the training and licensing needed to become a stylist as well as provide a makeover for someone in the audience. A flight attendant and a commercial airline pilot can talk about air safety and the hectic schedules that those jobs involve. Local government officials can provide information on how the township, city, or county operates. The Sheriff's Office Search and Rescue Unit or the Police K–9 Unit not only provides information but allows law enforcement personnel to be seen in a nonthreatening manner. The local chapter of the American Red Cross can provide a program on water safety and first aid. Your local Emergency Medical Services can also provide a program on first aid. If your community has an interest in boating, the Coast Guard or the local Power Squadron can talk about navigation and boating safety. If your library maintains a directory of community resources and clubs, start your search there.

Having an author visit your library is a great way to combine a guest speaker with a literature experience. Many authors and illustrators enjoy visiting libraries and talking with children, young adults, and adults who read their books. In addition to telling about the creative process, some authors and illustrators enjoy participating in young writers' festivals. However, just because someone is a good author or illustrator does not necessarily mean he or she is a good speaker. Inviting an author or illustrator may not be financially feasible for many libraries; in addition to providing an honorarium for these guests, libraries usually pay transportation costs as well as providing housing and meals for the speaker. Many more ideas on how to bring this type of program to fruition in your library are found in Kathy East's *Inviting Children's Authors and Illustrators: A How-To-Do-It Manual for School and Public Librarians* (New York: Neal-Schuman, 1995).

If your library is unable to secure funding for such an in-person visit, you may want to investigate arranging an electronic visit with the author via a chat on the Internet. Several publishing houses now have home pages on the World Wide Web; some of those pages include information on how to make electronic contact with their authors and illustrators.

The New York Public Library has been doing live online author chats as part of the summer library reading program for the past two years. Even if you miss the online chat, you can read transcripts of past sessions at http://summerreading.nypl.org/chats/index.cfm. On that page, there are links to the sessions with Ann Martin, Walter Dean Myers, Andrew Clements, and Jean Craighead George that were held as part of the 2004 program, Read, White and Blue. To find out about upcoming online author chats for children, check out http://kids.nypl.org/ or for teens, http://teenlink.nypl.org/. This is one of the ways that libraries can use technology and the Internet in an innovative, constructive, and appropriate manner.

Members of the community can also be called upon to provide programs about computers. Computer stores, both hardware and software, and local firms that teach computer skills may, on occasion, be willing to provide a program at the library. Many people still are computer illiterate and an introduction to computers at the library may be less threatening than going into a store where salespeople are trying to get prospective customers to buy. Many times the teens in your community have more computer skills than anyone else. If the library has computer equipment and software, the YAs can provide computer demonstrations on a regular basis. YAs can also serve as computer tutors for children and even for adults, helping them to negotiate your electronic public-access catalog and gain access to the local community computing network and the Internet. They can also help customize computerized reader-guidance programs. (See Reader Guidance section below.)

## *Guys Read*

According to research cited by Jane McFann in the August/September 2004 issue of *Reading Today*, boys take longer to learn to read than girls do. In addition to the fact that boys read less than girls, girls tend to comprehend narrative texts and most expository texts better than boys do. This may be because boys value reading as an activity less than girls do. According to a national survey conducted by the Young Adult Library Services Association (YALSA), a division of ALA, boys who averaged 14 years of age listed the following as their top obstacles to reading:

- 39.3 percent said reading is boring or no fun;
- 29.8 percent of the boys said they did not have time to read or they were too busy to read;
- 11.1 percent said there were other activities that they liked better than reading;
- 7.7 percent said they could not get into the stories; and
- 4.3 percent of the boys surveyed said they were not good at reading.[23]

Author Jon Scieszka, author of *The Stinky Cheese Man,* strongly believes that boys need extra motivation to become readers. He has started a movement, "Guys Read," which has the mission to motivate boys to read by connecting them with "materials they will want to read, in ways they like to read." To do this, we need to, "expand our definition of reading. Include boy-friendly nonfiction, humor, comics, graphic novels, action-adventure, magazines, Web sites, and newspapers in school reading. Let boys know that all these materials count as reading." In addition to allowing boys to choose what they want to read, we have to provide male role models involved in literacy activities.[24] Check the *Guys Read* Web site (www.guysread.com or www.penguinputnam.com/static/packages/us/yreaders/guysread/content1.html) for additional suggestions of how to involve boys (and men) in reading programs. Scieszka also provides a list of suggested readings that have special appeal to boys.

### Kitchen Chemistry

The Stow-Monroe Falls Public Library in Stow, Ohio, offers a four-week program for rising fourth- through seventh-grade students. Saturdays became special for these children and the teen volunteers who assisted at these programs. They explored scientific principles through cooking and other food-related activities. When they made butter, the participants learned about suspensions; when they made bubbles, they learned about solutions and surface tension; making rock candy, taught them about crystals. Everyone learned about the properties of yeast when the group made root beer. The session they enjoyed most was when everyone learned the freezing properties of salt by making ice cream.

### Outreach Programs—Have Program, Will Travel

The goal of outreach programs it to entice children and teens to visit the library. Learning about what the library has to offer in locations and venues that children already frequent provides an opportunity to educate them and attract them. The Laramie County Library System in Cheyenne, Wyoming, took its show on the road with its bookmobile. The outreach coordinator and bookmobile driver presented craft, storytime, and other programs at low-income apartments. Children and families were encouraged to get a library card, register for summer reading activities, and borrow books. Food coupons and enthusiastic staff persuaded children to attend.

This program increased total participation 93 percent and was so successful that the library extended the programming during the school year to a trailer park and continued it at the low-income housing complex. [25]

For years, the LeRoy Collins Leon County Public Library, headquartered in Tallahassee, Florida, has been aware that many children in their service area were not able to participate in the regular summer library programs that were offered at the main library and its branches. Many children participate in camps and other full-day programs that do not allow them to get to the library when the summer library programs were offered. Librarians in this system knew that children who read over the summer gained more in reading achievement than those who did not read. They decided that since the children could not get to the library, they would take the library to the children. And so, Park-It was born.

The Park-It program started in 1991 with funds provided through the State Library of Florida in the form of a Library Services and Construction Act grant. The project took library programs to the children who attended summer camps sponsored by the City of Tallahassee Parks and Recreation Department. Grant funds, provided again in 1992, were used to provide salaries for two part-time storytellers, to purchase audiovisual equipment, a portable puppet stage, operating supplies, and books. For several years following, Hank Rye, the owner of McDonald's restaurants in Tallahassee, supported the McDonald's Park-It programs with generous donations that covered salaries for the musicians/storytellers and a clerk for the program; the library provided the books and a van. Programs were presented twice each morning, five days a week, and changed weekly. Each of the ten city-park summer camps got one program each week for eight weeks. The program provided a 30- to 45-minute entertaining presentation of stories, songs, skits, and audience participation. The program was followed by browsing time when campers select books from large plastic bins (milk crates). Along with encouraging campers to borrow library materials, camp counselors were encouraged to select materials for use in their summer-camp program activities.[26]

Taking the summer library program on the road is also done by the Lancaster County (S.C.) Library. The library schedules bookmobile visits to camps and outreach centers. After a puppet show, the children each select two books from the bookmobile to check out. Library cards are issued to each site so the books can be kept on site. The bookmobile returns in two weeks and the campers return the books previously checked out and select more for the next two weeks.

The Garden City (N.Y.) Library trains teens to do story programs for younger children at the local pool. "Teens and Tots Storytime" has been presented at the Garden City Pool for the past 14 years. On average, every summer 50 young adults volunteer to be storytellers and story readers. Staff from the library train the teens who are going into grades 6 through 12. They attend two training sessions that orient them to the program and provide them with information and training on how to read aloud and select good books for storytimes. They also learn finger plays and age- and developmentally appropriate games. The children's librarians also demonstrate and teach the teens simple craft projects.

For five weeks during summer vacation, the teens and the children's librarian meet twice weekly at the pool. The teens are responsible for bringing their own books and a blanket for the children to sit on. An announcement is made on the public address system encouraging those who want to listen to a story to meet at the picnic area where the teens are set up for their storytimes. The teens decide in advance which age group they will work with that day: toddlers, preschoolers, kindergarteners, and children in first through third grade. The librarian helps the children get to the correct group. Children are treated to biweekly storytimes and the teens contribute to the community. At the end of the summer, the teen storytellers are invited to a party and are awarded certificates of achievement. They also receive a gift certificate for a visit to a local ice cream parlor or pizza place.

### Parents as Partners

While not all adults may want to participate on their own in a segment of the summer library reading program, libraries should encourage parents to be partners in their child's education. To that end, many libraries are finding ways to encourage parents in some unique ways. During the summer of 2004, the State Library and Archives of Florida began providing reproducible masters in the summer program manual that encouraged parent participation. Fliers were designed using art work from the program; text was kept to a minimum. When the font size is larger, when there is lots of white space on the page, and when the reading level of the text is low, even parents with low-literacy levels are encouraged to use the one-page sheets. These sheets have suggestions on ways parents and caregivers can become involved in reading, literacy, and learning activities. The suggestions help extend the learning opportunities available to the children over the summer, thus improving their learning outcomes. Figures 7–4 a and b are examples of the Parent Pages that public libraries throughout Florida used for their "Read Around Florida" program.

### Parties, Celebrations, Carnivals, and Festivals

Many libraries find that one of the best ways to generate interest at the beginning of the summer is to hold a large kick-off party. If you have sufficient space and enough staff, a party that features activities related to your summer library program theme, some musicians, lots of games, and, of course, food can create lots of excitement. Make certain that you have enough handouts about the summer library reading program for everyone who comes to the party. If you want participants to register for the rest of the summer program when they come to this event, have all your registration materials readily available. Make registration procedures so simple that they do not detract from the fun and excitement of the party. Make certain the activities at this party are developmentally appropriate for your target audience. If you are trying to attract teens to your summer library program, the party should be aimed at teens; if preschoolers are your primary target audience, your activities will be different. If families are your target, make certain that you offer a wide variety of activities so that there is something for everyone.

Festivals and other celebrations during the summer can help maintain interest in your ongoing program. All members of the community can be involved in putting

**Figure 7–4a**
**Parent Page (Teens)**

# Read Around Florida

## Lectura Alrededor de la Florida

Talk to your teen about graphic novels. They are more than just comic books.

Set aside one evening per week when the family sits down to dinner together and everyone talks about what they have read during the week – magazines, newspapers, books.

Plan a family trip. Use travel guides from the library to help you make your plans.

Listen to what your teen is saying.

Pick a book that you and your teen can read and discuss. Ask your local librarian for help in selecting an appropriate book.

Used by permission of the State Library and Archives of Florida.

**Figure 7–4b**
**Parent Page (Children)**

# Read Around Florida

## Lectura Alrededor de la Florida

Bake cookies to practice fractions and measuring ingredients. Make homemade ice cream and other foods to show them about the properties of salt, liquids, and solids, and how to measure temperature.

Use an outdoor thermometer to track weather, make predictions, and observe patterns.

Participate in a local recycling program.

Check out books from your local library that contain ideas for science experiments.

*These tips for parents are adapted from Center for Summer Learning, Inc., © 2002*

together a country fair. A small fair can be held in the library meeting room or at stations around the library. If you intend to have a large fair outside on the library grounds, check your insurance to see about liability coverage before you start to plan. The primary purpose of this type of program is to remind the community that the library is open all summer and that it provides recreation as well as information for people of all ages.

As much as possible, games, refreshments, and entertainment should relate to your theme. Whether you have a large fair or a minifair, you can have booths staffed by teens with games such as ring toss. If your theme is related to outer space, your ring toss can be Saturn's rings; if it is conservation related, it becomes toss the ring into the recycle container. Offer prizes of books, posters, and other incentives donated by people in the community. Face painting is always an enjoyable activity for the younger set. A roving clown or magician will enliven the event. Space permitting, acts from your talent show can also perform at this event. Some of the roving entertainers may be providing a sampling of a full program that they will be presenting later in the summer.

End of summer parties are a great way to celebrate your success and to remind the community of all that your participants have accomplished. It reminds all your participants that even though they had lots of fun and enjoyment over the summer, they also achieved some very important things: they learned more about the world, their community, their neighbors, the library, and themselves. They discovered new authors and new genres, developed new skills and enhanced ones they previously had. This is the time to announce to the entire community that you have reached your goal of $x$ number of people attending programs, that the library circulation increased by 25 percent over last summer, or that the entire community exceeded your goal of a cumulative total of 50,000 days of reading. Participants that contracted to read a specific number of hours should receive recognition for completing their contracts.

End of summer parties also are a way to say thank you to the rest of the library staff and all the volunteers (teens through senior citizens) who provided untold hours of service. End of summer parties are again a time when community partnerships are needed. The Mesa County (Colo.) Public Library held an "end of summer bash at an indoor roller skating rink." This party was cosponsored by the roller skating rink and a local radio station that broadcast live from the party. [27] Though not primarily designed as media events, all end of summer parties can take on that aspect and allow the library to tell how its resources and staff contribute to the quality of life in the community.

## Pen Pals and Key Pals

Pen pal projects have been around for years. They take a modicum of effort on the part of the adult organizing the program and provide an outlet for children's writing. Pen-pal programs can be arranged with children and teens from all over the United States and throughout the world. King County Library System in Seattle, Washington, is involved with four other libraries around the United States in a pen-pal exchange for children ages 9 through 11; they also sponsor a young adult pen-pal exchange with several libraries for ages 12 through 18.

A new and updated version of the pen-pal idea is "key pals." Children and teens are paired with each other over the Internet and use that electronic medium to correspond via e-mail. Besides allowing participants to learn about another area of the nation or the world and improve their writing skills, it also provides a very real reason to learn about computers and the Internet. A good place to post a message if your library is looking for key pals for the children and young adults in your summer library reading program is on the Public Libraries Young Adults and Children (PUBYAC) listserv. You must be a member of the list to be able to post a message; do a search on the Internet to get up-to-date information on how to join this list. Once you are a member, post a message regarding your interest in key pals or pen pals. Check the Teacher's Corner Web site (www.theteacherscorner.net) for leads on classes that wish to join either a pen-pal or key-pal program.

## Poetry Slams and Open Mikes

Over the past several years, there has been renewed interest in poetry. The Children's Book Council annually sponsors Young People's Poetry Week. This celebration, observed during the third week of April, provides a chance to celebrate poetry—to read it, hear it, write it, and enjoy it. Teens especially have been enticed into reading and libraries through programs known as poetry slams and open mikes—and not just during Young People's Poetry Week.

The open mike (or mic), sometimes called a cover slam, is an event at which the public is invited to read their poetry and listen to the poetry of others. The open mike is an environment for people to read brand-new work, to hear how it sounds, to get feedback, or to connect with other writers, sometimes for the first time. It's also usually the port of entry for people who have never read their work aloud before. For this type of event, you need a gracious host who needs to create a comfortable, encouraging, and safe environment for readers.

A poetry slam, on the other hand, is the competitive art of performance poetry. It puts a dual emphasis on writing and performance, encouraging poets to focus on what they're saying and how they're saying it. It provides a venue for new poets to read, gives poets a chance to try out new work and get feedback, and creates community. The competitive nature of this type of event has broad appeal for teens. A slam is an inherently competitive event, in which performance and literary skill are valued equally. It is also a participatory event, with the audience serving as judges and sometimes giving instant feedback in the form of cheers or jeers. In planning this type of program, remember that not every teen poet is ready to be a performer. Plan alternative approaches to sharing poetry to accommodate those who are shy or too hesitant to perform.

## Puppets and Puppetry

Puppet shows are another way to bring language and literature experiences into your library programs. Many times people think of puppetry as something designed to entertain only the youngest ones in the community. In other cultures, especially in Asia, puppetry is an art form that is enjoyed by adults more often than children. While many librarians are comfortable with hand puppets, there are numerous other types of puppets that can be used in library presentations.

Shadow puppets can range from simple to complex. They can be simple silhouette cutouts that are manipulated by the puppeteer behind a translucent screen that is back-lit to create the shadows. More complex shadow puppets can include hinged figures and puppets with textures added by fine cuts on the silhouettes. Action-packed stories work best with this type of puppet presentation.

Another form of Asian-style puppetry is Bunraku. A full-body puppet is used in this type of puppetry; it can take up to four people to manipulate these puppets, depending on their size and complexity. With this style of puppetry, the puppeteers are usually dressed completely in black; they even conceal their faces from the audience by using black net hats and veils.

Marionettes, or string controlled puppets, are yet another option for those that want to present puppet shows. However, these traditional puppets require more hands than many libraries can provide to manipulate them and the strings can get tangled making presentation difficult.

While some librarians may be comfortable presenting puppet shows or manipulating some of the more complex types of puppets, many feel that they want to maintain face-to-face contact with the audience. If this is the case, hand puppets or small Bunraku puppets can be used. A puppet that acts as a mascot for the summer library reading program can introduce every program all summer long. A Bunraku-style puppet can be given a place of honor in the youth section of the library so that program participants can visit with the mascot before and after programs. A stuffed animal that has been given a "puppetectomy" can also be used. A puppetectomy is an operation in which a small amount of stuffing is removed from the neck of the stuffed animal and the opening is then closed. This permits the puppeteer to move the head freely in a natural manner thus giving the object life.

Many times, youth librarians working more or less independently do not have a sufficient number of hands or time to properly present a puppet show. If you do not have the time to write puppet-show scripts, create puppets and scenery, and practice, you many want to invest your time in working with the teen volunteers, who can provide all the creative energies needed for such a venture. With proper guidance from library staff, teens can write original puppet-show scripts that highlight the library collection and its services. Original scripts can also integrate your summer library reading program theme. Teens relish the opportunity to perform for younger children.

## Read-To-Me-Programs

Not all of your summer library program participants are going to be readers. Some will be young children who have not yet acquired the skills to be independent readers. There may be others of many ages in your community who are learning English as a second language and would welcome the opportunity to hear other people read aloud. Even those people with good reading skills can benefit from hearing books read aloud; listening skills are two to three years ahead of instructional reading levels, and instructional reading levels are two years ahead of independent reading levels. Children and adults learning a new language learn usage, sentence structure, and pronunciation by listening to language.

Pairing readers with listeners is an activity that most libraries can sponsor. In addition to programs such as the one in Chappaqua, New York, that was discussed earlier, libraries can train senior citizens to read to children either individually or in groups. In their Prime Time program, the Broward County (Fla.) Division of Libraries was able to involve more children in summer library programs and provide an outlet for the energies of the community's senior citizens. Seniors were trained to present storytimes to children in child-care settings. Children benefited first by seeing that another older person, someone outside their family, cared about them; they also benefited by having additional language and literature experiences that could not otherwise be provided. Book buddies, teens listening to younger children, benefit both the teen and the younger child.

Children and teens who have difficulty reading aloud in class or other group situations may be more comfortable reading to stuffed animals or live ones. A program called "Paws for Reading" teams therapy dogs with children who want to read aloud. Several libraries around the US have programs that allow children to gain confidence in reading, learn how to interact with animals, and improve their overall reading skills. As a result of this program, libraries such as the Salt Lake City, Utah, and the Martin County Library in Stuart, Florida, report that children look forward to coming to the library to participate in the program. Catherine Sarette of the Whatcom County Library in Bellingham, Washington, reports that their program is called "Dog Days Afternoons" and is run in its entirety by a volunteer from the local Humane Society.

### *Reader and Materials Guidance*

Though many people may not think of this ongoing activity as part of the summer library reading program, reader guidance is a vital and integral part that, when done properly, ensures success of the program as a whole. Even if youth librarians cannot make personal recommendations to every child and young adult who comes to the library or to a library-sponsored program outside the library, there are many other ways to provide that needed guidance.

Reading lists and displays can assist those patrons you cannot serve through direct and personal contact. Not only do displays provide visual clues, these passive forms of reader guidance are available whenever the library is open, even when library staff are unavailable. They are also available to those patrons who are reluctant or too shy to ask for assistance. Reading lists and reviews by other readers when posted on the library's home page on the Internet provide guidance 24 hours a day.

Computer programs such as *Book Brain* can also provide reader guidance. Many of these electronic reader-guidance programs can be customized to each library's collection. Some also have the capability of letting readers add comments about the books they have read. Many library automation systems now allow for such online participation. Allowing readers of all ages to add reviews and recommendations not only provides an outlet for budding writers; it also permits members of the community to assist one another in selecting additional materials to read. Because of confidentiality laws in some states, you may need to make certain that names or other identifying characters are not included in reviews posted to the electronic system. Notebooks containing reviews written by local readers are a low-tech alternative.

Displays can incorporate collections from members of the community as well as books related to these collections. Displays should be mounted in such a way that the display items can be seen but are secure. Even if someone has a collection that coordinates perfectly with your summer library program theme, do not accept it for loan and display if you cannot adequately provide a proper, safe, and secure setting for the collection. Be certain that people who lend materials to the library for display sign a release form that renders the library harmless and unencumbered from any liability should something unforeseen happen to the collection while the library has possession of it.

Reading lists on topics related to your summer library program theme will help extend your program. Recommending books that children and teens might not find on their own will help you get the most out of your collection. Many times these reading lists and bibliographies are referred to weeks, months, or years later. Maintain a file of these bibliographies and update them as appropriate.

Library staff need to be knowledgeable not only about books but also about videos and DVDs, recordings, computer programs, magazines, and other materials that will interest their clients. Apart from reading, viewing, and listening widely, library staff should listen to what books, movies, and recordings their patrons are requesting, borrowing, and enjoying. Participating in book discussions with friends, colleagues, and patrons will aid library staff in expanding their knowledge of the collection and the reading interests of the community they serve.

## *Reading Camps*

As previously discussed, rather than providing a formal, punitive-inspired, traditional summer school, many school districts are providing a less academic setting during the summer that allows students the opportunity to enhance their learning in a less-structured setting. The Martin County Library System based in Stuart, Florida, was the recipient of a Library Services and Technology Act grant from the State Library and Archives of Florida to implement a Summer Library Reading Partnership Program during the summer of 2003. The library partnered with the county school district to set up a program to enrich children's summer learning experiences, to benefit children's school achievement, and to create and encourage lifelong readers. Following their morning summer school classes, the children in the program were transported to the public library to experience reading in a fun and relaxed way. Reading comprehension was stressed, and each session included read-aloud sessions, booktalks, and mentoring. The library received a National Association of Counties 2004 Achievement Award for their effort.

### *School Visits*

Though not technically part of your summer library program, school visits immediately prior to the start of summer vacation can guarantee a large audience for your summer programs. Dressing in costume related to the summer theme helps create excitement and makes you more visible, especially if you are doing an assembly program. See "Partnerships and Collaborative Effort with the Education Community" in Chapter 6 for information on this important part of your program.

### *Service Learning Programs*

While many libraries provide reading incentives, prizes, and rewards for reading, more and more libraries are incorporating service reading into their programs instead. Heifer International is an international organization that "works to end world hunger and save the earth." [28] Libraries and other organizations sign up. The Colchester-East Hants Regional Library in Truro, Nova Scotia, Canada, is one such library.

**Figure 7–5**
**Children who participated in the Martin County Library System's Summer Library Reading Partnership Pilot Program recieved a "Readers Rule!" T-Shirt.**

Participating children gather sponsors who pledge money for how much time or how many books the children read. In 2004, the children at this Canadian library raised $2,000 that was given to Heifer International to buy livestock for developing countries.[29]

## *Sleepover at the Library*

An exciting event that can be the highlight of your summer library program is an overnight at the library. The thrill of being in the library after hours is truly an adventure for many. For those children and YAs who are unable to go to overnight camp, this provides a refreshing, inexpensive alternative.

One of the first steps in planning this program is to check with the attorney for the library about whether staff and patrons can legally be in the library after hours without special liability insurance. If necessary, obtain such coverage, even on a temporary basis, for this program. Once this hurdle is cleared, the rest of the process should proceed smoothly.

As with other programs, you will need to decide who your target audience for this program will be. While many young children will want to participate, you may want to limit this program to middle school–age youngsters. A library sleepover is also a great end-of-summer reward for your teen volunteers.

Determine in advance the total number of people (participants, chaperones, and staff) that can be accommodated at your sleepover. Chaperones are a must; you need at least one adult chaperone for every five participants. Make sure that you have both men and women as chaperones. If you have determined that you have space to accommodate 12 sleepers at the library, that means that your program can have 10 youth participants and that you will need two adult chaperones, one male, one female, in addition to at least two staff. Besides having a sufficient number of chaperones in the library with you and program participants, inform local law enforcement authorities (police and sheriff) about your special program. They can provide additional security outside the building and can be on alert if you need assistance inside.

Once you have determined how many people you want to participate, you need to determine who will be invited to participate in this special program. Will registration be open to all, or will you limit registration to only the teen volunteers, or will there be other criteria to participate? After you determine who is eligible to attend, you need to establish your registration procedures. Every participant should have a slip signed by parent or guardian granting permission for him or her to take part in the library sleepover. The registration slip should have a place for parents to supply an overnight contact phone number should the need to get in touch with them arise. When participants register, they should be given all rules that you have established for this special program. This includes what participants need to bring with them (sleeping bag, toiletries, special snacks, etc.), what time they need to be at the library, and what time they need to be picked up the following morning. If the participants have any medical needs or dietary restrictions, there should be a place on the registration form for that information so library personnel are informed about those conditions. You don't want to serve pizza to a person who is allergic to yeast or tomatoes or only have pepperoni pizza if you have a vegetarian in your midst. Arrange to have participants in your library sleepover dropped off at the library after closing time one day and picked up before opening time the next morning. After serving a light breakfast of juice and cereal, have the participants assist with clean-up before they leave.

Storytelling for and by participants, especially ghost stories after lights out, playing group games, crafts, singing, viewing films and videos, reading, and eating are activities preferred by many participants. You need to plan and arrange to have more activities for participants than you think is actually necessary; many activities will go faster than you plan and the group will always want to stay up past what you think is a reasonable bedtime.

Establish, announce, and stick to a specific lights-out time. To help handle any difficulties that may arise, two adults should be awake and available all night long. Chaperones and library staff need to rotate times that they are up and patrolling the library.

Many libraries have undertaken this special program with rewarding results. Participants have a great time and lifelong memories about their night in the library.

## *Storytelling*

Storytelling is a wonderful way of integrating oral traditions from many cultures into your summer programs; it has long been considered an acceptable method of entertaining and educating members of the community of various ages. Storytelling is an excellent way to expose children, adults, and speakers of other languages to the intricate language patterns of spoken English. Without the use of visual clues that are found when reading from books or viewing movies and videos, telling stories provides motivation for developing good listening skills. Along with establishing a friendly relationship between the storyteller and the listener, storytelling helps the listener develop a sense of humor and imagination. Storytelling also helps the listener develop sympathy and empathy for the characters in the stories and translate these feelings to real life. "Storytelling bypasses the barriers of illiteracy and reluctance of nonreaders"[30] and is a vital link to remembering cultural heritage and preserving traditions.

Not only should adults tell stories as part of summer programs, children and young adults should be encouraged to learn literary tales. In addition to the use of literary tales, older community members can be invited to tell about what it was like in your community when they were growing up. Participants of all ages should be encouraged to commit their family stories to paper and audiotape so that others may share them. These stories can become part of a community oral history project.

Storytelling can add a multicultural aspect to all of your programs. One library that has added storytelling to its repertoire of outreach programs is the LeRoy Collins Leon County (Fla.) Public Library. With a grant from the Winn Dixie Foundation, the library created "Tanga Tanga" for the 1996 summer library program. "*Tanga Tanga*" is a Swahili phrase meaning to stroll from village to village telling tales. That is exactly what this library outreach program does.

"Tanga Tanga," a four-week summer program that originated during the summer of 1996, was part of the library's ongoing efforts to reach out into the community surrounding the Bond Library, an underutilized branch. The branch is located in a predominately African American neighborhood that has many low-income families and a high-crime rate. There are numerous reasons why the children in this community do not use the library: lack of transportation, fear of having to pay overdue fines for a lost or damaged book, not knowing that the library is more than just books, and fear that many of the books and other materials it has would not be right for them.

To overcome the reluctance of children and their families to use the library, weekly visits to four low-income housing projects featuring African American storyteller Oluesegun Williams and his talking drum were arranged. The Caribbean Dance Theater where Williams works donated many hours to teach children music and dances from other cultures. Some of the older children participating in the program brought life to African folk tales by acting out parts and characters as the storyteller told the tales. As the weeks progressed, many parents and older siblings started joining in just to experience the fun of learning a Liberian welcome dance or hear the talking drum.

Each week, paperback books, comic books, pencils, and bookmarks were given to the children who attended this special program. The library's literacy coordinator was on hand to talk with community residents about family literacy programs offered through the branch library in their community.[31]

### Storytime

Many of the individual programs you include as part of the summer library program will be traditional storytimes. Depending on the ages, developmental abilities, and interests of your participants, several books, a song or two, finger or hand plays can be included in each individual program. A puppet mascot can introduce the program and be used to encourage children who do not otherwise communicate orally to participate. When time and space permit, an appropriate art activity can be included. In addition to the books that are shared in storytime, additional books related to your theme should be available for participants and their families to borrow.

In addition to your traditional storytime programs, libraries are responding to the changing demographics of their communities by offering bilingual and multilingual storytimes. After holding auditions, the Pleasanton (Calif.) Public Library contracted with bilingual staff from libraries in surrounding communities. Eight individuals were provided a stipend for presenting a 30-minute storytime. Programs were offered in Japanese (1), Russian (1), Mandarin (2), Farsi (2), and Spanish (2).

### Teacher-Challenge Programs

Teachers in area schools should be encouraged to participate in your summer library reading program. As you present your school visits in late spring, recruit teachers as presenters for special programs and to be judges for contests. If you are tracking individual reading, invite teachers to participate in this activity. Students enjoy seeing how much their teachers read. You may even want to have teachers challenge the students who will be in their class in the fall to read a specified number of days. Together, if students meet this goal, then the teacher must publicly do something humorous or mildly outrageous, such as sit on the roof of the library or school and read aloud to the students, dye their hair a shocking color (temporary color, of course!), or kiss a pig. Male teacher, principals, and librarians involved in similar challenges have been known to shave their heads or shave off their beards and mustaches. If you are having a fair or festival at the end of the summer, you may be able to convince some brave soul to be the victim for a dunk tank or to be slimed.

### TV Tie-Ins

Teens especially are attracted to popular culture and programs that can tie into popular television game and reality shows. Using the game-show format that has been popular on television for more than a decade, libraries can have a *Wheel of Fortune* or *Jeopardy* tournament. Popular shows such as *Fear Factor, CSI,* or *Survivor* can be adapted for use at the library.

The Whatcom County Library in Bellingham, Washington, has created a program called "Survivor: Library Style!" Rather than voting people off the island, the library program became one in which members of the teams had to cooperate with one another. Several challenges can be presented at each program. One of the challenges that the library created was the "Treacherous Trail." For this challenge, there was a small obstacle course that the entire team had to complete. A step stool became a hill to climb; a piece of rope taped to the floor became a rope bridge that had to be crossed; tables draped with camouflage fabric were a cave to crawl through; and craft paper cut into stepping stones became a path and team members had to jump from one stone to another. Each team member is timed while trying to complete the challenge; times for the team are totaled. The team that survives each challenge is rewarded. At the end of the program, everyone receives a prize for surviving.

There are many activities that could be used to emulate the proliferation of forensic-science television shows such as *CSI* or *Crossing Jordan*. Natasha Forrester from the Winfield (Kans.) Public Library compiled a list of such activities and posted it on PUBYAC. Since observation is key to criminal investigation, be sure to talk about how important it is to observe things accurately. Provide program participants with a small notebook that they can use to write down what they observe. Place an assortment of items on a table and give them 15 to 20 seconds to study them. Cover them with a cloth and then have each person write down detailed descriptions of what they have observed. Compare the observations and then reveal what is actually on the table.

Let the evidence speak. Make invisible ink using lemon juice, onion juice, or equal parts baking soda and water mixed together. Using a Q-tip as a pen, have the participants write messages on plain white paper. Use a low heat source such as a light bulb or warm (not hot) iron to develop the ink. Baking soda ink can also be read by painting over the hidden message with grape juice.

To enhance the atmosphere in the program room, decorate the area with crime-scene tape. Another activity would be to have participants make pictures using finger and thumb prints reminiscent of Ed Emberly's thumbprint drawing books. To top off the program, invite a police investigator, state trooper, or state bureau of investigation officer to talk about solving crimes.[32]

### *Writing Activities*

Author Richard Peck says in many of his presentations to parents, teachers, and librarians, "Nobody but a reader ever became a writer." Not only should summer library programs promote reading, these programs should encourage and promote other literacy activities, too. Remember that literacy truly and broadly defined includes all aspects of language skills: listening, speaking, reading, and writing. One important activity that is often overlooked in library programs is writing. Libraries can encourage readers to write reviews, booktalks, or annotations for books they have read. Reviews and annotations can be compiled in a notebook or an electronic database to be shared with other patrons. Library staff can work with the teen volunteers to compile reviews and written booktalks for a literary newsletter that can be distributed to patrons of the appropriate age.

A successful writing project was initiated by Alan Nichter, branch librarian, Lutz Branch Library of the Tampa-Hillsborough County (Fla.) Public Library System. After presenting a series of booktalk programs at local middle and senior high schools, Nichter worked with language arts and English teachers and their students. Together they developed student-written annotated book lists that were distributed in the schools and the public library. While this program originated during the school year, there is no reason why programs similar to this cannot take place during your summer library program.[33]

Other libraries have had success with other types of writing activities. A library in Colorado sponsors a writer's workshop where middle school students write, illustrate, and bind their original manuscripts. They share their books during a final "Author's Reception" where refreshments are served. [34]

Budding writers may want to try their hand at creating scripts for readers' theater. This is a great way to involve many participants in activities that extend the literature experience.

To create a reader's theater script, the writer adapts a chapter or segment from a chapter book or an entire picture book. Dialog becomes lines for a character to read; description and comment provided by the author needs to become narration. Depending on the amount of narration, this can be split between several narrators. Several prepared readers' theater scripts are available online at author Aaron Shepard's Web site: www.aaronshep.com/.

Another writing activity involves readers creating their own ending to a story. Read up to a specific point in a short story or book or provide the beginning of a story from a collection of folk tales. Have the group discuss various endings and then allow them to create their own endings. Post the complete stories on the library Web site. This activity could also be done remotely by posting the story starter on the Web site and allowing people to submit their completed stories online.

### Zoo Mobiles and Wild Wings

Wild and native animals hold an attraction for many. Many communities have either wild-life rescue programs or a zoological garden of some type; most have educational units. Add these agencies to your list of community contacts as you plan your programs. Many of the animal rescue programs are able to bring injured animals out to educate the community about the treatment of animals. Cathy Henderson, children's librarian at the Seymour Library in Brockport, New York, had one agency bring a golden eagle to the library. "It was an awesome program; kids and adults alike raved about it."[35] Henderson also contacted the local zoo, the Senaca Park Zoo in Rochester, New York. This zoo has a mobile-zoo service. They have several programs that they can take on the road. The one that was presented at the Seymour Library as part of their 2004 summer program was "Creepy Crawlies."

## Endnotes

1. Gary H. Becker. 1994. "Copyright Considerations for Youth Librarians." *Developing Public Library Services for Young Adults*. Tallahassee, Fla.: Division of Library and Information Services, Florida Department of State, 14–24.

2. Becker.

3. Becker.

4. Becker.

5. Muzette Diefenthal, Barbara Kruser, and Ricki Nordmeyer. 2000. "Summertime and the Reading Is Easy (for Adults)." *Illinois Library Association Reporter* 18, no. 4 (August): 1–4.

6. E-mail from Pat Vasilik to Cheryl Weems, in response to a posting on PUBYAC, "Summer Reading Program query," August 2, 2004.

7. Elizabeth A. Poe, 1998. "Promoting Literature Discussions." In *Into Focus: Understanding and Creating Middle School Readers*, edited by Kylene Beers and Barbara G. Samuels. Norwood, Mass.: Christopher-Gordon, 163.

8. Poe, 167.

9. Carole D. Fiore, 1994. *Programming for Introducing Adults to Children's Literature,* New ed. ALSC Program Support Publications. Chicago: American Library Association.

10. Information about Booknic was provided by program originator Susan Oliver, Principal Librarian, Tampa-Hillsborough County (Fla.) Public Library in an unpublished program report, September, 1996.

11. R. C. Anderson, et al. 1985. *Becoming a Nation of Readers*. Washington, D.C.: National Institute of Education, 1985.

12. *Children's Books Awards and Prizes*. New York: Children's Book Council, annual.

13. Kathleen Staerkel, Linda Ward-Callaghan, and Nancy Hackett. 1994. *Newbery and Caldecott Mock Election Kit: Choosing Champions in Children's Books*. Chicago: Association for Library Service to Children, American Library Association.

14. Cathi Dunn MacRae. 1991. *Bookjack: Colorado 1991 Young Adult Summer Reading Program*. Denver, Colo.: Colorado Department of Education, State Library and Adult Education Office, 10.

15. "Prime Time Family Reading Time." *Louisiana Endowment for the Humanities Web site*. Available: www.leh.org/primetime/PThomepage.htm. Accessed November 19, 2004.

16. Rachael Fishbaugh. 2004. "Using Book Talks to Promote High-Level Questioning Skills." *The Reading Teacher* 58, no. 3 (November): 296.

17. Mary K. Chelton. 1976. "Booktalking: You Can Do It." *School Library Journal* 28, no. 8 (April): 39–43.

18. E-mail from Katie Kloop to Carole Fiore, November 16, 2004.

19. Virginia Miehe. 1992. "Send Your Books on Vacation." *School Library Journal* 38, no. 5 (May): 54.

20. Paula Morrow. 1985. "Library Treasure: A Summer Reading Program." *Top of the News* 41, no. 2 (Winter): 169–176.

21. MacRae, 1.

22. MacRae, 64–68.

23. Jane McFann. 2004. "Boys and Books." *Reading Today* 22, no. 1 (August/September): 20.

24. *Guys Read.* Available: www.penguinputnam.com/static/packages/us/yreaders/guysread/content1.html. Accessed November 7, 2004.

25. Walter Minkel. 2002. "Taking the Show on the Road." *School Library Journal* 48, no. 2 (February): 46–48.

26. Cay Hohmeister. 1996. "McDonald's Park-It Program: LeRoy Collins Leon County Public Library and Summer Outreach to Tallahassee Parks Day Camps." *Florida Libraries* 39, no. 4 (May/June): 67.

27. Diana Tixier Herald. 1996. "Buy More Books! & Other Bright Ideas from a Teen Advisory Board." *School Library Journal* 42, no. 7 (July): 26–27.

28. *Read to Feed.* Available: http://readtofeed.org/for_teachers_leaders_and_parents/. Accessed November 14, 2004.

29. E-mail message from M. Lynda Marsh to PUBYAC, posted November 12, 2004.

30. Gail De Vos. 1991. *Storytelling for Young Adults: Techniques and Treasury.* Englewood, Colo.: Libraries Unlimited, ix–x.

31. Unpublished program report by Sara Johnson, LeRoy Collins Leon County (Fla.) Public Library, September 1996.

32. E-mail from Natasha Forrester posted to PUBYAC, July 20, 2004.

33. Alan Nichter. 1994. "Literature for Today's Young Adults." *Developing Public Library Services for Young Adults.* Tallahassee, Fla.: Florida Department of State, Division of Library and Information Studies, 115–135.

34. MacRae, 9.

35. E-mail from Cathy Henderson to Carole Fiore, November 14, 2004.

## Recommended Reading

Baltuck, Naomi. 1993. *Crazy Gibberish and Other Story Hour Stretches.* Hamden, Conn.: Linnet.

Barban, Leslie. 1991. "Booktalking: The Art of the Deal." *School Library Journal* 37, no. 8 (August): 106.

Barchers, Suzanne I. 2000. *Multicultural Folktales: Readers Theater for Elementary Students.* Englewood, Colo.: Teacher Ideas Press.

Bauer, Caroline Feller. 1987. *Presenting Reader's Theater.* Bronx, N.Y.: H. W. Wilson.

Bodart, Joni. 1980. *Booktalk!* Bronx, N.Y.: H. W. Wilson.

———. 1985. *Booktalk! 2.* Bronx, N.Y.: H. W. Wilson.

———. 1988. *Booktalk! 3.* Bronx, N.Y.: H. W. Wilson.

———. 1992. *Booktalk! 4.* Bronx, N.Y.: H. W. Wilson.

———. 2002. *Radical Reads: 101 Young Adult Novels on the Edge.* Lanham, Md.: Scarecrow.

Braun, Linda W. 2003. *Hooking Teens with the Net.* Teens @ the Library Series. New York: Neal-Schuman.

Briggs, Diane. 1992. *Flannel Board Fun: A Collection of Stories, Songs, and Poems.* Metuchen, N.J.: Scarecrow.

Carle, Eric. 1998. *You Can Make a Collage: A Very Simple How-to Book.* Palo Alto, Calif.: Klutz.

Chupela, Dolores. 1994. *Ready, Set, Go! Children's Programming for Bookmobiles and Other Small Spaces.* Fort Atkinson, Wis.: Alleyside Press.

Crews, Kenneth D. 2000. *Copyright Essentials for Librarians and Educators.* Chicago: American Library Association.

Dailey, Susan M. 2001. *A Storytime Year: A Month-to-Month Kit for Preschool Programming.* New York: Neal-Schuman.

de Vos, Gail. 1996. *Tales, Rumors, and Gossip: Exploring Contemporary Folk Literature in Grades 7–12.* Englewood, Colo.: Libraries Unlimited.

———. 2003. *Storytelling for Young Adults: Techniques and Treasury,* 2nd ed. Englewood, Colo.: Libraries Unlimited.

de Vos, Gail, Merle Harris, and Celia Barker Lotteridge. 2003. *Telling Tales: Storytelling in the Family.* Edmonton, Alberta, Canada: University of Alberta Press.

Dickerson, Constance. 2004. *Teen Book Discussion Groups in the Library.* Teens @ the Library Series. New York: Neal-Schuman.

East, Kathy. 1995. *Inviting Children's Authors and Illustrators: A How-To-Do-It Manual for School and Public Librarians.* New York: Neal-Schuman.

Edgerton, Cathi. 1993. "Young Adult Summer Reading Games: A Source and Resource." *VOYA* 6, no. 3 (August): 134–141, 163–164.

*EZ Library Programs.* Available: http://midhudson.org/resources/ezorigram.htm. Accessed November 19, 2004.

Faurot, Kimberly K. 2003. *Books in Bloom: Creative Patterns and Props That Bring Stories to Life.* Chicago: American Library Association.

Feinberg, Sandra, Joan F. Kuchner, and Sari Feldman. 1998. *Including Children with Special Needs: A How-To-Do-It-Manual for School and Public Libraries.* New York: Neal-Schuman.

Feinberg, Sandra, and Sari Feldman. 1995. *Running a Parent/Child Workshop.* New York: Neal-Schuman.

———. 1996. *Serving Families and Children through Partnerships.* New York: Neal-Schuman.

Freeman, Judy. 1990. *Books Kids Will Sit Still For: A Guide to Using Children's Literature for Librarians, Teachers, and Parents.* New Providence, N.J.: R. R. Bowker.

*Gambit: Selected Programming Strategies for Young Adults.* 1988. Baltimore, Md.: Maryland Library Association, Public Services Division.

Gillelspie, John T., and Corinne J. Naden. 2003. *Teenplots: A Booktalk Guide to Use with Readers 12–18.* Englewood, Colo.: Libraries Unlimited.

Herald, Diana Tixier. 2003. *Teen Genreflecting: A Guide to Reading Interests.* 2nd ed. Genreflecting Advisory Series. Englewood, Colo.: Libraries Unlimited.

Honnold, RoseMary. 2003. *101+ Teen Programs That Work.* Neal-Schuman.

Jones, Patrick, Michele Gorman, and Tricia Suellentrop. 2004. *Connecting Young Adults and Libraries: A How-To-Do-It Manual,* 3rd ed. New York: Neal-Schuman.

Langemack, Chapple. 2003. *The Booktalker's Bible: How to Talk about the Books You Love to Any Audience.* Westport, Conn.: Libraries Unlimited.

Lenser, Jane. 1994. *Programming for Outreach Services for Children.* Chicago: American Library Association.

Libretto, Ellen, and Catherine Barr. 2002. *High/Low Handbook: Best Books and Web Sites for Reluctant Teen Readers,* 4th ed. Serving Special Needs Series. Englewood, Colo.: Libraries Unlimited.

MacDonald, Margaret Read. 1986. *Twenty Tellable Tales.* Bronx, N.Y.: H. W. Wilson.

———. 1992. *Peace Tales: World Folktales to Talk About.* North Haven, Conn.: Linnet.

———. 1993. *Storyteller's Start-Up Book: Finding, Learning, Performing and Using Folktales (Including Twelve Tellable Tales).* Little Rock, Ark.: August House.

———. 1995. *The Parent's Guide to Storytelling: How to Make Up New Stories and Retell Old Favorites.* New York: HarperCollins.

Maddigan, Beth. 2003. *The Big Book of Stories, Songs, and Sing-alongs: Programs for Babies, Toddlers, and Families.* Westport, Conn.: Libraries Unlimited.

McBride-Smith, Barbara. 2001. *Tell It Together: Foolproof Scripts for Story Theatre.* Little Rock, Ark.: August House.

McGrath, Renée Vaillancourt. 2004. *Excellence in Library Services to Young Adults,* 4th ed. Chicago: American Library Association.

Miller, Teresa. 1988. *Joining In: An Anthology of Audience Participation Stories and How to Tell Them.* Cambridge, Mass.: Yellow Moon Press.

Minkel, Walter. 1999. *How to Do "The Three Bears" with Two Hands.* Chicago: American Library Association.

Moss, Joyce, and George Wilson, ed. 1992. *From Page to Screen: Children's and Young Adult Books on Film and Video.* Detroit, Mich.: Gale Research.

National Storytelling Association. 1994. *Tales as Tools: The Power of Story in the Classroom.* Jonesborough, Tenn.: National Storytelling Press.

———. 1995. *Many Voices: True Tales from America's Past.* Jonesborough, Tenn.: National Storytelling Press.

Nespeca, Sue McCleaf, and Joan B. Reeve. 2002. *Picture Books Plus: 100 Extension Activities in Art, Drama, Music, Math, and Science.* Chicago: American Library Association.

Neuman, Susan B., Carol Copple, and Sue Bredekamp. 2000. *Learning to Read and Write: Developmentally Appropriate Practices for Young Children.* Washington, D.C.: National Association for the Education of Young Children.

Olness, Rebecca. 2005. *Using Literature to Enhance Writing Instruction: A Guide for K–5 Teachers.* Newark, Del.: International Reading Association.

Pellowski, Anne. 1984. *The Story Vine: A Source Book of Unusual and Easy-to-Tell Stories from around the World.* New York: Macmillan.

———. 1987. *The Family Storytelling Handbook: How to Use Stories, Anecdotes, Rhymes, Handkerchiefs, Paper, and Other Objects to Enrich Your Family Traditions.* New York: Macmillan.

———. 1995. *Storytelling Handbook: A Young People's Collection of Unusual Tales and Helpful Hints on How to Tell Them.* New York: Simon & Schuster.

Phlomm, Phyllis Noe. 1986. *Chalk in Hand: The Draw and Tell Book.* Metuchen, N.J.: Scarecrow, 1986.

Reid, Rob. 1999. *Family Storytime: 24 Creative Programs for All Ages.* Chicago: American Library Association.

———. 2002. *Something Funny Happened at the Library: How to Create Humorous Programs for Children and Young Adults.* Chicago: American Library Association.

Rochman, Hazel. 1987. *Tales of Love and Terror: Booktalking the Classics, Old and New.* Chicago: American Library Association.

———. 1993. *Against Borders: Promoting Books for a Multicultural World.* Chicago: American Library Association.

Schiller, Pam. 2001. *Creating Readers: Over 1000 Games, Activities, Tongue Twisters, Fingerplays, Songs, and Stories to Get Children Excited about Reading.* Beltsville, Md.: Gryphon.

Schiller, Pam, and Jackie Silberg. 2003. *The Complete Book of Activities, Games, Stories, Props, Recipes, and Dances for Young Children.* Beltsville, Md.: Gryphon.

Sierra, Judy, and Robert Kaminski. 1991. *Multicultural Folktales: Stories to Tell to Young Children.* Phoenix, Ariz.: Oryx.

———. 1997. *The Flannel Board Storytelling Book.* 2nd ed. Bronx, N.Y.: H. W. Wilson.

Sullivan, Michael. 2003. *Connecting Boys with Books: What Libraries Can Do.* Chicago: American Library Association.

*Teens Making a Difference: 2002 Programs for Teens from the Library of Virginia.* 2002. Richmond, Va.: The Library of Virginia.

Trelease, Jim. *The Read-Aloud Handbook.* New York: Penguin, 2001.

# 8

# Evaluating Program Success

## Evaluation as Part of Planning

An important and frequently overlooked aspect of the summer library reading program is the evaluation of the program. Evaluation is part of the planning cycle. Assessment of needs and goal setting occurs at the beginning of your program when you are determining the needs of your community. Goals and objectives make it possible to evaluate how well you have accomplished what you set out to do. Determining the outcomes you wish to achieve in advance will help you know if you have achieved those outcomes.

Evaluation should occur over the entire length of the summer library program. No matter how well planned, you may need to make some adjustments, even minor ones, in your strategies so that you can better achieve your goals. Evaluation at the end of the summer is done not just to see what you have accomplished and whether the program's objectives have been met, but as the first step in planning your next summer library program. As Douglas Zweizig, professor emeritus at the University of Wisconsin–Madison, frequently says, "Evaluation is not to prove, but to improve."[1] The true purpose of any evaluation activity should be to find out what can be learned in order to improve service in the future.

Knowing the outcomes of your program and communicating those results to all stakeholders in your community is just as important as delivering the service to your target audience.

Regardless of whether your library formally evaluates its services and programs such as the summer library program, informal evaluations will be done on an ongoing basis by everyone who has any interest in the service. The children and teens you wanted to participate in the program will let you know right away if you are on target. Comments and reactions by teachers, parents, and caregivers whose children use or do not use the service are an indication of how well your program is responding to the needs of your community. Taxpayers and funding agencies, both public and private, that underwrite the service will also be interested in how well you are meeting your announced goals. Other library staff and volunteers who observe the program and invest time and energy into its development and presentation are sure to let you know if they feel their efforts and talents are being used appropriately to meet the goals and objectives of your program. The governing bodies of the library that must make decisions about the services and programs that the library offers will also be observing your program and making judgments about it.

If the library and its staff do not design an evaluation for its own programs, others will do so for you. If library staff are not actively engaged in evaluating the services and communicating the contributions that service makes in the community and its effect on the lives of the members of the community, then decisions about that service and program will be made by others without the benefit of that information and knowledge.

There are numerous methods that can be used to evaluate your summer library program. Evaluation methods must be practical, useful, and efficient. If evaluation methods are difficult to implement, people will not use them. If evaluation methods are to be used, they must provide useful, practical information upon which future decisions can be made. Just because it would be *interesting* to know something does not mean that it should be part of your evaluation. If evaluation methods are so complex and time consuming that they interfere with service delivery, they can adversely affect your program. The purpose of this chapter is to introduce various methods that can be used to evaluate the summer library program as well as other aspects of the youth services program as a whole.

Various evaluation methods require different levels of effort and yield different types of information. It is up to the staff of each library as they design their summer library program to build in appropriate methods of evaluation that will help them determine the success of the current program and allow goals and objectives for future ones to be established. To be able to tell about your successes, you need to know in advance what you want to tell and to whom you will deliver the message. In other words, you need to know from the very beginning what outcomes you desire, how you will measure that achievement and success, and who needs to know the results of your program. Knowing what your goals and objectives are will help you determine what you will evaluate and how that evaluation will be done, what data will be collected, and why you are doing it.

## The Numbers Game

Though numbers by themselves give little information, numbers gathering has long been associated with evaluation. For numbers to be of real value, however, they must be compared with something else.

Counting up is a basic component of documenting the delivery of library services. Librarians are used to counting things related to library services. Automated systems provide circulation statistics; even libraries with manual circulation systems usually keep the most basic of circulation statistics—how many books are checked out each day. Most libraries count how many reference questions are asked; fewer count how many of those questions are answered to the patron's satisfaction. Many libraries even count the number of people who walk through the door, though few distinguish why people come to the library. Numbers can answer the question, "How many?" but cannot on their own answer the question, "How well?" Without comparing numbers over time, gathering numbers means little. Comparing numbers over several years provides information that can be useful in determining trends. Numbers-gathering is also used when tabulating questionnaire results. While a numbers-gathering approach to evaluation is limited in its ability to clearly reflect outcomes, it does provide logical indicators of a library's movement towards its goals.

One of the problems with numbers gathering is derived from the apparent abundance of statistics or data elements that libraries collect and the seeming uselessness of them. To make numbers gathering meaningful, you must determine several things in advance:

- what use the statistics will have;
- what is to be counted;
- how these data elements are defined;
- a sensible procedure for collecting the statistics;
- and how the counts will be tabulated.

Numbers gathering can be relatively unobtrusive, requiring no action on the part of the library patron, or intrusive, when patron effort is involved. Unobtrusive measures include staff counts of people attending programs or numbers of items borrowed or used in the library. An unobtrusive measure for the summer library program would be a count of how many children, young adults, and adults attend each program. Intrusive counts require staff, or whoever is doing the counting, to make a specific inquiry of the patron. Intrusive counts include calculating title, author, and subject fill rates because you must ask patrons, either verbally or using a written questionnaire or survey, if the material that was provided answered the question that they presented. If you want to see if your booktalk programs and reader-guidance efforts are having an effect on what patrons are checking out of the library, have the circulation staff ask patrons why they selected the materials that they are checking out that day. Is it because of a recommendation by the librarian, did the patron select it because it was on display, did the patron hear a booktalk by the librarian where that book was promoted, was it recommended by a friend or neighbor, did they read a review in the library newsletter or on the online system, or was it another reason? Staff needs to keep track of the responses so they can be accurately counted.

## Outputs

Many librarians are familiar with evaluation techniques that involve numbers gathering or counting up. The American Library Association, as part of the Public Library Development Program, has established a set of output measures that help libraries ascertain how their programs and services measure up. Many of these measures can be used to evaluate the success of your summer library program.

Basic measures related to the use of materials can help you evaluate your goal of having children and young adults read more. If that is one of your goals, this might have been one of your objectives:

*During the summer library reading program of 2006, circulation of materials from the children's and young adult collections will increase 15% over the same period the previous year.*

To measure this, the library needs to be able to count circulation by collection (children's and young adult) and within certain calendar ranges. However, just knowing how many books in the children's and young adult collections have circulated within a certain period of time is not enough; you must compare it either with another library of the same size or with your own library for a similar time period. This time period could be the same weeks the previous year, or the same number of weeks during another period of time during the year.

You might have had an additional objective related to materials use:

*Circulation of children's materials per child will increase from .7 books per child in 2005 to 1.5 books per child in 2006 for the period during which the summer library reading program occurs.*

These per child measures are based not on just the number of participants in your summer library reading program, but on the total number of children in your service area. The total juvenile circulation for a specific period of time is divided by the total number of children in your service area. This ratio gives a better picture of how many children in your community borrow books.

One of the easiest measures to track, even though it does not show the full impact of the entire summer program, is to count how many programs are given and how many people attend these programs. To get a better idea of the effectiveness of your programming efforts, you should compare the total number of program participants with the total size of your target audience. This figure of programs attendance per capita (total number of children or young adults in your service area, depending on your target audience) gives a clearer picture of how effective your programming has been in reaching your target audience. Comparing the program attendance per capita from year to year gives an even clearer picture of this service. For example, these might be your objectives regarding participation:

*Total program attendance during the 2006 summer library reading program will increase by 5% over summer library reading program attendance of the previous year.*

*Program attendance per child for the 2005 summer library reading program was 2.1; program attendance per child for the 2006 summer library reading program will increase to 2.4.*

When trying to determine program attendance, every person who attends any program designed as part of your summer library program for children (or young adults) should be counted, and every program should be counted. By counting programs attended per child, you eliminate the need to determine how many of the attendees are new people attending your summer library programs. It is not as necessary to find out how many individuals availed themselves of the opportunity to attend a variety of programs as it is to know how many people in the aggregate attended programs. A figure of 2.4 programs per child shows that, on the whole, every child in your service area attended 2.4 programs during the summer library program. This figure by itself, however, does not have as much meaning as comparing it with what the program attendance per child was during another time period, either last summer or over the entire year.

You might also want to measure how many children and young adults visit the library during the summer, whether or not they attend summer library programs. This is a good measure if one of your goals is to turn nonusers into library users. It is neither necessary nor practical for library staff to count each and every child, young adult, and adult who uses the library each and every day for the entire summer. Rather, you should sample library usage. Sampling is based on the premise that it is usually easier and more accurate to count things that are a representation of the whole rather than to count the whole.

There are two ways to draw your sample. First, you could count everyone who comes to the library for an entire week. The second way is to count one day each week over the course of the summer, thus ensuring that every day of the week that the library is open is accounted for. Thus, during week one, you would count everyone who comes to the library on Monday; week two, Tuesday; week three, Wednesday; and so on. By the end of six weeks (seven weeks if your library is open Sunday, too) you will have a complete sample of library use. Again, this figure by itself holds little meaning; it must be compared to a similar sample from the previous year or a sample done during the school year. While this library-use figure will not accurately tell if the people counted in this manner were previously nonusers, if the count increases annually, you can assume that you are reaching more people.

Figure 8–1 is a reporting form for some of the data that can be collected for summer library programs.

## Figure 8–1
## Statistical Reporting Form

### Summer Library Program Statistics

Date program started _____          Date program ended

_____

Number of children in service area _____  Number of YAs in service area _____

### I.  Programming

| | In-House Programs | | Out Reach Programs | | Total | |
|---|---|---|---|---|---|---|
| | Number of Programs | Attendance | Number of Programs | Attendance | Number of Programs | Attendance |
| **Children's Programs** | | | | | | |
| Storytimes | | | | | | |
| Puppet shows | | | | | | |
| Craft programs | | | | | | |
| Booktalk programs | | | | | | |
| **Young Adult Programs** | | | | | | |
| Booknic | | | | | | |
| Film programs | | | | | | |
| Booktalk programs | | | | | | |
| Library sleep over | | | | | | |
| **Family Programs** | | | | | | |
| Family storytimes | | | | | | |
| Kick-off celebration | | | | | | |
| **Community contacts** | | | | | | |
| **Media contacts** | | | | | | |

**Figure 8–1**
*Continued*

**II. Teen Volunteers**

Total number of teen volunteers _____

Total number of hours donated by TVs _____

**III. Circulation**

|          | Picture Books | J Fiction | J Non-fiction (total)* | J Paper-backs | Young Adult Fiction | Young Adult Non-fiction* | Young Adult Paperback | Computer programs |
|----------|---------------|-----------|------------------------|---------------|---------------------|--------------------------|-----------------------|-------------------|
| June     |               |           |                        |               |                     |                          |                       |                   |
| July     |               |           |                        |               |                     |                          |                       |                   |
| August   |               |           |                        |               |                     |                          |                       |                   |

(If you are targeting specific areas of your nonfiction collection, you may want to provide a complete breakdown of nonfiction categories on an addition sheet.)

## Outcome-Based Evaluation

In Chapter 3, "Planning the Program," outcome-based evaluation (OBE) was introduced as part of the planning process. The discussion that accompanied Figure 3–3 took you through the planning part of OBE. In this chapter, you will go through the final two columns on the LSTA Outcomes Plan.

The final two columns "Indicators" and "Sources/Methods" concentrate on the evaluation aspects of OBE. These two columns represent the evaluation part of your plan. To continue developing the outcome plan, you must look back to the outcome. The outcome statement identifies who achieves the outcome. It describes a change in knowledge, status, or condition of the client or patron who is receiving the service.

## *Indicators*

Indicators are statements that you make concerning the data you collect. These indicators show that the outcome has been achieved. They are similar to outputs, but there are differences. Each *indicator* shows that the outcome has been achieved at the individual level.

To determine what the indicators for the project should be, brainstorm with other people who are working on the project. Discuss what data you will be collecting over the course of the project. Are you collecting the number of programs you are offering and how many people attend? Can you determine how many new library cards are issued? Are you collecting circulation statistics? Does your circulation system have the ability to identify the age of the patron checking materials out?

You should generate a list of all possible indicators. While your objective here is not to try to measure every part of the outcome, you need to choose the most descriptive and powerful indicators to demonstrate the success of your project. You must have at least *one* indicator for *each* outcome; since you don't want to spend all of your time collecting and analyzing data, you should limit the number of indicators to no more than three for each outcome.

It is important to match the outcomes with the indicators. Taking time during the planning process at the beginning of the project will save you time and effort when you start to evaluate the success of the project. If you know what data you need to collect, you will eliminate frustration at the end of the project.

As was discussed earlier, raw numbers do not mean much. Therefore, each indicator should be stated as a number and a percentage (# and %). Setting targets provides a way to anticipate how many people you will serve or what changes you expect to see as a result of the project activities and participation. While you may be tempted to set a target by guessing and overestimating, you should not. The first time you prepare this segment of the plan, you may not be able to enter values as you might not be able to determine the target numbers. In the second and future years you implement your project, you should be able to determine the target figures.

### Sources/Methods

The final column on the outcome plan chart actually reflects two separate, yet related, things. The source identifies "who" will provide the information needed to measure the outcome. The method is "how" the outcome will be measured.

The sources you use should be unbiased. The people providing the service should not be the people measuring it. However, in many libraries, the staff implementing the summer library reading program is small; often the same person manages the project and paperwork, conducts the programs, gathers the data, and prepares the reports. Rather than trying to find someone else to provide the data, identify who is providing the data and recognize the limitations.

There needs to be at least one source for each indicator. You need to select methods that provide data that are detailed and precise enough to measure the indicator. Possible methods include questionnaires, interviews, focus groups, and observations by trained observers. These methods will be discussed later in this chapter.

Preferably, the methods you select to use will be tested and verifiable. There should be at least one method for each indicator, as shown in Figure 8–2. Figure 8–2 shows the relationship between outcomes, indicators, and sources/methods.

## Questionnaires

While questionnaires are an intrusive form of evaluation, they can yield significant amounts of information that cannot be obtained from just unobtrusive measures of

**Figure 8–2**
**LSTA Outcomes Plan**

## LSTA OUTCOMES PLAN

**Project Name:** _____  **Library:** _____

**Project Summary / Program Purpose:** _____

| INPUTS | ACTIVITIES | OUTPUTS | OUTCOMES | EVALUATION | | |
|--------|-----------|---------|----------|-----------|----------|----------|
| | | | | INDICATORS | SOURCES/ METHODS | |
| | | | Outcome 1 | Indicator 1-A | Source 1-A.1 | |
| | | | | | Source 1-A.2 | |
| | | | | Indicator 1-B | Source 1-B | |
| | | | | Indicator 1-C | Source 1-C | |
| | | | Outcome 2 | Indicator 2-A | Source 2-A.1 | |
| | | | | | Source 2-A.2 | |
| | | | | Indicator 2-B | Source 2-B | |
| | | | Outcome 3 | Indicator 3-A | Source 3-A.1 | |
| | | | | | Source 3-A.2 | |
| | | | | Indicator 3-B | Source 3-B | |

library usage, such as program attendance, circulation, and similar data elements. Questionnaires are one of the most prevalent techniques used in gathering data and one familiar to most librarians and many patrons. You can use questionnaires to obtain either oral or written responses. The person administering the questionnaire (interviewer) must make careful note of all oral responses. In effect, an oral questionnaire is a form of interview.

To whom a questionnaire is administered and the method by which responses are gathered greatly affects the results. By administering a questionnaire only to participants of the summer library program, you will not be able to find out why people do not participate; however, you can find out how they found out about the program, what they liked about it, and how they think it might be improved. To find out why people did not participate, you will need to identify who in the community did not participate in the summer library program, and then administer a different questionnaire to them. By talking with nonparticipants, you may be able to find out about conflicting programs, schedules that are incompatible with certain individuals or families, activities that are perceived as inappropriate, themes that are not embraced by the community, and other areas of concern that were not taken into account during the planning process. Written questionnaires, as opposed to oral questionnaires, limit responses to people with a certain level of literacy. Personal interviews (which orally administered questionnaires really are) allow the library to reach individuals who are not likely to respond in writing.

The construction of a questionnaire is extremely important. While constructing a questionnaire, you should remember what you like or don't like about them yourself:

- Employ the KISS strategy: Keep It Simple Sweetheart. The less complicated it is to administer, the easier it will usually be to tabulate and analyze.
- Keep your questionnaire—whether written or an interview, as short as possible. Try to keep written questionnaires to only one page. Focus on what you really need to know. One of the most important things to remember about questionnaire construction is to ask only for the information that you absolutely need rather than collecting data and information because it seems interesting. Avoid asking questions just because it would be interesting to know something.
- Don't ask people to make impossible choices such as "I attended the craft program and the storytelling program? Yes or No." Some patrons may have attended one program and not the other. Even though you want to keep the questionnaire short, patrons may not be able to answer both segments of such questions with a simple yes or no.
- Don't use library jargon. Make the questionnaire user friendly. Use words, terms, and phrases that the users know and use.
- Use fixed-response questions (checklists and rating scales) when possible, but do include some open-ended questions, too. Fixed-response questions are easier to tabulate than open-ended ones. However, people may feel boxed in when being asked to check off a fixed response; therefore, if you cannot anticipate the full range of responses, allow participants to respond "other" and fill in the

blank. If the range of responses to a question cannot be anticipated in advance, allow for an open-ended response.

An essential step when designing a questionnaire is to pretest it to ensure that you obtain the information that you are seeking. Administer the questionnaire to a small number of people who are similar to those whom you will be surveying. Let them review the wording and language to make certain that it is understandable and that it elicits the information that you are seeking. If extensive changes are needed after this initial pretest, a second pretest is necessary. This helps establish the validity of the survey instrument.

Soliciting responses from summer library program participants will help you improve your program. Figure 8–3 is a sample questionnaire that can be used with program participants. Adapt and revise this to meet the needs of your program and the goals and objectives that you have established for your program.

Besides surveying the children and young adults who participated in your summer program, you may want to survey the parents or primary caregivers of the participants. Again, think about the information that you need, not just what is interesting to know. Figure 8–4 is a sample survey that can be completed by the parent or guardian. Another group to survey might be the teachers in the community. Several weeks after the start of school in the fall, ask teachers if they noticed better language skills and reading retention in certain students and cross-check their responses with your list of summer library reading program participants.

## Interviews

Whether structured or unstructured, interviews can be done with groups or individuals. Structured interviews consist of specific questions that are asked in a designated order; unstructured interviews are more like a conversation in which the interviewer has specific areas to be explored and discussed. While more time consuming to administer and interpret than questionnaires, there are several advantages. The only skill needed by the respondent is the ability to speak. Since each interviewee receives personal attention by the library or its agents, interviewing can also have a positive public-relations effect. On the other hand, personal interviews can be time consuming and, therefore, costly. When interviewing speakers of other languages, make sure the interviewer can conduct the interview in the other language and report it in English.

Interviews are useful when working with children, young adults, and adults with limited reading skills because they eliminate the need for the interviewee to read the questionnaire. By doing interviews with people other than those with limited reading skills, the stigma of being treated differently is eliminated.

To ensure valid results from the interviews, interviewers must be trained. Training is necessary to assure that there is consistency in how the questions are asked, how the interviewer responds to the interviewee, and how the information is recorded.

---

**Figure 8–3**
**Sample Questionnaire for Summer Library Program Participants**

---

Circle your answers or fill in the blanks.

1. I am a boy.                    I am a girl.

2. How old are you? _____

3. What school will you be going to in September? _____

   What grade will you be in? _____

4. How did you find out about the Summer Library Program?  Circle all the ways you heard about it.

My teacher told me.                              The media specialist at school told me.

My parents told me.                              I found out when I came to the library.

My friends told me.                              I just wandered into a program and stayed.

Another way – tell me how? _____

5. I though the theme this summer was:

Awesome!            Cool          O.K.          Boring              Dorky!

6. The best part of the summer program was:

_____

7. The thing I would like to change about the summer program is :

_____

---

**Figure 8–4**
**Sample Survey of Parents/Guardians**

---

Adapt this survey to the goals and objectives of your program. The final survey should be only one page!

**Thank you in advance for taking a few minutes to complete this survey about your child's participation in our Summer Library Program. Check or circle all appropriate replies. If you have more than one child, please complete one survey form for each child. Thank you!**

1. How old is your child? _____

2. Did your child participate in the Summer Library Program sponsored by the
   _____ Library?   Yes _____   Please go to Question 3
   No _____   Why not?  Please check all that apply.
   _____ Did not know about the program.
   _____ Programs were at an inconvenient time.
   _____ The program appeared too young for my child.
   _____ The program appeared too old for my child.
   _____ My child went to summer school, camp, out-of-town over the summer.
   _____ Other:  Please specify _____

3. What did you like about the summer library program?
   _____ My child liked the weekly programs.  (Which ones?) _____
   _____ I liked the reading incentives.
   _____ The price was right – free!
   _____ I liked the weekly puzzle sheets, coloring sheets, and other handouts.
   _____ It encouraged my child to read new books.
   _____ I did not like the program.  Why not? _____
   _____ Other:  Please specify _____

4. What didn't you like about the program?
   _____ There were too many rules.          _____ Not enough rules.
   _____ My child did not receive enough individual attention.
   _____ My child was discouraged because of the number of books required to complete
            the program.
   _____ Program registration was too limited; my child was denied membership in the
            program.
   _____ I did not like the theme of the program.  Why not? _____
   _____ My child did not receive enough help in finding books; the librarian was too busy.
   _____ Other:  Please specify _____

**Figure 8–4**
*Continued*

5. What did you observe about your child?
    _____ My child's reading skills improved during this summer.
    _____ My child spent more time reading this summer than previous summers.
    _____ My child read a greater variety of books this summer than previously.
    _____ Other: Please specify _____

6. Is this the first time your child has participated in the Summer Library Program? Yes _____

      or

My child has participated in the Summer Library Program for _____ years.

7. Do you want your child to participate in the Summer Library Program next year?

    _____ Yes. Why? _____

      or

    _____ No. Why not? _____

**Thank you for completing this survey.**

## Focus Groups

A group-interview technique that is frequently used is the focus-group interview. This technique uses and takes advantage of the process of group dynamics. For focus groups to be effective, the interviewer must prepare an interview guide or schedule in advance of the group session.

The interview schedule is a list of five to ten questions and additional probes that is prepared in advance of the focus-group interview. This schedule is used to keep the interviewees on the topic that is being investigated. The first question should be one that allows the participants to relax and become comfortable with the group. Questions two through the next to last relate to the topic under investigation. The last question must bring the interview to closure for both the interviewer and the interviewees.

When conducting focus groups with children and young adults, you may want to include an opportunity for them to respond nonverbally; ask a question for which they have to draw a picture and then probe for the meaning of the drawings.

The following interview schedule is an example that can be used to determine whether promotional materials and programs were appropriate for your target audience. Your focus group participants should be a representative sample of participants and nonparticipants of the age you wished to reach in your summer library program. It is assumed that this group interview is taking place in the fall, after the summer library program has ended and school has started again.

1. Tell me about your new class, school, or teacher.
2. Who participated in the summer library program at the _____ library? What attracted you to the summer library program?
   Probe: Did someone from the library visit your school last spring to tell your class about the program?
   Probe: Which of the materials—bookmarks, pencils, bags, posters, prizes and incentives—and programs made you want to be part of the summer library program?
3. For those of you who did not join the summer library program, why didn't you join the program?
   Probe: Were there too many books to read?
   Probe: Did you think the theme was too babyish?
   Probe: Is the library too far away from where you live?
   Probe: Were the programs at times you could not get to the library? Are there better times to have programs?
   Probe: Have you ever been part of a library program?
4. I'd like each of you to draw a picture that shows what you want the library to have for you during the summer. It could be the type of programs you want the library to plan. Or, are there special things you want in the library—like computers, DVDs and other stuff?
   Probe: Ask about what each person drew and why it is important to that person.
5. What can the library do to get you and your friends to use the library during the summer?

The second step in working with focus groups is to recruit participants. For your summer library program, you may want to have several groups: elementary school—age students, middle school and high school—age students (either together or in separate groups), parents and teachers, library staff, and community supporters. Group size should range from 8 at a minimum to 12 at the maximum. Remember to get parents to sign a permission slip when interviewing children either individually or as part of a focus group.

Once you have recruited participants, you can conduct the interview. The focus-group interview runs between one and two hours, depending on how many people are involved and how in-depth the participant responses are. A small, cozy area where the participants and the interviewer can be undisturbed is best. Casual seating arranged in a circle where all participants are viewed as equal helps set the tone for the group. The interviewer needs to be a good facilitator, a person who likes people and enjoys talking with and listening to others.

Along with the interviewer, it is recommended that there be another person, not one of the participants and not someone directly involved in program delivery, to act as the note-taker or recorder. By freeing the interviewer from the responsibility of being the recorder, the interviewer is allowed to be more fully involved with listening to the discussion. It is not necessary for the note-taker to make a word-for-word transcript of the focus-group session. This person should, however, get the salient points down on paper; this will assist the interviewer in preparing the final report. While many people may think that machine recording of these sessions is useful, it really is not. Past experience has shown that the most important comments are usually made when the tape is not running or that all you get recorded on tape is paper shuffling and people coughing. Even if voices are clear, having to listen to the tape and make notes later is time consuming. Sufficient information is gleaned from the notes taken during the session. The note taker should be asked to be alert to and be prepared to write down as exactly as possible brief, salient comments. A few direct quotes will give the product credibility and interest. At the end of the focus group, after all the participants have left, both the note-taker and the interviewer should take five minutes to individually write down their overall and significant impressions. A few minutes should be taken after that to compare these impressions.

Ideally the interviewer and note-taker will not be people directly affiliated with the program that is being investigated; they should be people who are neutral. Therefore, it is best if, when doing focus groups about the summer library program, the youth services staff are not involved in the focus groups. If possible, people running the focus group and acting as note-takers should not be from the local library. Trade your services as an interviewer or note-taker to another library and have staff from that other library provide similar services in yours.

## Observation

One of the most overlooked forms of evaluation is observation. Observation is done on a regular basis in the library and during library programs and results in anecdotes and stories about library activities. When incidental observation goes beyond this natural occurrence and moves to a more-structured process in which there are clear definitions of what is to be observed and when, then it becomes structured observation.

The goal of observation is to report what is seen or heard, not to draw inferences about what is observed. It is desirable to employ observers who are not familiar with seeing the activity and who will not interrupt what they are observing. Good observers are unobtrusive, yet just by being there and taking notes, even though they are not participating in the activity, they may affect the actions of the participants.

Depending on the behavior that you want to observe, you will need to determine the observation schedule. Some behaviors, such as who comes to the library, need to be observed during a varied range of hours that the library is open. While staff may report through informal observation that young adults only use the library between 3:00 PM and 5:30 PM, structured observation may reveal quite a different picture.

Structured observation takes into account the number of observations, the length of time of each observation, and when the observations are done. In the example above, staff may not be looking to see if teens use the library during the day; they may assume that they are occupied during the morning hours and do not come to the library at that time. If, on the other hand, the observation is structured so that staff or volunteers are stationed at the library entrance during the entire day for one week and told to record the number of young adults who enter the library during specified time ranges, the result will, more than likely, be quite different.

Other behaviors may relate to specific programs and can be observed by focusing your observations on that event. For example, if you want to find out how many people attend the weekly family storytimes that are held on Tuesday evening, then a staff member must be present to count participants at that specific program. While this is a count, it is obtained through observation.

Another less-formal type of observation but one that is of equal value is the use of a log or journal. Library staff and others involved with your summer library program can add anecdotes and stories about what they observe about the program. When a nine-year-old boy tells you that he thinks the poster for the summer library program this year is the best one yet and asks if he can have one to put in his room, make a note of that in the log. If you present a storytime and have success with the creative dramatics activity that you included, make note of that. Record children's reactions and comments and differentiate them from your impressions. You also have to include in the log the negative comments that you observe, such as hearing from a senior citizen that there are too many noisy children in the library or a comment from a circulation clerk that there were far too many books checked out after a program. You may want to editorialize and make a rebuttal comment of your own, but the log is not the place for that. The log is for observations. Having summer library program participants keep track of what books they read or how long they read on a reading log is actually asking them to observe their own reading behavior and report that behavior to you.

## Telling Your Story

Why is it important to have an evaluation component in your summer library program or any other program? You need to be able to report to your supervisor; your library administrators; your governing body; funding agencies; the residents, citizens, and taxpayers of your service area what the results and impacts of your program are. Most of these groups are aware of the inputs into the program—staff time, funds for materials, facilities, and so forth. They want to know what their investment has yielded. In your planning, you indicated what you expected and hoped the outcomes would be. Now, after measuring and evaluating, you need to communicate the results and the impact of the program to everyone. To be able to make the link between the inputs, outcomes, and impact of your summer library program requires that you employ a variety of evaluation methods and communication tools.

Communication is the key to telling your story. You must determine who wants to know and who *needs* to know the results of your program. Each audience needs to know about your program, but different audiences need to know different things about it.

Internal audiences may be the easiest to reach and to inform, but many times they are left out. As with planning, all staff need to know the results of the summer library program. You don't want staff to rely on the grapevine or to be left in the dark about what happened, especially if you will want their continued support, cooperation, and assistance again next summer or on another project.

External audiences include the community as a whole. Use the media to communicate with the community. As with the promotion of your program, a news release will help you tell your story, such as telling how you met the goals of your program, how many children participated, and how many hours the community read over the summer. External audiences also include your funding agencies, such as your city or county council or commission, private foundations, and the state library agency. Funders as well as library support groups, such as the Friends of the Library, are interested in seeing not only how the money was spent but how this investment improved library service. They also want to know how it improves and benefits the quality of life for the people in your service area.

Not everyone needs the same information or needs the same amount of detail. Usually, the more important the individual, the less they want to know. Boil down your evaluation into a brief bulleted list of results. Make this list as concrete as possible. Make sure you tailor the message you are delivering to the person receiving the message. A business person who provided sponsorship of your program will be interested in knowing how many people were exposed to his message, while members of the local board of education will want to know how many children from each school participated and how many hours they read. Your professional peers will want you to tell about "how you run your summer library program good" and may not be as interested in the human interest story about the child talking to the puppet as would the local press. Other library staff are usually interested in only one thing: "how this program affects my job."

When you are communicating the success of your summer library program, keep in mind the goals, slogans, and themes that are dominant in the public arena in your community, especially the ones that come into play in the use of public funds. If education is a hot issue, communicate about your program in terms of how the summer library reading program supports and enhances local education programs and coordinates with the efforts of the local schools. If economic development is the hot issue, talk about your program's success in terms of how it prepares the youth of the community to be employable and begins to prepare them for flexibility in the work place through learning how to learn.

The most important part of the evaluation of the summer library program is learning what parts of your program worked and which were not as successful—and why. From the evaluation, you can begin again to plan for next year. You can take parts of your summer library reading program and integrate them into the ongoing operation of the youth-services department. Programs that were unsuccessful can be reworked and tried again. If the program was right but you presented it to the wrong audience, you might want to present it to a different group at another time. You can look back at the program and see where you made strides in forging new partnerships with other youth-serving agencies, and think of ways to extend and expand these partnerships.

You can determine which of your promotional efforts yielded the most publicity and participants and which were not worth doing again. You can tell your story to the community and gain additional support as you start the planning cycle all over again and determine how best you will make the youth of your community a part of a nation of readers.

The Indianapolis-Marion County Public Library annually produces a report on their summer program. In 2003, the theme of the summer program was "Summer Reading Toon-up!" This was a tribute to Garfield, the wise-cracking fat cat with an insatiable appetite for lasagna and good books. Jim Davis, creator of Garfield, is a native son of Indiana and agreed to let the library use his four-legged child as the mascot. The orange cat graced the annual report and added some pizzazz to what could otherwise be just another document. Important outputs are shared in the eight-page, full-color report to the community. Corporate sponsors are recognized and expenditures are summarized. The introduction summarizes the important accomplishments, achievements, and outcomes. In addition to the narrative, the report includes many charts and graphs that help readers visualize the impact of the program on the community.

## Endnote

1. Douglas Zweizig, Debra Wilcox Johnson, Jane Robbins, with Michele Besant. 1996. *The TELL IT! Manual: The Complete Program for Evaluating Library Performance.* Chicago: American Library Association, 5.

## Recommended Reading

Durrance, Joan C., Karen E. Fisher, with Marian Bouch Hinton. 2005. *How Libraries and Librarians Help: Assessing Outcomes in Your Library.* Chicago: American Library Association.

*Evaluation of the Public Library Summer Reading Program: Books and Beyond . . . Take Me to Your Reader! Final Report, December 2001.* 2001. Los Angeles, Calif.: Evaluation and Training Institute.

Johnson, Debra Wilcox. 1995. *Evaluation of the Role of the State Library of Florida in Youth Services.* Tallahassee: Fla. Department of State, Division of Library and Information Services.

Lance, Keith Curry, et al. 2004. *Counting on Results: New Tools for Outcome-Based Evaluation of Public Libraries.* Denver, Colo.: Library Research Service.

*The LSTA Outcome-Based Evaluation Toolkit: September 2004.* 2004. Tallahassee: Florida Department of State, Division of Library and Information Services. Also available at www.lstatoolkit.com.

McClure, Charles R., Amy Owen, Douglas L. Zweizig, Mary Jo Lynch, and Nancy A. Van House. 1987. *Planning and Role Setting for Public Libraries: A Manual of Options and Procedures.* Chicago: American Library Association.

*Measuring Program Outcomes: A Practical Approach.* 1996. Alexandria, Va.: United Way of America.

National Center for Education Statistics. *Services and Resources for Children and Young Adults in Public Libraries.* 1995. Washington, D.C.: U.S. Department of Education, Office of Educational Research and Improvement.

"Outcome-Based Evaluation: Viburnum Literacy Conference OBE Presentation." *Resources for Librarian.* Texas State Library and Archives Commission. Available: www.tsl.state.tx/ld/pubs/ obe/. Accessed August 28, 2004.

Pennsylvania Library Association, Youth Services Division. N.d. *Evaluating Summer Reading Programs.* Harrisburg: State Library of Pennsylvania.

Robbins, Jane, Holly Willett, Mary Jane Wiseman, and Douglas L. Zweizig. 1990. *Evaluation Strategies and Techniques for Public Library Children's Services: A Sourcebook.* Madison: School of Library and Information Studies, University of Wisconsin–Madison.

Robbins, Jane, and Douglas Zweizig. 1988. *Are We There Yet? Evaluating Library Collections, Reference Services, Programs, and Personnel.* Madison: School of Library and Information Studies, University of Wisconsin–Madison.

Steffen, Nicolle O., Keith Curry Lance, and Rochelle Logan. 2002. "Time to Tell the Whole Story: Outcomes-Based Evaluation and the Counting on Results Project." *Public Libraries* 41, no. 4 (July/August): 222–228.

Walter, Virginia A. 1995. *Output Measures and More: Planning and Evaluating Public Library Services for Young Adults.* Chicago: American Library Association.

_____. 1992. *Output Measures for Public Library Service to Children: A Manual of Standardized Procedures.* Chicago: Illinois: American Library Association.

Zweizig, Douglas, Debra Wilcox Johnson, Jane Robbins, with Michele Besant. 1996. *The TELL IT! Manual: The Complete Program for Evaluating Library Performance.* Chicago: American Library Association.

# 9

# Summer Reading Programs
# in the Spotlight

The previous parts of this book discuss why summer library programs are needed and important; how they contribute to summer learning; how to organize, plan, and design them; how to implement, promote, and evaluate them. Numerous real-life examples have been woven throughout this volume. Brief mentions and descriptions have been included throughout to provide models that can be emulated.

This part provides a more detailed look as some unique programs from the past several years. These descriptions provide more than the overviews and brief mentions in the previous parts of this volume. All of the information in this section was provided directly by the libraries listed. These programs have practices and procedures that are worthy of notice. They build on the traditions that have made summer library reading programs a staple of public library programming, yet they reach to the future through partnerships that enhance the library and the community as a whole. They promote literacy and learning. Whether named simply or elaborately, they all promote reading and libraries. They have an impact on the community by creating a new generation of readers and library users. There are programs from various sizes of libraries, serving communities of various sizes. These libraries serve both urban and rural communities. The people in these communities range from low literate to highly educated. The economy in these communities range from poor to affluent. The programs range from those that can be run on a dime to those that take deep pockets. They all have elements that can be replicated in other libraries regardless of budget size. Much of the theory and philosophy behind many of the elements of these programs have been discussed earlier.

While I highlight just 25 programs, they are just a sampling of the programs that can be found in libraries and outreach settings all over. Please keep these programs and practices in mind as you plan summer programs for your community. As you plan and implement summer library reading programs, share your experiences with the rest of us. To help maintain and expand the profession's knowledge base, please complete the form in Appendix D, "Outstanding Summer Library Reading Programs," and submit it to the author through the publisher. These submissions may be included in future updates and expansions of this book.

## "SLRPP"
## Alachua County Library District
## Gainesville, Florida

The Alachua County Library District is a centralized library system with a headquarters library located in downtown Gainesville, Florida. Two urban branches are located in the northwest and southwest areas of Gainesville; the system also has seven branches serving rural areas of the county. In addition to these facilities, the district operates two bookmobiles and provides library service to the inmates of the Alachua County Jail through an interlocal agreement with the Alachua County sheriff. The library district offers borrowing privileges free of charge to any resident of the State of Florida. Through reciprocal borrowing agreements, Alachua County citizens may borrow free of charge from library systems in 11 surrounding counties.

The mission of the Alachua County Library District states that residents of Alachua County are provided: access to materials in a variety of formats to meet their needs for general information, popular topics and titles, and recreational reading; assistance and instruction in using library resources to acquire information and enrichment; information about the community and community issues and access to free civic, cultural, and entertainment activities; and resource support for students in formal education, home schooling, vocational, and preschool programs.

During the summer of 2003, the Alachua County Library District (ACLD) received a grant from the State Library and Archives of Florida to initiate a special summer reading program in conjunction with the state's annual summer library program, the Florida Library Youth Program (FLYP). The Summer Library Reading Partnership Pilot (SLRPP; pronounced "slurp") project was initiated by the State Library and Archives to support Governor Jeb Bush's "Read to Learn" project. The aim of that program is to ensure that all Florida students are reading at grade level before they enter the fourth grade. This pilot project is being phased into libraries throughout Florida over a three-year period. Libraries received grant funds from $2,500 to $10,000 for one year based on the population of the service area. After the initial year of funding, libraries are continuing the project with local funds and through partnerships with the local school district and other community agencies.

To support the "Read to Learn" program, the ACLD targeted third-grade students who failed the reading portion of the Florida Comprehensive Assessment Test (FCAT) and were being retained in third grade. The federal Library Services and Technology Act grant allowed ACLD to hire temporary summer staff and purchase books for the students. Staff were able to make weekly visits to a school with a highly mobile and sometimes homeless population. During these weekly library outreach visits, staff presented a library program and gave each student an exciting, age- and developmentally appropriate book to keep. During the weekly programs, the library staff were also able to make these low-achieving students aware of the resources that were available to them at the library. Staff also introduced them to materials that were fun, interesting, and exciting. Making reading fun and providing an enjoyable literacy experience was something that these students had not previously experienced.

One of the most exciting parts of the weekly programs was the book give-away. Knowing that access to books was important in creating readers, the library wanted to be able to provide the start of a home library to these students. The Junie B. Jones series was one of the best-liked books, with the Captain Underpants series coming in a close second.

In addition to partnering with the school system, the library also provided programs to every recreation center through the City of Gainesville Parks Department. Again, children who would otherwise not have access to summer library reading programs were able to get this service through outreach services from the library.

In evaluating SLRPP, library staff said that targeting services to under- and low-achieving students made a significant impact. To be able to continue this project, the library was planning on requesting funds from the Friends of the Library. One of the positive impacts of the program was the enhanced relationship with the school district. While the ACLD has a good relationship with the school district and had shared author programs in the past, this was the first time they sat down together to plan a program. Meetings with the school principals, media specialists, teachers, and curriculum specialists resulted in support for the activities provided by the library.

For additional information about the library and its programs, go to the library Web site at www.acld.lib.fl.us/; the youth services page at www.acld.lib.fl.us/acld-new/branches/hq/YS/YS.html; or contact Roseanne Russo, Youth Services Manager, at rrusso@exchange.acld.lib.fl.us. For information about the SLRPP grant program, contact Carole Fiore, Youth Services Consultant, State Library and Archives of Florida, cfiore@dos.state.fl.us.

## "Reading Rocks/Young Adult Summer Reading Program"
## Allen County Public Library
## Allen County, Indiana

The Allen County Public Library, headquartered in Fort Wayne, Indiana, operates 14 buildings but is still experiencing growing pains. Currently, the main library is being enlarged and is operating out of a temporary facility. All but two branches are being replaced or renovated; each building has children's and young adult sections.

The YA summer reading program is an expression of the library's mission statement: as a public service institution, the library is concerned with the education, information, entertainment, and cultural enrichment of the community. The library also subscribes to the principle that the origin, age, background, or viewpoint of a library user does not deny or abridge that person's right to full use of the library. The YA summer reading program builds on that philosophy.

Responding to research cited by Walter Minkel in the February 2004 issue of *School Library Journal*, the library set out to design a program that would incorporate activities to enhance developmental assets for teens. Planning involved developing an outcome plan, otherwise known as a logic model.

The purpose of the young adult summer reading program is to encourage young adults to read during the summer. The program is advertised through local middle and high schools as well as public service announcements.

A series of programs was designed that provides teens from many areas of the community with innovative activities. The interactive programs stimulate creative thinking and build on the current interests of teens.

"Miniature Mayhem" is a program that requires an initial investment, but once the supplies are on hand, it is an inexpensive program to continue. The program is designed so that teens paint small metal and plastic miniatures. The miniatures range from science fiction to comic-book characters and fantasy-based miniatures. The program has built repeat usage and has introduced YAs to the magazine and art collections and to the YA collection itself.

Another program in this series brings joy to a chocoholic's heart. During "Sweet Chocolate Art," teens learned to mold chocolate treats. Preregistration for this program was required so that enough supplies would be available; even so, a maximum of 20 teens was set so that there would be sufficient interaction and supervision, ensuring participants would have a successful experience. Teens learned about the candy-making process and made several molded treats, decorated chocolate suckers, and made bark. This experience really made an impression on the teens who participated. One teen was so pleased with her finished product and so proud of her new skills that she announced to the entire group that she knew what she wanted to do for a career— she wanted to work at DeBrand's (a local chocolatier ) and make chocolates. Several were so proud of their accomplishments that they were going to give the boxes of candy that they created as birthday gifts to significant people in their lives.

"Plugged-In Players," another element in the YA summer program, provides a supervised time and space for teens to play video games. When the program began, the library borrowed a Play Station from a staff member; after the success of the program, the library purchased a Play Station 2 and several games. Because the teens are in a supervised setting, there are limits on the language the teens are permitted to use and on the games that can be played. This program encourages teens to socialize during what is often a solitary pastime. It also encourages communication and informal peer mentoring as the teens share their expertise in the game playing.

Other individual programs that make up the overall YA summer program include:

- "Beads, Beads and More Beads:" Teens make items such as necklaces, bracelets, or book-thongs.
- "Mad Libs!" Teens fill in the blanks with appropriate parts of speech and then read them back with hilarious results.
- "If It Glitters, It's Good: Body Image and Art Workshop:" Self-esteem and positive body image are stressed.
- "Zine Workshop:" Introduces teens to the basics of beginning a zine.

Promotion of the programs included traditional posters and bookmarks all around town where parents and teens would be likely to see them, such as grocery stores and neighborhood Boys and Girls Clubs. The twist was that the Teen Advisory Board prepared a four-minute video for schools that had morning video-news programs.

## "Splish Splash Read" and "Splish Splash Read to Me"/ Children's Summer Reading Programs
## Allen County Public Library
## Allen County, Indiana

Realizing that children and teens do not relate to the same programs and promotional materials, the Allen County Public Library created a separate program for preschool and elementary school–age children. While the library for many years has had a summer program for children, they recently added two new components. The first was to split the program book into two sections—one for readers and a new section for prereaders. The reader segment of the book contained the usual summer program: game board, activities, bibliography, and calendar of events. The new prereaders section included activities for caregivers and parents to do with their children. The activities were based on the six skills outlined in the PLA/ALSC "Every Child Ready to Read @ your library" program and were called "Smart Start Activities." The prereaders had their own game board. On each of the four trails of bubbles there was a bubble where the parent or caregiver had to do a Smart Start Activity of their choice to complete the trail.

The second new component is the "Read Away Your Fines" component of the program. Children had to read one item from five of seven categories of books: award books, magazines, nonfiction, poetry, folk and fairy tales, audiobooks, and holidays. Upon completion of this challenge, readers are given a $15.00 coupon that can be used to reduce their fines.

For additional information about either the children's or YA programs from the Allen County Library, visit the library's Web site at www.acpl.lib.in.us, or contact Nancy Magi, Branch Youth Services Coordinator, nmagi@acpl.lib.li.us.

**Figure 9–1 a and b**
"Reading Rocks" promotional materials and game card used bright neon green and purple
to attract the attention of the teens they were targeting in this summer program.

**Figure 9–2**
"Splish Splash Read!" The Allen County Public Library's game board for young readers not only helped them track how long they read but promoted other related activities. To fill in one of the bubbles on the game board, children had to read for 20 minutes, attend a program, or "go fish." Go fish activities included memorizing a favorite poem, tell a fish story, learn to spell the name of their favorite fish in sign language, and several other activities.

## "Title Wave"
## Andover Public Library
## Andover, Kansas

The Andover Public Library (APL), a small library in the affluent community of Andover, Kansas, just east of Wichita, targets preschoolers to middle and high school students for their summer library program. The summer reading program supports the library mission by helping improve individual, family, and community life. The program also supports the APL's commitment to encourage lifelong learning among its patrons. The library, its board, and the staff are committed both to outreach and to the expansion of the variety of children's programming. The summer library reading program addresses outreach and growth of programming for youth.

A relative newcomer to summer programming, the APL began its summer reading program in 1999. By 2003, over 750 in this community with a total population of 8,000 participated in the program, recording over 19,000 hours of reading. Although the general consensus in the library community is that teenagers won't participate, APL has found that if the right incentives and activities are offered, teens will read and participate. Twenty-one percent of the readers in 2003 were over 12 years of age.

Prizes for teens include cameras, CD players, gift certificates, bean bag chairs and they are awarded on the basis of how many hours the participant reads. No limits are imposed on the type of material or the source. While teens are encouraged to read or listen to books on tape from the library, materials can be obtained from other sources. Hours spent watching a movie adapted from a book cannot be counted for reading hours. The program closes the gap between the end of school in the spring and its reopening in the fall.

Program activities enhance many of the developmental assets youth need to succeed in life. The summer program has clear rules and consequences or rewards. The children and teens become actively involved in learning opportunities while still having fun. Children report having high self-esteem as a result of participating in the program.

At the end of a summer filled with lots of programs and other activities, the Andover Public Library celebrated a 30 percent increase in participation in the summer reading program. The Harry Potter Birthday Bash was designed to attract the whole family. Activities at this end of summer party included face painting, photos with Professor Dumbledore, and crafts to create Harry Potter realia. A magic show thrilled wizards of all ages as did the fantastic door prizes, including a Harry Potter quilt, a set of Harry Potter books, and many other items. During the party, tired parents were even able to take advantage of a free chair massage. This final program was supported by donations from the Friends of the Library, Pizza Hut, and other local businesses. Two television stations covered the end of program celebration.

Because of the publicity generated by the summer program and the numbers involved, the library and the Friends group anticipates increasing their fund-raising efforts for the summer program and other library activities. The population of Andover has increased substantially in the past few years, and the library is feeling the pinch of the limited space the current building affords them. With the success of the summer program and the visibility the program affords the library, the library expects support for building a new, larger facility.

Additional information about the library can be found on the library's home page at http://andoverpubliclibrary.org, or contact Carol Wohlford, Library Director, carol@andoverpubliclibrary.org.

## "The Envelope Please . . . A Tribute to Hollywood"
## Billerica Public Library
## Billerica, Massachusetts

A growing town of nearly 40,000 people, Billerica is situated in Middlesex County, just 40 minutes north of Boston, Massachusetts. The population is predominantly white, with small numbers of blacks, Asians, and Hispanics. Forty-one percent of the households in the community have children 18 years of age and under.

The Billerica Public Library strives to provide responsive library service to its residents through free access to diverse materials, programs, and information. The roles of the library are to provide current, high-demand, high-interest materials for the leisure reading of all age groups; to encourage and foster an interest in reading by children; to serve as a support center for both formal and informal learning pursuits, and to do so in a cost-effective manner. To meet that mission, the library provides a variety of services, including services to teens.

In 2001, the library developed a program that attracted a record number of teens. "The Envelope Please . . . A Tribute to Hollywood" had several elements that played off the movie theme.

The first part of this blockbuster summer was for the teens themselves to plan, direct, and tape several video commercials that would be shown at schools. The local cable-provider lent cameras for this effort. A group of ten teens met with library staff early every Monday morning for five weeks of planning and taping. Two hours of brainstorming and taping (plus editing time afterwards) resulted in a 20-second commercial each week. One commercial was a takeoff on the *Brady Bunch* titled the "Library Bunch." Another commercial was titled "Who Let the Books Out?" where library books mysteriously jump off the shelves and run out of the library, hoping to be caught by a patron.

Another program lasted four weeks. During "Lights, Camera, Action!" another group of teens prepared for a reenactment of *Hollywood Squares*. During week one of the program, each participant decided on a star to portray, and they all began working on their costumes. They also had to prepare a short biography of that person. During week two, each person came up with 20 questions using library resources. There were specific types of questions that the teens were required to construct:

1. a quote,
2. one fact from the *Guinness Book of World Records,*
3. one fact from an encyclopedia,
4. one question about a book or an author,
5. one historical question,
6. one sports question,
7. one true/false question,
8. one question about a cartoon,
9. one movie question, and
10. one music question.

The remaining ten questions could be about anything the teens chose.

During week three of this segment of the program, the set was created and there was a dress rehearsal. Week four was the actual game day. With an audience of fifth- and sixth-grade students in attendance, the game was a great success. The volunteers created memorable characters. On the top row were portrayals of Charlie's Angels. Row two had Pop-star Hoku in the left square and Mary-Kate and Ashley in the right surrounded Whoopie Goldberg in her usual place in the center square. The bottom row of squares was filled with Haley Joel Osment, Julia Roberts, and Jennifer Lopez. The teens all said that it was "Hip to Be a Square at the Library."

Teens also constructed a library float that was part of a community parade. Building on the interest in the Harry Potter books, teens cut, painted, glued, glittered, and constructed a four-foot by four-foot castle to be placed on the Harry Potter float. The teens also made wizard hats for the marchers and hundreds of magic wands that were handed out to people along the parade route.

In addition to these activities, teens were invited to read books and earn prizes. For every book they read, teens were awarded raffle tickets that could be placed in containers for specific prizes. Prizes were drawn at the end-of-summer party, the Academy Award of Good Reading Junk Food Party. The more the teens read, the better their chances of winning any of the numerous prizes. Prizes were donated by local businesses; refreshments were paid for by the Friends of the Library. At this Hollywood-themed party, teens came dressed in fancy or funny ball gowns and suits and feasted on Skittles, M&Ms, licorice, and other junk food. Prizes ranged from free video rentals at Blockbuster Video, Beanie Babies, graphic novels, a walkman, food from many local restaurants, and gift certificates that ranged from $5 to $50 for various local businesses. Grand prizes were a Jimi Hendrix Skate Board and a free limousine ride to the first day of school for the winner and four of the winner's friends. These prizes and the invitation to the junk food party kept teens reading over the summer. Even in this small community, over 150 teens participated in this event.

The program provides opportunities for teens to work together in an environment conducive to learning and having fun. It encourages teens to read during the summer and provides opportunities for them to contribute to the library and community through the service project (float construction for the parade).

For additional information about the Billerica Public Library, visit the library Web site at www.billericalibrary.org, or e-mail Michelle Paquin, Children's and Young Adult Librarian, at Mpaquin@mvlc.org.

## "BLAST" Extended Year Program
## Carnegie Library of Pittsburgh
## Pittsburgh and Allegheny County, Pennsylvania

The eleventh-largest library in the nation, the Carnegie Library of Pittsburgh serves the citizens and residents of Pittsburgh and Allegheny County, Pennsylvania. Serving a total population of over 1.2 million, the Carnegie Library of Pittsburgh is a state-supported public library and serves as a resource center in the fields of science, technology, and business for all libraries in the Commonwealth of Pennsylvania. It is comprised of a main library, 18 neighborhood locations, the Library for the Blind and Physically Handicapped, five Reading Centers in public-housing communities, as well as deposit collections in senior-citizen centers. The library has as one of its goals to provide service to children both in the library and through outreach. Participation in the extended year program provides the library the opportunity to reach children who would not otherwise have the opportunity to participate in the library's regular summer library reading program.

BLAST stands for "*Bringing Libraries and Schools Together.*" This school-outreach program partners the public library with the Pittsburgh Public Schools. Started in 2002, the program has expanded each year since then, with the school system's asking the library system to visit more schools each year. Targeting students in kindergarten through fifth grade from schools in low-income neighborhoods, the BLAST staff visit each school in the program weekly. The library maintains a database of children and teens who have registered for the regular summer library reading program and is able to determine if the students are registered for that program. In 2003, the library was able to determine that 94% of the children in this outreach program were not registered for the in-house library program. By providing this outreach experience, children in low-income neighborhoods were able to participate in a summer reading experience that they would otherwise not have had.

The weekly programs offered at the schools by library staff include several components. The structured storytimes presented at the schools use the same read-aloud techniques that teachers in the classroom use. Children are asked open-ended questions as the books are read aloud. They also concentrate on two new vocabulary words selected from the story and participate in reinforcement activities. The program also offers incentives for children to read and provides time for book selection.

Teachers are asked to complete an evaluation for the program. Teachers provided the following comments that show the educational value of this program:

- As a teacher, what was the best part of the Carnegie Library Extended-Year Program?
  o Giving the children an opportunity to take a book home.
  o Exposing children to rich vocabulary.
  o It encouraged students to read books and helped students meet the "25-book" standard in the school district.
  o This program motivated students to enjoy reading. It gave them a diversion from the more structured activities/lesson plans. I thought it was great!

- What benefits did your students gain from participating in the program?
  o The students began to be excited about "borrowing" books and they started to talk about what they were reading.
  o The students gained a better understanding of language as well as using their comprehension skills through question/answer periods and vocabulary development.
  o The students had an opportunity to hear stories of different genres and gain an appreciation of cultural contributions to amazing stories.

The library was complimented on the selection of books for this program. The books selected, while being age- and developmentally-appropriate, challenged the students to listen and focus on what was being read. Activity sheets, though useful in some classrooms, were not used in others. Teachers made several suggestions to improve the program. In addition to suggesting that there be a field trip to take the students to the library, the teachers wanted the library to take the program to the schools twice weekly. They also suggested that each child be registered to get a library card.

For additional information about the library, check them out at www.carnegielibrary.org; for information about the summer program and BLAST, go to www.carnegielibrary.org/kids/booknook. Georgene DeFilippo is the youth services coordinator in charge of this project. She can be reached via e-mail at defilippog@carnegielibrary.org.

**Figure 9–3**
**Carnegie Library of Pittsburgh. The BLAST School Outreach Program offered by the Carnegie Library of Pittsburgh was funded in part by the Grable Foundation and the Pittsburgh Foundation.  Shown are two of the handouts that teachers used as follow-up to the school visits by library staff.  The brochure in the center is distributed to teachers and parents.**

## "Reading . . . Naturally!"
## Cass District Library
## Cassopolis, Michigan

Located between Kalamazoo, Michigan, and South Bend, Indiana, the Village of Cassopolis, population 1,740, is one of 53 Michigan communities that received funds from Andrew Carnegie for a public library. Cass District Library's legal-service area includes the Cass County townships of Calvin, Howard, Jefferson, LaGrange, Mason, Milton, Newberg, Ontwa, Penn, Pokagon, Porter, and Volinia and serves a population of slightly over 51,000. The communities served have a high level of education: 72.3 percent of residents of Cass County graduated from high school and almost ten percent have a bachelor's degree. Branches are located in Cassopolis, Edwardsburg, Howard, and Mason/Union; the library district operates an affiliated computer learning center at the Cass County Council on Aging in Cassopolis. The mission of the Cass District Library is to provide a center for information, education, culture, and recreation for all patrons throughout their life span using the library's collections, programs, and special services.

"Reading . . . Naturally!" was designed to promote community awareness to the youth of Cass County through fun and exciting learning opportunities centered on nature and the environment. Through a partnership with several community agencies, programs were developed around environmental topics such as rainforests, groundwater and its conservation, recycling, animals native to the area, and learning about nature through hands-on activities. Programs were provided by the Curious Kids' Museum, the Cass County Conservation District, Sarett Nature Center, Cass County Parks Department, and the Southwestern Michigan College Museum. An inventive program featuring educational songs by the Banana Slug String Band rounded out the programs.

When children and teens signed up for the summer reading program, they were each given a calendar that showed when all the programs are and where they will be presented. Program participants were also instructed to use the calendar to track how much time they spent reading each day. When they returned to the library, the times were added up. Children were given a prize for every hour they read. For the first hour read, children got an animal clicker; the second, an activity book; the fifth hour, a pencil and topper; for every hour read past that, they received a raffle ticket. Teens received food coupons for every two hours spent reading; after reading six hours, they too got raffle tickets. The raffle tickets were for larger prizes that were awarded at the end of the summer.

Door prizes were also given away at each program. Throughout the summer, program participants had the option of going to a Kid's Nature Workshop.

In addition to providing educational opportunities where children and teens were engaged in learning, the summer reading club provided situations for parental involvement, creative activities, and stimulated reading for pleasure.

After collecting statistics related to program attendance and circulation of materials over the summer and soliciting comments from program participants and their parents and caregivers, library staff made presentation to the Cass District Library Board of Trustees, the Cass County Board of Commissioners, the Cass County Youth Council, and the local Rotary Club about the success of the summer reading program.

For more information on the Cass District Library and the summer program, visit the library Web site at www.cass.lib.mi.us/index.php, or e-mail Marilyn Smith, mjsmith@cass.lib.mi.us.

## "Summer Reading Club"
## Central Arkansas Library System
## Pulaski and Perry Counties, Arkansas

Serving Pulaski and Perry counties with a total population of over 300,000, the Central Arkansas Library System has a main library of 132,000 square feet and nine branches that have a total of 95,000 square feet. The system has as its overall goal to provide information to members of the community. The summer reading club helps the library meet its goal of providing information by providing a variety of programs that bring not only children to the library, but their parents and caregivers as well. The programs introduce children to recreational reading and other library resources. To do this, they target children from 18 months to 15 years of age. As reading is the foundation for all learning, the library focuses on getting children to read, thereby opening the door to all areas of education.

The financial support for the summer reading club comes from two primary sources. Slightly less than half of the funding comes from general library funds. In addition to that $9,000, an additional $10,000 is provided by the Friends of the Library. This combined total of $19,000 is used for posters, bookmarks, book bags, reading records, and stickers that are placed on the reading record each week as the child visits the library. Not willing to rely only on press releases to be published on a space-available basis, funds are used to purchase ads in local parenting magazines. Realizing the amount of staff time and energy needed to implement a full-scale summer program, the library also uses the funds to hire two traveling programmers from within the community. These temporary positions are usually filled by school librarians or teachers who are off for the summer. They work during the eight weeks of the summer reading club. Each of the programmers prepares several preschool programs and travels to all of the branches, thus lightening up the load on the regular library staff.

In addition, a local skating rink, Skate Connection, provides an in-kind donation that attracts many nonusers to the program. A special free skating program is provided at the rink for all program members as a reward for participation.

Rewards are an important part of this program, but competition is not. Rewards are given to participants who reach a goal that they set for themselves at the beginning of the summer. Preschoolers and children with learning disabilities who aren't reading independently yet are allowed to count any book that is read to them. Their older siblings and other reading partners can count not only the books they read independently but the ones they read to other children. This encourages children to read books to one another; this creates a win-win situation in which children, parents, and the library all work together to promote reading. Children are asked to estimate how many books they will read (or listen to) during the summer—anything from 250 picture books for preschool and primary students to 3 books if an older student want to read the Lord of the Rings trilogy. Children are permitted to recalculate their goal midway during the summer. The library makes certain that every child who participates and reads gets a medal when they stay with the program for the duration of the program.

For more information on the library, check out their Web site, www.cals.lib.ar.us, or contact Betty Fowler Kerns, Assistant Director for Youth Programs and Services and Head of Main Library, bkerns@cals.lib.ar.us.

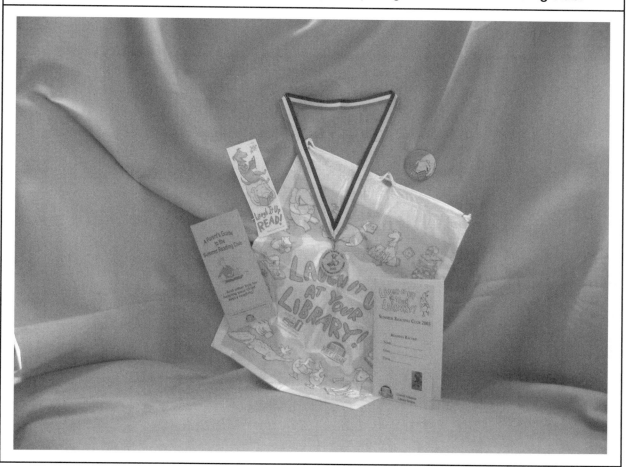

**Figure 9–4**
**Central Arkansas Library System Promotional Materials. The Central Arkansas Library System rewarded readers with a medal for participating in the summer reading club.**

## "Daycare Summer Reading Program"
## Clermont County Public Library
## Batavia, Ohio

Not every summer library reading program targets school-age children. And even those that do target school-age children no longer rely on family groups to attend programs during the day. The Clermont County Public Library (CCPL) located in Batavia, Ohio, targets their program to the preschool through fifth-grade children who spend their summer days in childcare facilities. Batavia is a community east of Cincinnati and is considered part of the Appalachian Region of Ohio. There are 27 childcare facilities in the county that are eligible for the Daycare Summer Reading Program. Census data indicates that 15% of the county's population is under ten years of age.

The mission of the CCLP states that the library strives to provide innovative access to information and services that stimulate the diverse educational, informational, and recreational needs and interests of the community. It goes on to say that the library seeks to be an integral part of the community in cooperation with other community organizations. The summer reading program relates directly to the library's mission to provide access to services to meet the needs of the community while working in partnership with other community partners.

The "Daycare Summer Reading Program" supports the education of the children involved in the program by encouraging them to maintain the reading skills they developed in school during the previous school year. Additionally, the preschool children who are working on emergent-literacy activities are supported in their efforts through this program. The activities the library provides as part of this program continue the process of getting them ready to enter a formal educational setting. The program allows library staff the opportunity to model reading behaviors for the childcare providers and teachers, and also encourages them to model those same reading behaviors for parents. Many of the children who participate in this project have never visited the library or read voluntarily, especially over the summer.

Program planning was done by the library in partnership with childcare agencies at the county level. Comprehensive Child Care (4Cs), Head Start, and Child Focus all met to decide how best to implement this library literacy program. After planning was completed, each individual childcare agency was invited to participate. Participating agencies received deposit collections from the library that they could use during the program; at the conclusion of the summer, the childcare centers were able to keep the books. In addition, the Clermont County Department of Jobs and Family Services encourages their providers to participate in the program. They deliver materials to homes and provide new books for use by in-home childcare providers, a group that is usually difficult to reach with library programs.

In 2003, children at the childcare agencies were to read 15 minutes per day, and each classroom group kept track of their progress as a class on a giant reading game board. Library staff visited the centers biweekly to deliver reading incentives and a short program. They also collected information on how much reading the groups had done since the last time the library visited. In 2004, the program changed to counting pages with the goal of the entire community contributing to the effort to read one million pages. To encourage the childcare centers to participate and to make record keeping easy for them, it was decided to count 15 minutes of reading as equal to 32 pages, the average length of a picture book.

The program takes place over eight weeks during the summer. The program has a countywide focus and includes all ten branch libraries and their communities.

Community support for this program has grown. Many of the businesses that provided donations to support the project in 2003 willingly volunteered to participate again in 2004. County agencies also were enthusiastic and again partnered with the library to provide this service.

For additional information on this project and the library, visit the library Web site at www.clermont.lib.oh.us/kidz.html, or contact Leslie A. Massie, Co-Director of Public Services, masseyle@oplin.org.

## "Step to the Beat—READ!"
## Emmet O'Neal Library
## Mountain Brook, Alabama

Serving a population of 20,600, the Emmet O'Neal Library is located in Mountain Brook, Alabama. A member of the Jefferson County Library Cooperative, the library maintains its autonomy, as do all members of the cooperative. The members of the cooperative work together to provide services to all county residents; the mission of the cooperative is to foster, encourage, enable, and coordinate services and resource sharing among the public libraries of Jefferson County. The cooperative contracts with the Birmingham Public Library for the provision of certain countywide services, such as automation, books-by-mail, delivery-van services, cataloging, and training.

The Emmet O'Neal Library adapts the statewide theme for use in their community; Alabama is part of the Southern States Summer Reading Cooperative Program along with Georgia, Virginia, Mississippi, and South Carolina. As each participating library is given artistic license to interpret the theme, the Emmet O'Neal Library chose a game-show format.

Playing off the "Step to the Beat" statewide theme, the library rewarded children who played their version of *Name That Tune*. The "Step to the Beat Feat" program gave weekly prizes to those who played the theme-related game. Beginning at the Musical Feats Board, children had to push a button to listen to a prerecorded sound byte and correctly identify the musical instrument making the sound. After finding the instruments in the Children Department, they took a token to the children's services desk that allowed them a chance to spin a colorful game wheel. The color upon which the wheel stopped determined which color button they would push. Once they push that button, they had to identify the song. Prizes were given for correctly identifying the song. The buttons, prizes, and songs were changed weekly.

The Junior Women's Committee of 100, the Friends of the Emmet O'Neal Library, the merchants of Mountain Brook and the Mountain Brook School System all contribute to the success of the summer program. The schools publicize the program by distributing reading logs and calendars and awarding Summer Reading certificates during school assemblies in the fall. Funds raised by the Junior Women's Club and the Friends of the Library provide materials for the collection and prizes for the program.

To help promote the program, three over-the-road banners are placed over the main traffic area in a triangle formation at a major intersection and remains on display for the entire summer. In-ground signage is placed in front of the library to promote specific programs. A summer reading bag filled with promotional items is given to each child at registration. The promotional items include reading logs, a summer reading program cup with sponsor's name on it, a kazoo, bookmarks, food coupons, and stickers featuring summer program art. Staff wear T-shirts with theme art to help decorate the library and promote the program to anyone who visits the library.

Additional information about the library can be found on their Web site at www.eolib.org, or contact Carol Melton, Children's Department Head, carolm@bham.lib.al.us.

## "Summer Library Program"
## Fairbanks North Star Borough Public Libraries and Regional Center
## Fairbanks, Alaska

The Fairbanks North Star Borough Public Library, also know as the Noel Wien Public Library, is located in Fairbanks, Alaska. A branch of the borough government, the library system has a main library facility in Fairbanks, a branch in North Pole, and provides van and homebound delivery and regional services to communities without libraries. The library provides a full range of services for the 82,840 people who live in the area; over 30 percent of the population is 19 years of age or under. The library has a collection of over 300,000 items in a wide range of forms and approximately 400 newspaper and magazine subscriptions. Reference service by phone and in person is available during all hours the library is open. The library also provides Internet access, on-site and remote access to databases, word processors, game computers, a homework center, as well as access to typewriters.

Throughout the system, an emphasis is placed on children's programming. The library cooperates with other community agencies and organizations, and formally networks with other libraries in the area. The Noel Wien Library coordinates the local-area summer library reading program for several libraries, including other branch libraries, the Ft. Wainwright Post Library and the Eielson Air Force Base Library.

The library builds their summer program around the "Collaborative Library Summer Program" that the Alaska State Library provides to public libraries in the state. A variety of programs for toddlers to teens enhance the "Discover New Trails @ Your Library" theme. A craft club was offered three times during the summer program. Children and teens could participate in a library search/scavenger hunt. Clues were provided in covered wagons that were located throughout the library. When they located all the covered wagons, participants received a reward. In addition to regular storytime programs, the summer program offered a Harry Potter movie and book discussion. A potluck dinner was held for participants and their families. Two parties, a pajama storytime and an end-of-summer program that featured the dedication of the new story garden, rounded out the program.

Teens participated in separate programs. The libraries in Fairbanks and North Pole offered a wilderness-survival course. Fairbanks provided an orienteering course and North Pole held a bookmaking program. To reward participants, a Mystery Night was held where pizza was served and the teens received free books.

Each participant had a shoeprint to represent his or her membership in the program; the shoeprints were displayed in the library window to promote the program. As participants reported on the books they read each week, they received small incentives related to the program theme. Incentives included a bookmark, an assemble-it-yourself diary and pencil, theme-related incentives that were purchased through Upstart, Pioneer Park train passes, and McDonalds food coupons. At the end of the six weeks, children who completed the program earned a free paperback book of his or her choice. These books are purchased with grant funds provided by a local oil refinery, Flint Hills Resources. Formerly Williams Alaska, Flint Hills Resources has provided grant funds for the past six years; they support community projects, especially those associated with children and literacy.

For more information about the library and its programs, visit their Web site at http://library.fnsb.lib.ak.us/ or send an e-mail to Susan Jones, Youth Services Librarian, susan.jones@fnsb.lib.ak.us.

## "Summer Reading Game"
## Free Library of Philadelphia
## Philadelphia, Pennsylvania

The Free Library of Philadelphia has several roles. It provides current materials of high interest in a variety of formats for persons of all ages. It also provides timely, accurate information and reference services employing a highly qualified staff who provide the link between library materials and users in a congenial and professional manner and support the educational goals of Philadelphians by providing materials and programs for children, as well as for their parents and caregivers. The library system provides services to 1.5 million people across an area of 135 square miles through 50 branch libraries, 3 regional libraries, a central library, and the library for the blind and physically handicapped. All libraries have a meeting room and a children's area, including a preschool center. The young adult areas are generally shelving spaces only.

Incorporated in 1891, the Free Library of Philadelphia has been providing summer reading programs for youth since 1906; the library considers summer programs for youth one of its signature programs. It grows and changes through the years and is an essential part of the future for this large, urban library system. Summer reading provides a bridge from school-based reading to the broader use of the public library.

In a city where more than 85 percent of the public schools are failing, the Free Library of Philadelphia provides a summer reading program that encourages reluctant or poor readers to participate in activities that make reading pleasurable; they want these students to give reading another try. The goal is to bring children and teens who are nonreaders and nonusers of the library into the library. Widespread publicity and the program's structure and components are designed to achieve this goal.

Children have the opportunity to earn an unlimited number of stickers each week during the summer for reading activities; for every week youth participate in the program they earn an incentive prize. Children record books read and collect stickers in folders. The overall program is loosely structured so that each of the 55 agencies can adapt it to fit the needs of the local communities they each serve. For example, some libraries offer youth the opportunity to win bigger raffle prizes through increased participation. Children visit the library any time the branch is open to talk with staff and collect stickers and prizes. The "Teen Summer Reading Game" focuses on local and citywide raffles, with students submitting one raffle ticket for each book read.

Knowing that many children are enrolled in other full-day summer programs, the library takes the summer reading game to camps, recreation centers, and other summer programs. The library's outreach specialists regularly visit more than 90 summer schools so that students enrolled in those programs may also participate.

An important facet of this program is the partnership that the public library has with the School District of Philadelphia. Both the School District of Philadelphia and the Free Library of Philadelphia believe that children involved in the summer reading game maintain or improve their reading skills during the summer vacation. Using Branch Associates, an independent evaluation group, the library learned that children involved in the "Summer Reading Game" are more likely to see themselves as learners and readers; this improved self-image makes it more likely that these children will succeed in school. Students reported in the pre- and post-summer reading program surveys that the program helped them in school. Parents and teachers also report seeing positive differences in youth who participate in the program.

The superintendent of the public school system and the director of the library send a letter that they both sign to all schools and again to all summer schools encouraging participation; this is followed up with in-person visits to the schools. Local librarians and support staff visit all 450 public, private, and parochial schools in Philadelphia; talk with the students; and distribute bookmarks and other promotional materials. Letters are also sent to community organizations, camps, and recreation centers to promote participation. Information is also posted on the library Web site and is listed in the city's "Summer Activity Directory."

The Free Library of Philadelphia and the summer reading program offer opportunities to read and participate in library and literacy-related activities with a positive focus on youth development. Because the program is geared to nonreaders and non–library users, the library provides opportunities for youth to improve several development assets they need to become successful in life. The library provides friendly positive words of encouragement; has high expectations for youth; and helps youth meet and exceed these expectations. The library sees youth as resources and valuable assets to the community and provides youth with interesting volunteer and work opportunities. The library provides adult role models and positive peer interaction and influences. The "Summer Reading Game" is an opportunity to introduce and reinforce the library's role as a safe place and welcoming environment in the community.

While computers are not integral to the "Summer Reading Game," children can do a computer activity to earn a sticker and a weekly prize. Many of the branches offer technology programs as part of their summer activities. The library also links to the Pennsylvania state summer reading Web site so students can participate there.

Funding for this citywide program provides for publicity (bookmarks, posters, folders, and one banner for the central library); incentives and prizes; staff (an assistant for the development office and 12 outreach summer workers); evaluation; and other related items. Funding and in-kind services come from many sources, including numerous corporate sponsors: Wachovia, PKG Foundation, AMETEK Foundation, Inc., Sunoco, the Franklin Institute Science Museum, Verizon, and many others.

For additional information on the Free Library of Philadelphia, visit the library's Web site at www.library.phila.gov, or contact either Hedra Peterman, Chief, Office of Public Service Support, packmanh@library.phila.gov, or Betsy Orsburne, Youth Specialist, orsburne@library.phila.gov.

## "Get Wrapped Up in Reading!" Jefferson County Public Library Jefferson County, Colorado

Jefferson County Public Library (JCPL) serves several communities in the foothills just west of Denver, Colorado. Included in the library system's service area are Evergreen, Lakewood, Arvada, Columbine, Golden, and several other communities. In addition to providing services and programs from the bookmobile, the system has ten service outlets.

The mission statement for the JCPL is to enrich the quality of life for all people in the county by providing resources for information, education, and recreation. To accomplish this, the library provides free services that are equally accessible to all; they pay special attention to the learning needs of children; they provide personal assistance from a well-trained, service-oriented staff; it has a broad diverse collection of books and materials in varied formats, and it provides confidentially in the use of resources. The library also uses current technology and modern practices in public library services. And, the library strives for excellence in all endeavors.

Related to JCPL's mission are the ongoing goals of the summer reading club: to encourage the love of literature, to introduce children to the library and its staff, to provide a venue to introduce school-age children to the variety of resources available in the public library and to fight alliteracy. The summer reading club presents reading as an experience for fun and recreation to help children maintain their reading skills and to develop a pattern of regular library visits for the whole family.

The summer reading club is organized by the children's librarians' roundtable, a workgroup consisting of the heads of children information services for each branch library. Children are asked to read for eight hours to earn a new paperback book. Participants range in age from birth through fifth grade. The library system hosts a separate teen summer reading program for students in sixth grade and above in cooperation with the Colorado Young Adult Advocates in Libraries (C'YAAL). See the section in this chapter on Pikes Peak Library District for information about this cooperative program.

Each child who wishes to participate in the reading club is given a tally sheet that is used to record the number of hours the child reads in 15-minute increments. Children are encouraged to bring the tally sheet to the library during their regular library visits so that staff can stamp each full hour read as a visual measure of progress. While computers do not play a significant role in the program, children may include time spent reading information from the Internet as part of the eight hours they read to gain a reward. Books on tape and CDs also count.

Participants are challenged to contribute to a worthy cause by reading enough hours to meet a staff-determined, communitywide goal. The 2003 countywide goal was 100,000 hours. When that goal was reached, the Jefferson County Public Library foundation donated $1,000 to purchase books to stock the library in a shelter for homeless teens. In 2004, the goal was increased to 110,000 hours. In addition to providing the donation to encourage the service reading project, the foundation funds an annual grant to provide performers for many of the programs that are scheduled throughout the system.

The summer reading club program also has a contest element. Each library hosts a weekly candy-jar guessing contest. Children are asked to estimate the number of pieces of candy in the jar. The closest guess wins the contents of the jar, which changes weekly. In addition to free paperback books as prizes and incentives, local amusement parks, recreation centers, sporting goods stores, and restaurants donate coupons and services. Each library hosts a Book Award Day at the end of the program to celebrate the program participant's success.

The library tracks the total number of hours read online with an Excel-generated form, making reporting at the end of the program easy. Comparisons from year to year are also possible.

Publicity for the program is provided by JCPL's Public Information Office and Graphics Department. Through this office's support, promotional bookmarks and posters are sent to the schools in late spring before schools are dismissed for the summer. This office also prepares a full-color, slick brochure/calendar that lists all children's programs that are held throughout the summer; they also help create the "Summer Reading Club" Web page.

Additional information about the library and the summer reading club can be found on the Web at www.jefferson.lib.co.us, or by contacting either Shannon Van Hemert, Head, Children's Information Services at the Columbine Library, shannonv@jefferson.lib.co.us, or Robyn Lupa, Head, Children's Information Services at the Arvada Library, rlupa@jefferson.lib.co.us.

## "Manchester Reads"
## Manchester Public Library
## Manchester, Connecticut

The primary role of the Manchester Public Library is service to children. The library encourages youngsters from preschool through high school to develop independent intellectual growth and a lifetime love of reading, and it especially encourages young children to develop an interest in reading and learning by providing services for those children and for parents and children together. Located ten miles east of Hartford, Connecticut, the Manchester Public Library serves the nearly 55,000 people in the community through a main library and one branch. Despite its "blue collar" reputation, Manchester is, based on circulation, the fourth-busiest public library in Connecticut; the library circulates close to 350,000 children's items per year. The library employs four children's librarians. By attracting children to the library, they also bring in their parents, siblings, other relatives and friends, all of whom have contributed to the near tripling of the library's circulation over the past decade.

In 2002, the library decided to expand their regular summer library reading program from a children-only program to an intergenerational program. This expansion of the program mirrored the library's mission of meeting the lifelong educational needs of the community. By having a program that would attract a broader age range, the 2002 summer reading program reinforces the concept of family literacy for Manchester residents.

"Manchester Reads" is the theme that encompasses three individual summer reading programs: one for children birth through grade 5, one for teens in grades 6 through 12, and one for adults. There were programs for each group at the library.

Thousands of children attend weekly programs, such as "Picnic Storytime" (an al fresco bring your own brown-bag lunch); "Family Night" (multicultural storytellers and other performers); "Marvelous Mondays" (camp-like experience for 8- to 12-year-olds); and "Beat the Heat" craft programs.

Hundreds of teens attend weekly "Teen Nights" and "Teen Chess Club" programs. Teen Night encompassed themes such as a book-and-movie night. Teens read a book in advance and then watch the movie at the library and discuss which they preferred.

Adults attend author-visit programs and an end-of-summer punch-and-cookies social, during which valuable prizes are given away in a raffle. Adults receive their raffle tickets for each book they read over the summer.

Ongoing incentives for all ages included attractive T-shirts bearing the town seal and the "Manchester Reads" logo, and other prizes donated by local businesses. To receive the prizes and incentives, readers record the titles of the books they read on a reading log. Prereaders can be read to by adults or other children in order to receive their prizes.

Framed 36-inch by 24-inch posters with the "Manchester Reads" logo and local celebrities, such as the mayor, the chief of police, and the superintendent of school, reading their favorite books are printed and distributed through the town. This part of the project is popular with the town board of directors and other influential people in town as it gives them a chance to demonstrate their commitment to literacy.

A large component of "Manchester Reads" is the collaboration with the public schools. Prior to dismissal for summer vacation, library staff visit every public and parochial elementary school in town to advertise and promote the summer reading program to the students and the teachers. Public librarians help develop the recommended summer reading lists that are sent home with students along with the library's summer reading log. Along with the lists and logs, a letter signed by the library director and the superintendent of schools is sent home with students encouraging them to participate in the summer reading program. The library also sends hundreds of its books to the summer school program so that students have access to books and can participate in the summer reading program; since the school libraries are closed during the summer, the students would not have ready access to reading materials without this effort. This collaboration serves to integrate the schools' goal of maintaining reading skills over the summer and the library's goal of attracting more children to the summer program. The summer reading logs from the library are signed by the parents and returned to the students' new teachers in the fall, emphasizing parental involvement as well as the integration of school and public library programs. The library's summer reading logs can be substituted for reading logs from the "Governor's Summer Reading Challenge," a statewide campaign from the Connecticut Department of Education.

"Manchester Reads" continues to be an important program promoting family and community literacy for the town of Manchester. The 2002 theme continued into 2003, as did the intergenerational aspect of the program. A new community-service aspect was added in 2003; the "Community Knitting Project" began. Children, adults, and senior adults met weekly at the library to knit teddy-bear sweaters for stuffed animals that are given away by police officers to children in distress. Participation in the adult summer reading program grew by 40 percent from 2002 to 2003, reinforcing the belief that by creating an active program of children's services, an increase in adult usage follows. The popularity of the library's program of service and the resulting severe space and parking shortages have contributed to the town board of directors' recommendation that the library begin a long-term space-needs study with an eye to a new main library building.

For additional information about the Manchester Public Library, visit the library's Web site at http://library.ci.manchester.ct.us/missionroles.html; for information about "Manchester Reads," visit http://read.ci.manchester.ct.us/; or e-mail Ramona Harten, Assistant Library Director, rharten@ci.mancester.ct.us.

**Figure 9–5**
Manchester Public Library, "Manchester Reads." *Manchester Reads* T-shirts could be seen all around town on readers of many ages. T-shirts have become a popular reward for program participants. The summer program in this community also supports the Governor's Summer Reading Challenge.

## "Summer Reading Program"
## Multnomah County Library
## Portland, Oregon

The Multnomah County Library, headquartered in Portland, Oregon, and the oldest public library west of the Mississippi, reaches back to 1864. The system is comprised of a central library and 16 branches. Each library has at least one public meeting room that can also be used for programming, a children's area, and a young adult area. A reciprocal agreement with the public libraries in a four-county region in Oregon and two nearby library systems in Washington state allows all residents to use any one of over 40 public libraries located in these counties.

One goal of Multnomah County Library's strategic plan is that the library will provide emergent-literacy and reading programs to youth of all ages. Another strategic goal states that library books and services will support children and youth and satisfy their personal reading interests and educational needs. The summer reading program encourages readers and prereaders of all ages to experience and enjoy reading of their own choice over the summer. The library program is designed to encourage reading over time. The program lasts for three months and encourages readers to select their own reading materials with library staff assisting them to find what interests each participant most.

Each participant who signs up for the "Summer Reading Program" receives a game board to track his or her reading over the summer. As participants progress around the game board, the readers earn incentives such as Beanie Babies, free swim passes, food coupons, and other fun items. Participants can read on their own or be read to; parents have the flexibility to change the amount of time required to read according to the individual child's needs. Teens have their own game and read to earn chances in a weekly drawing. Prizes for the teens include shopping sprees, Portland Trailblazer basketball tickets, and movie party packs. All players who finish the game can choose between a free T-shirt or a coupon for a free book; all who complete the game are entered into a contest for the grand prize drawing for a family trip to Disneyland. At any point in the game, participants can choose to forgo their prizes in exchange for a "Discovery Dollar" that goes toward the purchase of materials for children in homeless shelters and child-care centers. In addition to the independent reading games, each of the branch libraries in the system offers numerous weekly cultural, artistic, entertainment, and reading-promotion programs, including storytimes, book groups, puppet shows, musical performances, and art classes.

Rather than waiting for the youth of the community and their families to find the library and its programs, staff actively seek out programs and events to promote the summer reading program. In addition to annual participation in the Junior Rose Festival parade, the library has hosted kick-off celebrations at a local amusement park. The Multnomah County Library summer reading program has both television and radio sponsorship, resulting in hundreds of commercials airing over the course of the summer.

Over 500 youth and adult volunteers log over 10,000 hours annually. Their efforts help to manage this enormous project by distributing prizes, doing data entry, and maintaining prize inventories. By providing these volunteer opportunities, the library is allowing teens to contribute back to their community, an important part of youth development.

The library's LIBROS (*LIBR*ary *O*utreach in *S*panish) program, which promotes and connects Spanish-speaking patrons with library service brings new life to the summer reading program. Working with in-house bilingual experts, the library is able to create program materials in Spanish. The library is also able to provide outreach to community organizations and summer-care sites to help Spanish-speaking babies, children, and teens all summer long. The library also provides materials, such as a parent-information sheet, in multiple languages—English, Spanish, Chinese, Russian, and Vietnamese.

In addition to involving the library's Early Childhood Resources office in the program, the library also has a "Books 2 U" program that takes the summer reading program directly to thousands of school-age children at community centers, housing authority sites, schools, Boys and Girls clubs, free-lunch sites, and other places where youth spend their time.

The Multnomah County Library Summer Reading Program enjoys a 99.8% approval rating from parents. Not only do the families like the prizes, but they say that the game motivates the family to read.

Additional information about the Multnomah County Library Summer Reading Program can be found on the library's Web site at www.mutlcolib.org/summer, or by contacting Katie O'Dell, Reading Promotions Coordinator, kodell@multcolib.org.

**Figure 9–6**
**Multnomah County Promotional Materials. The summer reading program at the Multnomah County Library provides multilingual promotional materials to reach their diverse community. Two of the game boards the library uses to encourage reading and participating are shown. To fill in the stepping stones along the trail, children count time they read or time spent listening to some one read to them.  Other library and literacy related activities are also included. Children are rewarded with prizes and incentives.  They also have the opportunity to place a bookplate honoring their reading achievement in a library book.**

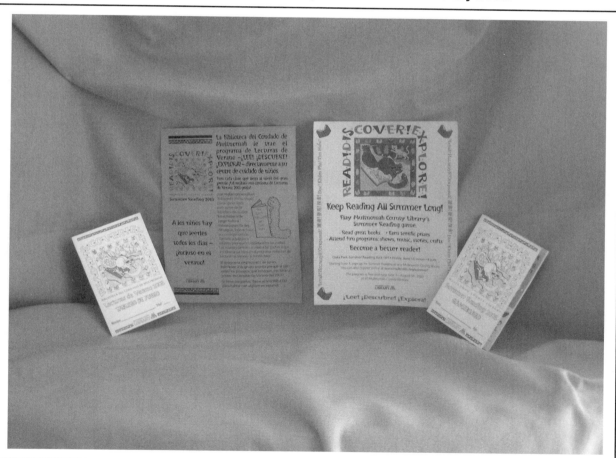

## "Unlock the Mystery"
## Nashville Public Library
## Nashville, Davidson County, Tennessee

Serving Nashville, Tennessee, and the surrounding Davidson County area, the Nashville Public Library system consists of 20 branch libraries, the downtown Main Library, Metropolitan Government Archives, Special Services for the Deaf and Hard of Hearing, and the Talking Library, a radio-reading service for the print disabled. Eight of the library locations have separate areas for teens. With a population increase of 11.6 percent from 1990 to the 2000 census, Nashville is experiencing high-job growth in the publishing, music production, higher education, automobile, and health care industries. Highlighting the cultural diversity of the community that the library serves, "Community of Many Faces" was created in partnership with the Global Education Center and Friends of the Library. It showcases the African, Chinese, Irish, Native American, Polynesian, Scottish, and South Indian cultures found in the community.

As stated in the mission of the Public Library of Nashville and Davidson County, the library is committed to extending the benefits and joys of reading, lifelong learning, and discovery to all people through collection and services; providing an environment that is welcoming to all people and that serves as a gathering place within the community; providing emerging technologies and instruction as a gateway to information resources within and beyond the walls of the library, and preserving and sharing across generations the wisdom, culture, and history of the community.

To accomplish this, service to teens has become a priority with the library.

"Unlock the Mystery" was developed by the eight members of the Young Adult Committee of the Nashville Public Library System and was carried out at each of the 21 public library locations in the system. The teens had two ways to complete the program: read 18 hours or complete a mystery-trivia sheet. To complete the trivia sheet, teens had to unlock a secret code or answer the questions by researching them. To track reading, teens completed three reading logs, each one containing space to track six hours of reading. Each log that was turned in was entered into a drawing for weekly prizes at each branch. To have more chances to win, teens read more than the required 18 hours and turned in additional reading logs, improving their chances to receive prizes. Teens were also encouraged to complete book-review forms that were then displayed in a binder. In keeping with the mystery theme, the review forms had the following rating system:

- I detect a winner!
- Evidently well written.
- There's a good motive to read this book.
- The plot was elementary.
- It's a mystery how this book ever got published.

Special programs just for teens were offered at individual branches. Many were directly related to the program theme; others were of general interest to teens. Programs included a Clue tournament, speakers from the Tennessee Bureau of Investigation, henna tattoos, Web-design class, Christmas in July snow-globe craft, and a murder-mystery night.

Upon completion of the program, each participant received several rewards: a T-shirt featuring the "Unlock the Mystery" logo and a free pass to either the local wave pool or the Tennessee Sports Hall of Fame. In addition, teens also received two tickets to the Kourtyard Karaoke Party that the library planned for the teens.

The Kourtyard Karaoke party was held at the main library as the grand finale party for all program participants who had met the requirements of the program. The party included a scavenger hunt, pizza, more prize drawings, and karaoke.

The program is designed to provide opportunities to enhance the developmental assets teens need to grow into healthy adults. The library staff provides opportunities for teens to see that there are adults outside of their family who care about them. The craft programs encourage teens to express themselves creatively. The library becomes part of a caring neighborhood by providing a safe place where teens can hang out and participate in constructive activities. Teens learn about responsibility; they track their reading and turn in their reading logs in order to receive credit for the time they read. Their self-esteem is improved by completing the program.

The "Unlock the Mystery" program provides Nashville's teens with an enjoyable incentive to continue reading during the summer months, helping to eliminate summer learning slide. By encouraging students to sign up for the summer reading program and log their required and recreational reading, the library helps teens complete their school summer reading requirements while emphasizing the importance of reading for fun.

The program is popular and attracts more teens each year. It is popular with the teens because they get to choose the books they want to read, and they get rewarded for it. Plus, the free library programs give them fun, productive things to do during the dog days of summer.

For additional information about the teen program at the Nashville Public Library, check out the library Web site at www.library.nashville.org, or send an e-mail message to Jessica.Trinoskey@nashville.gov.

## "Summer Mural Sidewalk Chalk Contest"
## New City Library
## Rockland County, New York

New City is located in Rockland County, New York. The library is a member of the Ramapo Catskill Library System and serves a community of 75,000 with its 31,000-square-foot building. The community the library serves is composed of predominately well-educated, upper-middle class to affluent people; there is a growing population of recent immigrants and working-class families. The mission of the New City Library is to provide materials that will aid in personal enrichment; encourage lifelong self-education; and supplement formal study, support cultural and recreational activities, and stimulate thoughtful awareness in world affairs. The library makes special efforts to address the needs of particular groups within the services area. The library works to attract underserved audiences and turn them from potential to actual users.

While the New City Library uses the theme and promotional materials provided by the New York State Library, the library staff designs individual programs that meet the needs of the local community. To address the part of the library mission that relates to providing recreational activities, the library has created a low-cost program that attracts families.

Families who wish to participate in the annual "Summer Mural Sidewalk Chalk Contest" are assigned an area in a roped-off area of the library's back parking lot. The library provides each family with a bag full of sidewalk chalk. Families have 1.5 hours to create a sidewalk mural based on the summer reading club theme. Children and parents alike enjoy this family activity. It provides an opportunity for the families to work together as a unit and allows them to communicate with each other. To determine the big winners, the library director acts as the judge. Three finalists are selected: one for the most colorful design, one for the best use of space, and another for best interpretation of the summer reading program theme. To allow more people to experience the art work that has been created, photographs are taken and displayed in the library. Everyone who participates in this activity receives a small prize and is considered a winner. The families whose creations are judged best receive gift certificates for the local ice cream parlor or passes to the local art museum as prizes.

This program is a tradition at the New City Library. To encourage family participation, the program is held in the evening, from 6:00 PM to 8:00 PM, while it is still light. Families have fun working together on this project. The young people and their parents have an enjoyable experience at the library and with the summer library program; they are encouraged to return for other programs. Since families must develop their creations based on the summer reading program theme, many of the entries draw on favorite characters from books the families have shared together or scenes of the library.

As this is an annual program, the library can take advantage of sales on the only supplies necessary for this program—sidewalk chalk. Prizes are donated by local merchants and the museum.

For information on the New City Library, visit the Web site, www.newcity library.org, or send an e-mail to Susan Schuler, Children's Services Librarian, sschuler@rcls.org.

## "Summer Reading Program"
## New Jersey Library for the Blind and Physically Handicapped Trenton, New Jersey

The primary audience for this program are the special-needs students who are served by the New Jersey Library for the Blind and Physically Handicapped (NJLBPH). The library works in cooperation with the National Library Services to provide recorded, Braille, and large-print books to residents of the state. It is the only source in New Jersey for children and teens with print disabilities to obtain popular, unabridged books on cassette tape from an all-inclusive and up-to-date talking-book collection read by professional narrators. The mission of the library is to encourage lifelong literacy. The summer reading program helps learning disabled, dyslexic, or students with print handicaps to develop the love of reading. Young or beginning readers are introduced to the wide variety of Braille and recorded books. The summer program offered by the NJLBPH piggybacks on the statewide theme that the state library provides to public libraries.

Children's and teens who are served by the NJLBPH set their own reading goal of 6, 12, or 18 books. At the start of the program, youth who are enrolled with the NJLBPH receive the *Rap Sheet*, a newsletter that tells about the program and provides a list of recommended books. Go to www2.njstatelib.org/lbh/youthsrv.htm to see the latest *Rap Sheet*. To participate in the program, the youth call their reading advisors on a toll-free phone number and talk about at least six of the books they have read. This call in is an important part of the program as this program is not site based; there is no library for the members of the program to visit. In addition to reporting on the books, this provides the reading advisors with information that allows them to recommend other books that the members might enjoy reading. Incentives—gifts that are theme-related—are mailed to members three times over the course of the summer program to encourage their participation. In addition to the incentives and more books to read, members are sent activity and fun sheets to complete. When children complete the program by reporting on six books and reading their goal number of books, they receive a certificate of achievement signed by the governor and the state librarian and a special prize. This program serves the entire state of New Jersey reaching approximately 2,000 children and teens with various disabilities that prevent them from reading conventional print. The NJLBPH also provides a chapter on serving children with special needs in the New Jersey's statewide summer reading program manual.

For more information about the New Jersey Library for the Blind and Physically Handicapped, visit www2.njstatelib.org/lbh/index.htm, or send an e-mail to Karen Messick, Head, Youth Services, kmessick@njstatelib.org.

## "Lights, Camera, READ!"
## Normal Public Library
## Normal, Illinois

An independent library in the city of Normal, Illinois, the Normal Public Library has selected several service responses that the summer library reading program supports, including Formal Education Support Center, Independent Learning Center, and Lifelong Learning. The three-level library building is located across the street from the campus of Illinois State University. The young adult area is located on the first floor of the building; the children's department on the second. Programs are held in the library's community room, which is located on the lower level of the library; on the lawn in front of the library; or at local parks, schools, or nearby college facilities.

The summer reading program at the Normal Public Library has many distinctive and separate aspects. While the program primarily targets children, adults are a secondary audience. Children and adults receive recognition for reading and program participation. The program is organized to work with five distinct target groups; participants receive prizes when reading slips are handed in.

- Rookie Readers (preschoolers) listen to five books every week.
- Kindergarteners through third-grade students read five books that are on grade level or read for 2.5 hours per week.
- Fourth through sixth graders read three books on grade level or 2.5 hours per week. Sixth-grade students have the option to participate in the teen program.
- "Cinema Teen Scene" is the theme for the teen reading program and is open to junior and senior high school students. Participants earn a free paperback book as they reach each one of five reading goals. All readers who complete the program get a prize plus a chance to enter a raffle for special prizes.
- A.R.K.S. (Adults Reading Kids' Stuff) targets people 18 years of age or older. These adults read up to 25 books in various genres and receive prizes as they reach their reading goals.

In addition to these categories, the library has a separate activity titled G.R.A.B. Great Read-Aloud Books encourages parents and children to share good chapter books to build a lifelong love of reading. The library developed a bibliography of some of the staff's favorite read-aloud titles and distributes this list to participants; families are not limited to these titles.

The rewards that participants earn are book bucks that can be redeemed for a variety of prizes and incentives. Prizes for purchase with the book bucks are donated by various businesses and community agencies. In addition to providing a Ronald McDonald magic show, the local McDonald's franchise provided coupons for ice cream cones. The Normal Parks and Recreation Department provides free admittance to one of the town's pool or waterslide facilities on one of two specific days. To maintain participation in the program, tickets for certain special events were only available to those who had turned in a certain number of weekly reading logs.

Additional information about the library and its summer programs can be found on the library Web site at www.normal-library.org, or e-mail the children's department at normallibrary@normal.org.

## "FLYP 2003: Hats Off to Reading!"
## NOVA Southeastern University
## Fort Lauderdale, Florida

The Alvin Sherman Library, Research and Information Technology Center at NOVA Southeastern University in Fort Lauderdale, Florida, is distinctive in that it is a joint public library/private academic library facility. While staff are hired by the university under the joint operating agreement, the library is also considered part of the Broward County Division of Libraries. The library seeks to advance information literacy not only for university faculty and students, but for all Broward County residents, too. To meet this goal, the library provides information-literacy training and develops and provides research-based instruction to students in Broward County Schools.

The Alvin Sherman Library is physically the largest library in Florida, occupying 325,000 square feet. There are multiple computer labs, one of which is dedicated to use by youth. This new facility has a 500-seat auditorium, which is run by the Broward Center for the Performing Arts and will soon host a children's theater. The public-service reference desk is on the first floor of this five-story building; the academic reference desk is on the second floor. The children's area is brightly decorated; the children's program room contains both carpeted and tiled areas and a video/computer projector.

This new library presents programs using the statewide theme of "Hats Off to Reading!" The primary audience for this eight-week series of programs is school-age children and teens. Children report their reading on reading logs designed by the State Library and Archives of Florida. By reporting their weekly reading, children are able to earn a different prize each week. Weekly programs entice children and families to visit the library weekly. Programs include "Kids Club," "Culture Club," "Bedtime Stories," "Storytime Fun," "Software Storytime," "Young Author's Guild," "Friday Freeplay," and "Saturday Specials." Programs for teens are offered throughout the summer at various times. The teen programs include a continuation of the library's ongoing Shakespeare Club; the library also offers craft and literature-based activities. Teen volunteers assist in presenting programs. The teens also formed an active puppet troupe.

The "Hats Off to Reading!" program provides students with educational enrichment through literature-based activities, multicultural crafts, and other enrichment activities. One activity that attracts much attention is the "Young Authors Guild."

For this segment of the program, the children and teens meet weekly in the dedicated youth computer lab. The youth librarian presents the weekly session using PowerPoint. The goal of the program is to provide an adult-style creative writing workshop that also teaches technology skills. Program participants receive training in various technology skills, including computer basics, such as mouse and keyboard skills; navigating in a Windows environment; online research skills; MS Word; saving to disk; and printing files.

Half of the children who participate in the program do so because they have a passion for writing. They have the opportunity to write their own "book" and find ways to publish it. The other half of the children participate in hopes that this program will prepare them for the writing portion of the Florida Comprehensive Assessment Test.

During the weekly sessions, the students individually practice free-flow writing. They then break into small groups to share their writing and critiquing each other's work. All of this is part of the creative process in which the participants create individually written and illustrated "books." The children and teens also work on writing their books at home. At the final session, the new authors receive a combbound copy of their book, autograph a copy for the library (the books are added to the library collection), receive praise and recognition, and feast on punch and cookies.

This technology program for youth supports several developmental assets. During the critiquing sessions, students provide service to others; they are encouraged to constructively offer criticism to their peers, and are trained on exactly what that means. The project provides a learning opportunity with participants working on their books at the library (caring out-of-home climate) and at home. This project also makes participants aware of deadlines and responsibilities.

Publicity for this program is provided by the Broward County Division of Libraries through their monthly calendar of events, *Bookings*. The library pays for advertising in *South Florida Parenting Magazine*; this is very effective in recruiting participants. They also distribute fliers to local schools and display them in the library. Librarians also appear on the morning video announcement programs at local schools to promote this and all FLYP programs.

To fund this new program, the library applied for a grant from the *Sun Sentinel* Children's Fund. The application included an outcomes-based evaluation plan.

For more information about this joint-use library, look them up on the Internet at www.nova.edu/library/main, or send an e-mail message to Anne Leon @ anneleon@nova.edu.

## "Fourteeners"
## Pikes Peak Library District
## Colorado Springs, Colorado

The Pikes Peak Library District, based in Colorado Springs serves one of the fastest growing populations in Colorado. It provides resources and services to inform, empower, inspire, and encourage respect for individuals and ideas. To that end, the library has selected several service responses: current topics and titles, general information, lifelong learning, local history and genealogy, and cultural awareness. Services and programs to support these service responses are provided through the library's 11 branches and two bookmobiles. The library is tax supported and funded as a special district; it also receives funding from specific ownership taxes, fines and fees, interest earnings, gifts, and private fund-raising efforts. The Pikes Peak Library District (PPLD) was one of the first libraries in Colorado to encourage a proactive, visible, and well-integrated Teen Services Team as part of its adult services staff. The team coordinates booktalks in local schools, plans teen programming, works with the Youth Advisory Council, and spearheads a statewide collaboration effort with other Colorado library young adult advocates.

Targeting middle and high school students, the PPLD developed the C'YAAL (Colorado Youth Adult Advocates in Libraries) "Fourteeners" theme for its own use and made printed materials available to other libraries through the C'YAAL Web site, www.aclin.org/~cyaal/. This teen program has various aspects that encourage respect and recognition for teens among staff and throughout the community. Community businesses and organizations support and recognize the significant efforts of the teens by donating prizes and incentives. Staff in all library branches are involved in and promote the program; teen services liaisons at the branches administer the program. The youth-serving staff state that the summer library reading program provides helps develop a positive relationship between the teens and the adults who serve them. Teens are empowered to participate in the planning of the program by choosing artwork, selecting activities and programs, helping at programs, and more.

Teens who participate in "Fourteeners" are asked to read 10 books and do 10 activities to complete the program. Teens who complete the program are awarded a "Fourteeners" T-shirt; they are also entered into a drawing for several prizes: ski tickets, free water-world coupons, and two grand prizes of $100 gift certificates to the mall. Participants record their progress on a Fourteeners Log and earn prizes at 5 and 10 books and 5 and 10 activities. Building on the ski culture of the area, the log also included 20 additional Black Diamond Challenges. Teens who complete 10 of these challenges receive a special embroidered patch. Special prizes are also awarded for reading the *All Pikes Peak Reads* book, *Frankenstein* by Mary Shelley, and for completing a Blue Spruce (state award) ballot.

For those teens who want to continue reading after completing the regular reading log, they fill out a Beyond Fourteeners Log. For each book read, the Ent Federal Credit Union donated $1.00 to the El Paso County Search and Rescue. Rather than reading for prizes, teens raised $1,163 for Search and Rescue.

This entire program enhances many developmental assets teens need to succeed in life.

- Teens receive support from library staff in selecting their books, researching trivia answers, and reporting on books and receiving prizes, thereby enhancing nonparent adult relationships (adult role models, other adult relationships, and a caring neighborhood).
- The program is based on treating teens as a valued resource for the community. It also helps them feel empowered by the recognition they receive from program rewards created especially for their age group. In addition, members of the Teen Advisory Council help to develop the programs as well as attending and assisting at various programming events during the summer (community values youth and self-esteem).
- The reading, activities, programming, and trivia portions of the program all contribute to actively engaging teens in learning. Reading for pleasure is one of the main goals of the program (reading for pleasure, achievement motivation).
- The "Fourteeners" program is designed so that it challenges those who read easily as well as those who read reluctantly. PPLD required 10 books and 10 activities to complete the program during the summer; it also offered incentives at lower benchmark levels for those who are unable to complete the loftier levels (high expectations).

In addition to the printing services and staff time that PPLD includes in the regular library budget, the library provided an additional $8,500 to support the program. Over $4,000 was spent on T-shirts, $1,700 for programs and prizes. Community sponsors contributed cash and coupons worth $50,000. This included a donation from the Ent Federal Credit Union of $1,000 towards the "Beyond Fourteeners" portion of the program for the El Paso County Search and Rescue. The local Imax theater also donated 1,000 tickets (free entry with the purchase of an adult ticket) to the program. The library is planning to use an online tracking system in the future.

Additional information on this program can be found at the library Web site, ppld.org, or by contacting Bonnie Phinney, Acting Teen Services Coordinator at the Pikes Peak Library District, phinney@ppld.org.

## "Book Counting/Hour Counting"
## Round Rock Public Library
## Round Rock, Texas

Located north of Austin, Texas, the Round Rock Public Library serves a community of 75,000 people. The community boasts an educated, middle-income population; there is a low-income housing project near the library. The library serves a substantial bilingual population.

The library serves as a gateway to the community. Its mission is to provide the highest-quality educational, informational, recreational, and cultural resources and services to a diverse population. The reading program and the special events surrounding it provide opportunities for youth of many ages to improve their education and have recreational and cultural experiences.

While the reading program has different programs for various age groups, there are similarities. For children who cannot read yet, those learning how to read, and those who still enjoy picture books, there is the "Book Counting" program. These children read or listen to 25 books. Children who enjoy reading chapter books join the "Hour Counting" program. The goal for these children is to read for five hours. The teen program is for 13- to 16-year-olds; older YAs and adults have their own separate programs and read in five-hour increments.

Readers who participate in the "Book Counting" and "Hour Counting" programs earn certificates and recognition, incentives, and coupons for reaching four levels of completion. "Book Counting" incentive levels are 25, 50, 75, and 100 books; "Hour Counting" levels are 5, 10, 15, and 20 hours of reading. Readers who reach the top level receive a free book.

Teens and adults receive coupons and flashlight key rings for completing five hours of reading. For each additional five hours they read, they receive prize-drawing slips that make them eligible for random drawings for various prizes.

In addition to the reading program and regularly scheduled toddler story times, preschool story times, and the weekly "Books and Beyond" program, the library has special programs, such as a magic show, a marionette puppet show, musical performances, and live-animal programs.

The Friends of the Round Rock Public Library provide $4,000 for the program to supplement funds provided in the general library budget. Funds from the Friends are used for printing, T-shirts for teen volunteers, and prizes and incentives. Library

**Figure 9–7 a and b**
Pikes Peak Library District, "Fourteeners." Teens participating in the "Fourteeners" summer program read with "Attitude @ Altitude." T-shirts emblazoned with the program graphic were a popular reward. The back of the T-shirt displayed program sponsors. Teens became walking billboards for the program and the sponsors.

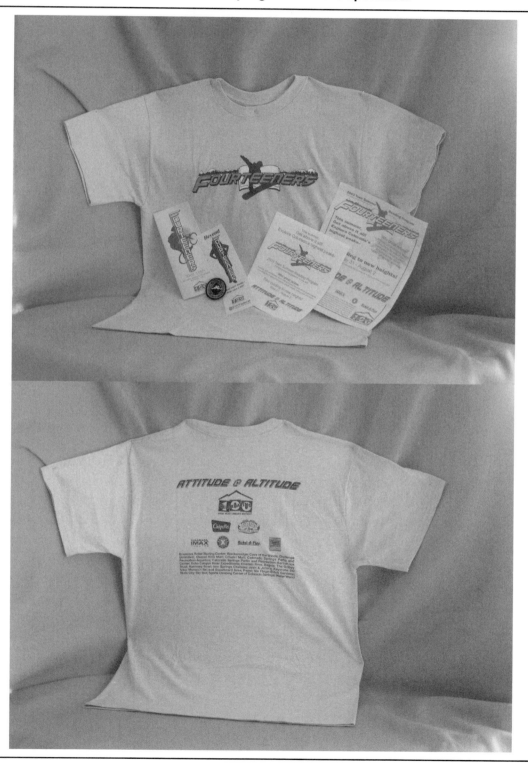

funds are used to supplement the supply of prizes and incentives and to pay to bring guest performers who appear at special programs. In addition, local businesses provide other prizes including food coupons.

In addition to the programs described above, the library has a teen-volunteer program. The teens work at the summer reading table most hours the library is open. They manage program registration and hand out packets of prizes when children bring their reading logs back to the library.

For additional information about the Round Rock Public Library, visit their Web site at www.ci.round-rock.tx.us/library/library.html; specific information about the summer reading program is at http://www.ci.round-rock.tx.us/library/children/summerreading/summerreading.html, or contact Janeette Johnson, Children's Services Manager, jj@round-rock.tx.us

## "Books! Wow! Read!"
## St. Louis Public Library
## St. Louis, Missouri

The St. Louis Public Library in Missouri serves a population of 340,000 people. The population is 50 percent African American and 45 percent white, and includes over 30,000 Bosnian, Afghani, and Turkish refugees. They are served through four regional libraries, eight neighborhood branches, one central library, and two mini-branches. All but the mini-branches have meeting rooms. All outlets have children's materials and space, though only the central library and two of the four regional libraries have distinct children's rooms. All library outlets have materials for teens, though none have adequate reading or program areas for them. Teen services is a shared responsibility of branch library staff and the teen services department, which provides programs and outreach throughout the city.

The city of St. Louis has a very high illiteracy rate. Over 40 percent of the city population has not completed high school. Poverty level is high; 85 percent of the children in the city are eligible for free or reduced lunch. Many parents do not read; they do not bring their children to the library, nor do they model positive literacy behaviors. The "Books! Wow! Read!" program is a way to bring the library and reading to the children in locations where they are during the summer. This supports the mission of the library: the St. Louis Public Library will provide learning resources and information services that support and improve individual, family, and community life. By taking the summer program to the community, the library is hoping to begin to break the cycle of reading aversion. Program activities help youth identify reading as something that is part of their lives.

Over the past several years, the St. Louis Public Library has partnered with Head Start, summer schools, the YMCA and other youth-serving agencies. As reading is becoming a more important part of the summer school program, the school district is seeking out the library for involvement in their programs. By the library's partnering with the school district, more children are being exposed to reading; the more comfortable the children are with reading, the more they will read.

Library staff models excitement for reading through the "Books! Wow! Read!" program not just for the students but for the teachers and leaders. This effect carries over into the regular school year, with teachers sharing literature year round. As many children are unable to attend summer programs at the library, the library takes the programs to the summer schools. After the initial contact with the program director at each location, a visit is made to enroll the children. Teachers and leaders provide a list of the children and their grade levels. Youth librarians present story programs, booktalks, and reading rallies to excite the children and teachers about reading. Groups are encouraged to schedule visits to the library to participate in enhanced programs that are not provided in the outreach setting.

In addition to presenting programs, the library helps to improve access to books by supplying each group with a deposit collection of age-appropriate books. Teachers read some of these aloud to the children in his or her charge and allow children free time to read independently. Each teacher or leader sets their own reading goals for his or her group. This can be to read 15 books aloud to the group, have each child read independently for 15 minutes per day, or some other goal that meets the needs of the children, teachers, and programs.

Record keeping is the responsibility of the teachers. They track the reading and report to the library when the group meets their goal. All of the children in the school or center receive their prizes at the same time. This is usually done at a special ending visit, when the librarian shares more stories and songs. The program builds excitement and becomes a pep rally where the children's accomplishments as readers are celebrated.

Prizes are small, but they promote the library. Approximately ten percent of program participants "double dip"; that is, they read at summer school or the centers and at the library to be eligible for more prizes. However, for most of the children, this outreach program is their only summer reading experience. To encourage their participation, teachers and leaders receive special recognition gifts. The library staff reports that imprinted highlighters, fancy bookmarks, and stress balls successfully encourage teachers to participate.

For more information about this and other youth programs at the St. Louis Public Library, visit the library Web site at www.slpl.lib.mo.us, or contact Patty Carleton, Director of Youth Branches, pcarleton@slpl.lib.mo.us.

## "Celebrate Ohio"
## Stow-Munroe Falls Public Library
## Stow and Munroe Falls, Ohio

Serving two suburban Akron, Ohio, communities, the Stow-Munroe Falls Public Library is listed as one of Hennen's Top American Public Libraries in its population group for 2004. The mission of the library is to provide excellent service to all who seek access to information and recreational, educational, and cultural materials of any format. It also aims to promote the well-being of the community through programs and cooperative efforts with other community agencies, public and private. To

**Figure 9–8**
St. Louis Public Library Program Materials. Using the theme of Books! Wow! Read! the St. Louis Public Library worked to entice not only children and teens to be part of the program, but to encourage participation and cooperation from the school system. Teachers were rewarded with a tricolor highlighter for working with the library. To-do-list pads were another adult encouragement. Readers of all ages received colorful pins. Rather than using full-page certificates, readers received a bi-fold, credit card-sized certificate.

accomplish this, the library helps create a community where ideas, culture, and knowledge thrive by providing materials, equipment and services to all people.

The library has two computer labs—one on each floor of the library building. Free computer classes are offered year round. In addition to the children's room on the second floor, there is also a storytime room and a large meeting room.

The library adapts the statewide theme to meet the needs of the two communities. For the "Celebrate Ohio" theme commemorating the state's bicentennial in 2003, the library created a game board that used the familiar Bingo format. To cover a square, program participants had to read books from various genres, attend a program, visit the local history room, read a book about one of Ohio's sports teams, read a Reading Rainbow book, watch a nonfiction video, or complete an activity in one of many other categories. As with a regular Bingo game, to win, children had to complete a row of five squares either down, across, or diagonally. Parents were charged with initialing each box as the child completed the book or activity. Readers put their name, age, and phone number on the form and deposited it in the Book Bingo drawing box; children could enter as many times as they wished. Drawings were held weekly, and children received coupons for McDonald's, Applebee's, and other restaurants.

In addition, children reported how many hours they read. For every five hours read, children were given various Ohio stickers to put on a cardboard bicentennial barn. School-age children who read 30 hours were eligible to enter a drawing for one of two donated bikes; preschoolers who were read to for 15 hours could enter a drawing for a large stuffed dog.

For additional information about the library and its programs, visit the library's Web site at www.smfpl.org org, or contact Elizabeth Adams, Children's Program Coordinator, stowkids@oplin.org.

## "Reading Road Trip U.S.A."
## West Bloomfield Township Public Library
## West Bloomfield, Michigan

West Bloomfield is an affluent, highly educated community near Detroit, Michigan. The West Bloomfield Township Public Library provides service to the 64,000+ residents in two buildings. The township is culturally diverse, including families from Japan, Germany, France, and middle Eastern and Spanish-speaking countries. In 1997, township residents approved a $10.8 million bond issue to renovate both the Main Library and West Acres Branch. The renovations for the Main Library were completed in May 2000, and for the West Acres Branch, July 2001.

The West Bloomfield Township Public Library provides its diverse community access to information and resources that support both lifelong learning and lifelong enjoyment. The library is committed to providing the best materials, resources, and programs for library customers of all ages, including children on the cusp of reading and those who are perfecting their reading skills. The summer library program keeps evolving to meet the mission of the library and its annual plan of service. In 2002, the library added an online reading log to the program.

To reach all children in the community, the library designed a summer reading club for children up to rising sixth-grade students. The young adult department ran a different program; both programs used the same theme, "Reading Road Trip U.S.A."

To promote the summer program, outreach visits to local schools were made during the weeks before summer vacation. While visiting the schools, librarians left program flyers with information about the summer reading club, including the kick-off date and time, programs, and general information about the summer program, and they showed a promotional video that the library created. Taking advantage of the popularity of the *Survivor* television program, the library created a promotional video that could be used to promote the summer program. Keith Famie, a resident of West Bloomfield who was a contestant on the show, graciously agreed to star in the video. The video featured local school children rapping about the upcoming summer reading club and a special program with Famie encouraging viewers to join in the fun at the library.

The local schools are excited to have library staff visit the schools, especially to promote the summer reading club. The teachers realize the benefit to the students when they participate in the reading program at the library over the summer.

These school visits have the goal of informing large numbers of students about the summer reading club, when it starts, and the minimum requirements to complete the program. For every three books read, children earn a sticker. When they finish 12 books, the participants receive a $5 gift certificate to a bookstore. The library also runs weekly contests in which children and teens are able to win new books and other prizes.

The summer program provides activities that help youth develop assets that will help them grow into healthy adults. Children know what is expected of them—they need to finish 12 books and select their own paths to reading success. Children are charged with the responsibility of selecting their own books; they do not need to follow a set reading list. Children are made to feel welcome. Throughout the summer, the library offers age- and developmentally-appropriate programs for babies through elementary school–age children, as well as summer reading club theme programs for crafts, performers, puppetry, and more for elementary to middle school–age students.

To be able to increase participation in the program, the library has recently added on online-tracking component to the summer reading club. As many families in the community go away on vacation during the summer or children attend camp, and children want to participate in the program, the library has devised a way for them to take advantage of the summer reading club remotely. Children register in person at the library. They are given a choice of how they wish to track their reading—either online or with a traditional, printed reading log. Staff enter the children's names into a database for accurate record keeping and statistics gathering. The database software allows for remote access, giving children, teens, and their parents an option of tracking their reading from library computers or from computers at home or elsewhere.

Online participants are assigned a username and password and enter the database through a link on the library Web site. This online tracking system is attractive to the older readers who are not interested in getting stickers. Instead of stickers, the online participants receive online incentives. For every three books read and recorded in the database, participants receive a link to fun Web sites, such as puzzle and game sites. The children and teens can visit the links as many times as they want. They can also enter the weekly contest by clicking on a button on their personal login pages.

All participants, in person and online, are able to participate in an Internet Scavenger Hunt during the summer reading club. Through the library's home page, children are given a series of questions and a list of Web sites holding clues to the answers. When club members find the answers, they complete an online form and e-mail it to a librarian. Children who complete the Internet Scavenger Hunt get an extra sticker to put on their paper reading log or an acknowledgment for that accomplishment on their online record.

For more information on the West Bloomfield Township Library, visit their Web site at www.wblib.org/, or send an e-mail to Wendy Wilcox, Youth Services Coordinator, wilcoxwe@wblib.org.

**Figure 9–9**

West Bloomfield Township Program Materials. Children became licensed road readers during the West Bloomfield Township Public Library's Reading Road Trip.  Readers who fill their tank by reading 12 or more books receive a $5.00 gift card from Borders and a reading certificate. For every three books read along the trip route, participants get a sticker.  Bonus stickers are awarded for using the library's new self-check-out machines or completing the Internet Scavenger Hunt.  Weekly drawings are also held.

# Appendix A

## Statewide Summer Library Program Themes by State

This compilation of summer program themes was originally prepared by Mary Jackson of the Nebraska Library Commission and has been updated by Grace Green, Vermont Department of Libraries; Carole Fiore, State Library and Archives of Florida; Jim Rosinia, State Library of North Carolina; and then again by Carole Fiore. As a service to its members the Association of Specialized and Cooperative Library Agencies (ASCLA), State Library Agency Section, Consultants for Library Service for Children and Young People Discussion Group of the American Library Association keeps this list updated. The themes listed have been compiled from lists provided by the state library agencies as well as manuals in library collections. The themes and slogans are included to provide suggestions and inspiration. They can be adapted in many ways to be responsive to the needs of local libraries. Many of these manuals are included in several library collections and may be requested through normal interlibrary loan procedures.

| State | Contact/Web Site | Year | Theme |
|---|---|---|---|
| Alabama | Children's/YA Consultant<br>Alabama Public Library<br>6030 Monticello Dr.<br>Montgomery, AL 36130<br>www.apls.state.al.us | 1990 | "Sir Al and His Summer Knights" |
| | | 1991 | "Al's Amazing Summer Circus" |
| | | 1992 | "Al's Wacky Summer Vacation" |
| | | 1993 | "Totally Terrific Time Treks" |
| | | 1994 | "The Summer of Champions" |
| | | 1995 | "Rock, Rhythm, and Read" |
| | | 1996 to 2003 | *No theme reported* |
| | | 2004 to 2006 | *Member Southern States Summer Reading Cooperative* |
| Alaska | School Library/Youth Services Coordinator<br>Alaska State Library<br>344 W. Third Ave., Ste. 125<br>Anchorage, AK 99501<br>www.library.state.ak.us/srp/home.html | 1980 | *No statewide program* |
| | | 1981 | "Tailspinners" |
| | | 1982 | "Great Alaska Reading Race" |
| | | 1983 to 1999 | *No statewide program* |
| | | 2000 to 2006 | *Member Collaborative Summer Library Program* |
| Arizon | Public Library Development Consultant<br>Arizona State Library<br>Archives and Public Records<br>1700 W. Washington, Ste. 200<br>Phoenix, AZ 85007<br>www.lib.az.us | 1990 | "Have Books Will Travel" |
| | | 1991 | "Read Arizona" |
| | | 1992 | "Rainbow Earth" |
| | | 1993 | "Rainbow Earth" |
| | | 1994 | "Get a Clue at the Library" |
| | | 1995 | "Pandemonium at the Library" |
| | | 1996 | "Read for the Gold" |
| | | 1997 | "Readers of the Round Table" |

| State | Contact/Web Site | Year | Theme |
|---|---|---|---|
| | | 1998 | "Read Arizona" |
| | | 1999 | "Bridges to the Future" |
| | | 2000 | *No theme reported* |
| | | 2001 | "2001: A Reading Odyssey" |
| | | 2002 | "Books and Pets: Our Friends for Life" |
| | | 2003 | "Lights, Action, Read!" |
| | | 2004 | *No theme reported* |
| | | 2005 to 2006 | *Member Collaborative Summer Library Program* |
| **Arkansas** | Library Program Advisor Arkansas State Library One Capitol Mall, 5th Fl. Little Rock, AR 72201 www.asl.lib.ar.us/ | 1990 | "A Beary Special Summer" |
| | | 1991 | "Book Buffet—All You Can Read" |
| | | 1992 | "Discover New Worlds—READ" |
| | | 1993 | "Nature Trek—A Reading Adventure" |
| | | 1994 | "Get a Clue . . . READ!" |
| | | 1995 | "Hats Off to Books" |
| | | 1996 | "Blast Off with Books" |
| | | 1997 | "Books under the Big Top" |
| | | 1998 | "Splash into Reading" |
| | | 1999 | "Go West! Blaze a Reading Trail" |
| | | 2000 | "Time to Celebrate! Time to Read!" |
| | | 2001 | "2001: A Reading Odyssey" |
| | | 2002 | "Arts Alive! @ your library" |
| | | 2003 to 2006 | *Member Collaborative Summer Library Program* |

| State | Contact/Web Site | Year | Theme |
|-------|------------------|------|-------|
| **Colorado** | Public Library Consultant<br>Colorado State Library—CDE<br>201 E. Colfax Ave., Rm. 309<br>Denver, Colorado 80203<br>www.cde.state.co.us/index_library.htm | 1990 | "Summer Time, Anytime, Book Time" |
| | | 1991 | "Be a Super Sleuth—Investigate the Library" |
| | | 1992 | "READisccover Planet Earth" |
| | | 1993 | "Books and All That Jazz" |
| | | 1994 | "Caught in the Book Web" |
| | | 1995 | "Take Me Out to the Book Game" |
| | | 1996 | "Readin' Round the Rockies" |
| | | 1997 | "'97 Bazillion Ways to Read" |
| | | 1998 | "Book Feast" |
| | | 1999 | "Title Wave" |
| | | 2000 | "Book Play" |
| | | 2001 | "Once upon a Time" |
| | | 2002 | "Reading, Rhythm, and Rhyme/Lectura, Ritmo, y Rimas" |
| | | 2003 | "Chews to Read/Elije Leer" |
| | | 2004 to 2006 | *Member Collaborative Summer Library Program* |
| **Connecticut** | Connecticut State Library<br>231 Capitol Ave.<br>Hartford, CT 06106<br>www.cslib.org | 1990 | "Make Tracks to Your Library" |
| | | 1991 | "Reading: Your Window to the World" |
| | | 1992 | "Leap into the Unkown" |
| | | 1993 | "Read: "Jest" for the Fun of It!" |
| | | 1994 | "Reading Is a Magic Trip" |
| | | 1995 | "Solve Mysteries—Read" |
| | | 1996 | "Everyone's A Winner—Read" |
| | | 1997 | "Exploring Nature's Tails and Trails" |

| State | Contact/Web Site | Year | Theme |
|---|---|---|---|
| | | 1998 | "Reading Renaissance" |
| | | 1999 | "Summer Splash—Dive into Books" |
| | | 2000 | "Read Rings 'round the Universe" |
| | | 2001 | "Libraries—Your Passport to the World" |
| | | 2003 to 2004 | *No theme reported* |
| | | 2005 to 2006 | *Member Collaborative Summer Library Program* |
| **Delaware** | Delaware Division of Libraries State Library 43 S. DuPont Hwy. Dover, DE 19901 www.state.lib.de.us | 1990 | "Make Tracks to Your Library" |
| | | 1991 | "Reading: Your Window to the World" |
| | | 1992 | "Leap into the Unkown" |
| | | 1993 | "Read: "Jest" for the Fun of It!" |
| | | 1994 | "Reading Is a Magic Trip" |
| | | 1995 | "Solve Mysteries—Read" |
| | | 1996 | "Everyone's A Winner—Read" |
| | | 1997 | "Exploring Nature's Tails and Trails" |
| | | 1998 | "Reading Renaissance" |
| | | 1999 | "Summer Splash—Dive into Books" |
| | | 2000 | "Read Rings 'round the Universe" |
| | | 2001 | "Libraries—Your Passport to the World" |
| | | 2002 to 2006 | *Member Collaborative Summer Library Program* |
| **Florida** | Youth Services Consultant State Library and Archives of Florida R. A. Gray Bldg. 500 S. Bronough St. Tallahassee, FL 2399-0250 http://dlis.dos.state.fl.us | 1990 | "Summer Bookaneers: Sign On with Captain Book" |
| | | 1991 | "Summer Safari: Book Your Adventure with Safari Sam" |

| State | Contact/Web Site | Year | Theme |
|-------|------------------|------|-------|
| | | 1992 | "Into Books . . . and out of This World!" |
| | | 1993 | "Silver Summer Scrapbook" |
| | | 1994 | "C.O.L.O.R.—Celebrate Our Love of Reading" |
| | | 1995 | "Once upon a Tale" |
| | | 1996 | "Rhythm and Books—Feel the Beat" |
| | | 1997 | "Communication Station—Tune in at Your Library" |
| | | 1998 | "Exploration Explosion" |
| | | 1999 | "Readers on the Prowl" |
| | | 2000 | "Libraries: Your Passport to Adventure" |
| | | 2001 | "Start @ the Library/Go Anywhere" |
| | | 2002 | "Color Your World with Books" |
| | | 2003 | "Hats off to Reading!  Nos quitamos el sombrero ante la lectura" |
| | | 2004 | "Read around Florida/Lectura Alrederdor de la Florida" |
| | | 2005 | "Read around Florida/Lectura Alrederdor de la Florida" |
| | | 2006 | "Book Feast" |
| **Georgia** | Georgia Public Library Service 1800 Century Pl., Ste. 150 Atlanta, GA 30345 www.georgialibraries.org | 1990 | "Escape into Books" |
| | | 1991 | "Reading Safari" |
| | | 1992 | "Catch the Reading Express" |
| | | 1993 | "Feast on Books" |
| | | 1994 | "Itzareader" |
| | | 1995 | "Book the Wave" |

| State | Contact/Web Site | Year | Theme |
|-------|------------------|------|-------|
| | | 1996 | "Solar Summer" |
| | | 1997 | "Follow the Reading Trail" |
| | | 1998 | "Think Big . . . Read" |
| | | 1999 | "Chill Out with Books!" |
| | | 2000 | "Open a Book—Jump In!" |
| | | 2001 | "Extra! Extra! Read All about It!" |
| | | 2002 to 2006 | *Member Southern States Summer Reading Cooperative* |
| **Idaho** | Idaho State Library 325 W. State St. Boise, ID 83702 www.lili.org/isl/ | 1990 | "Celebrate Idaho!" |
| | | 1991 | "The Great Book Hunt" |
| | | 1992 | "Read for It! Read!" |
| | | 1993 | "Read . . . Funtastic" |
| | | 1994 | "Critter Tales" |
| | | 1995 | "Read around the World" |
| | | 1996 | "Reading Is a Picnic" |
| | | 1997 | "Timeless Treks" |
| | | 1998 | "Ride a Wild Tale" |
| | | 1999 to 2006 | *Member Collaborative Summer Library Program* |
| **Illinois** | Illinois Library Association 33 W. Grand Ave. Chicago, IL 60610 | 1990 | "Station Read: 1990 on Your Dial" |
| | | 1991 | "This Is Reading Country" |
| | | 1992 | "Discover Read" |
| | | 1993 | "Amazing Book Capers" |
| | | 1994 | "Celebrate Reading" |
| | | 1995 | "Reading Is Tremendous" |

| State | Contact/Web Site | Year | Theme |
|-------|-----------------|------|-------|
|  |  | 1996 | "Travel the Reading Highway" |
|  |  | 1997 | "Team IREAD" |
|  |  | 1998 to 2004 | *No theme reported* |
|  |  | 2005 | "Superheroes—Powered by Books!" |
|  |  | 2006 | *No theme reported* |
| Indiana | Indiana State Library 140 N. Senate Ave. Indianapolis, IN 46204 www.statelib.lib.in.us | 1990 | "Wild about Reading" |
|  |  | 1991 to 2006 | *No statewide theme since 1991* |
| Iowa | Youth Services Consultant State Library of Iowa 1112 E. Grand Ave. Des Moines, IA 50319 www.silo.lib.ia.us | 1990 | "Silly Dilly Summer" |
|  |  | 1991 | "Super Summer Reader" |
|  |  | 1992 | "Books 'n' Stones 'n' Dinosaur Bones" |
|  |  | 1993 | "Story Spinners" |
|  |  | 1994 | "Footloose" |
|  |  | 1995 | *Member Collaborative Summer Library Program* |
|  |  | 1996 | "Iowa Mania!" |
|  |  | 1997 to 2006 | *Member Collaborative Summer Library Program* |
| Kansas | Kansas State Library Library Development State Capitol, Third Fl. Topeka, KS 66612 www.skyways.org/KSL/ | 1990 | "Affection Connection: Our Animal Friends" |
|  |  | 1991 | "Feed Your Mind—READ" |
|  |  | 1992 | "READ: Discover in 1992" |
|  |  | 1993 | "Read, Renew, Recycle" |
|  |  | 1994 | "Whale of a Tale" |
|  |  | 1995 | "Arts on Parade" |
|  |  | 1996 | "Kansas Kids Read" |

| State | Contact/Web Site | Year | Theme |
|---|---|---|---|
| | | 1997 | "'97 Bizillion Ways to Read" |
| | | 1998 to 2006 | *Member Collaborative Summer Library Program* |
| Kentucky | Youth Services Consultant Kentucky Department for Libraries and Archives 300 Coffee Tree Rd. Frankfort, KY 40601 www.kdla.ky.gov | 1990 | "Reading Is Dino-Mite" |
| | | 1991 | "Summer Splash" |
| | | 1992 | "READiscover Kentucky" |
| | | 1993 | "Together Is Better—Read" |
| | | 1994 | "Read around the World" |
| | | 1995 | "Solve Mysteries—READ!" |
| | | 1996 | "Everyone's A Winner—READ" |
| | | 1997 | "Book a Trip to the Stars" (done in cooperation with Arizona) |
| | | 1998 | "Readers of the Round Table" (done in cooperation with Arizona) |
| | | 1999 | "The Art of Reading" |
| | | 2000 | "It's about Time" |
| | | 2001 | "Wild about Reading" |
| | | 2002 | "Celebrate Books" |
| | | 2003 | "Reading Expedition" |
| | | 2004 | "A World of Readers" |
| | | 2005 to 2006 | *Member Collaborative Summer Library Program* |
| Louisiana | State Library of Louisiana 701 N. 4th Ave. P.O. Box 131 Baton Rouge, LA 70821-0131 www.state.lib.la.us | 1990 | "1990 Louisiana Libraries: Celebrate Festivals of Reading" |
| | | 1991 | "Summer Treasure: Find It at Your Library" |
| | | 1992 | "Grins and Giggles . . . the Library" |

| State | Contact/Web Site | Year | Theme |
|---|---|---|---|
| | | 1993 | "All Aboard for Summer Fun" |
| | | 1994 | "A Star-Spangled Summer" |
| | | 1995 | "Reading Roundup: Rope a Good Book" |
| | | 1996 | "Go for the Gold . . . Read!" |
| | | 1997 | "The Great Big Feast" |
| | | 1998 | "Wild about Reading" |
| | | 1999 | "Let the Good Books Roll! Laissez les Bon Livres Rouler!" *Louisiana Summer Reading Fete '99* |
| | | 2000 | "Zap into the Past: Read!" |
| | | 2001 | "Zap into the Future: Read!" |
| | | 2002 | "Silly Chilly Summer at the Library" |
| | | 2003 | "Footloose in Louisiana Libraries" |
| | | 2004 | "Buggy about Books" |
| | | 2005 | "Splish-Splash: Read!" |
| | | 2006 | *No theme reported* |
| Maine | Maine State Library 64 State House Station Augusta, ME 04333 www.state.me.us/msl/ | 2004 to 2006 | *Member Collaborative Summer Library Program* |
| Maryland | Maryland State Department of Education Division of Library Development & Services Youth Specialist 200 W. Baltimore St. Baltimore, MD 21201 www.marylandpublicschools.org/divisions/lds.html | 2000 | "Reading Rhythms" |
| | | 2001 | "Buggy about Reading" |
| | | 2002 | "Race to Read" |
| | | 2003 | "Blast Off to Reading" |
| | | 2004 | "Readers Rule" |
| | | 2005 | "Wild about Reading" |

| State | Contact/Web Site | Year | Theme |
|---|---|---|---|
| **Massachusetts** | Eastern Massachusetts Regional Library System | 1990 | "Wizard Read" |
| | Western Massachusetts Regional Library System | 1990 | "Make Tracks to the Library" |
| | | 1991 | "Read for a Spell" |
| | Central Massachusetts Regional Library System | 1990 | "Summer Feast" |
| | Starting in 1991, all regional library systems in Massachusetts worked in partnership to create one statewide theme.  Contact information for all of the six regional libraries can be found at http://mblc.state.ma.us/mblc/regional/index.php | 1991 | "Summer Safari" |
| | | 1992 | "Reach for It. Read!" |
| | | 1993 | "Sail on a Sea of Books" |
| | | 1994 | "Ticket to Read" |
| | | 1995 | "Reading Is Natural" |
| | | 1996 | "Catch the Summer Spark! Read" |
| | | 1997 | "Celebrate! READ" |
| | | 1998 | "Unlock the Mystery! Read!" |
| | | 1999 | "Funny Things Happen When You Read!" |
| | | 2000 | "Open Books! Open Frontiers!" |
| | | 2001 | "First of All . . . Read!" |
| | | 2002 to 2006 | *No theme reported* |
| **Michigan** | Youth Services Specialist Library of Michigan 702 W. Kalamazoo P.O. Box 30007 Lansing, MI 48909-7507 | 1991 | "Read on the Wild Side at Your Local Library" |
| | | 1992 | "Read, Rock and Rap: Tune into Summer Reading" |
| | | 1993 | "Make a Splash—Read!" |
| | | 1994 | "Camp Read" |
| | | 1995 | "Books under the Bigtop" |

| State | Contact/Web Site | Year | Theme |
|---|---|---|---|
| | | 1996 | "Wide World of Library Kids" |
| | | 1997 | "Discover Summer—Be Eager about Reading (BEAR)" |
| | | 1998 | "Discover Summer—Reading is Dino-mite" |
| | | 1999 | "G'day for Reading" |
| | | 2000 | "Score Big with Books" |
| | | 2001 to 2006 | *Member Collaborative Summer Library Program* |
| Minnesota | Summer Library Reading Program Coordinator MELSA—Metropolitan Library Service Agency 1619 Dayton Ave. Ste. 314 St.Paul, MN 55104 www.melsa.org | 1990 | "Wheel 'n' through Summer" |
| | | 1991 | "Hats Off to Libraries" |
| | | 1992 | "Library All Stars" |
| | | 1993 | "Hook a Book" |
| | | 1994 | "Go Wild For Libraries" |
| | | 1995 | "Sky's the Limit at Your Library" |
| | | 1996 | "Get in the Game at Your Library" |
| | | 1997 to 2002 | *Member Collaborative Summer Library Program* |
| | | 2001 | "Wolfin' Down Books @ Your Library" |
| | | 2002 | "Discover a Hoppin' Place @ Your Library" |
| | | 2003 | Children's—"Explore Bright Ideas at Your Library" Teens'—"Wise Up at Your Library" |
| | | 2004 | Children's—"Track It Down at Your Library" Teens'—"Gear Up at Your Library" |

| State | Contact/Web Site | Year | Theme |
|-------|------------------|------|-------|
|  |  | 2005 | Children's—"What's Buzzin' at Your Library" Teens'—"Tune In at Your Library" |
|  |  | 2006 | *No theme reported* |
| **Mississippi** | Mississippi Library Commission 1221 Ellis Ave. Jackson, MS 39209 www.mlc.lib.ms.us | 1990 | "Summer Splash" |
|  |  | 1991 | "Sizzlin' Summer Celebration" |
|  |  | 1992 | "Read to Win" |
|  |  | 1993 | "Camp Read-a-Lot" |
|  |  | 1994 | "Cool Kids—Hot Books" |
|  |  | 1995 | "Passport to Reading" |
|  |  | 1996 | "Supper Sports Summer" |
|  |  | 1997 | "Fantasy Quest" |
|  |  | 1998 | "Wild About . . ." |
|  |  | 1999 | "Mississippi Magic" |
|  |  | 2000 | "On the Go with Books" |
|  |  | 2001 | "Orbit the World with Books" |
|  |  | 2002 | "Reading Is a Picnic" |
|  |  | 2003 to 2006 | *Member Southern States Summer Reading Cooperative* |
| **Missouri** | Children's Services Consultant State Library of Missouri Box 387 Jefferson City, MO 65102-0387 www.sos.mo.gov/library/development/services/youth_srs.asp | 1990 | "Check Out Kids Country" |
|  |  | 1991 | "Undercover Readers" |
|  |  | 1992 | "Leap into Books" |
|  |  | 1993 | "Read Up a Storm" |
|  |  | 1994 | "Celebrate! Read!" |
|  |  | 1995 | "Rock Your World—Read!" |

| State | Contact/Web Site | Year | Theme |
|-------|------------------|------|-------|
| | | 1996 | "READiscover Missouri" |
| | | 1997 | "Open Door to Fun, Facts, and Fantasy" |
| | | 1998 | "Summer Readers = Adventure Seekers" |
| | | 1999 | "Reading Time '99" |
| | | 2000 | "Turn Over a New Leaf: READ" |
| | | 2001 | "2001 Places to Go" (Ages 0–12)<br>"Book Your Summer" (Ages 12–18) |
| | | 2002 | "Mysterious Summer" (Ages 0–12)<br>"Book Your Summer" (Ages 12–18) |
| | | 2003 to 2006 | *Member Collaborative Summer Library Program* |
| Montana | Publicity/Youth Services Specialist<br>Montana State Library<br>1515 E. 6th Ave.<br>P.O. Box 201800<br>Helena, MT 59620-1800<br>http://msl.state.mt.us/ | 1990 | "Many Faces, Many Stories" |
| | | 1991 | "Get the "Bear" Facts—READ" |
| | | 1992 | "Dragon Tales" |
| | | 1993 | "Many Faces, Many Stories" |
| | | 1994 | "Reading Is Natural" |
| | | 1995 | "Get a Clue—Read!" |
| | | 1996 | "Everyone's A Winner—Read" |
| | | 1997 | "Happy Tales to You" |
| | | 1998 | "The Good, the Bad & the Bugly" |
| | | 1999 | *No theme reported* |
| | | 2000 to 2006 | *Member Collaborative Summer Library Program* |
| Nebraska | Coordinator, Children and Young<br>Adult Services<br>Nebraska Library Commission<br>1200 N St., Ste. 120<br>Lincoln, NE 68508<br>www.nlc.state.ne.us/libdev/child.html | 1990 | "Summer Safari:  Stalk a Story" |
| | | 1991 | "Western Frontier!" |
| | | 1992 | "Dive into a Good Book" |

| State | Contact/Web Site | Year | Theme |
|---|---|---|---|
| | | 1993 | "Books Come in All Flavors" |
| | | 1994 | "Books Make the World Go Round" |
| | | 1995 | "Adventure Begins at Camp Read-a-Lot" |
| | | 1996 | "Peer-Amid Books" |
| | | 1997 to 2006 | *Member Collaborative Summer Library Program* |
| Nevada | Nevada Literacy Coalition 100 N. Stewart Carson City, NV 89701 www.NevadaLiteracy.org | | *No statewide program prior to 1997* |
| | | 1997 | "Reading Rodeo Roundup" |
| | | 1998 | "Search for Hidden Treasure" |
| | | 1999 | "Reading Is a Fine Art" |
| | | 2000 | "READiscover Nevada" |
| | | 2001 to 2006 | *Member Collaborative Summer Library Program* |
| New Hampshire | Youth Services Coordinator New Hampshire State Library 20 Park St. Concord, NH 03301 www.nh.gov/nhsl | 1990 | "Get That Reading Rhythm" |
| | | 1991 | "Some Enchanted Reading" |
| | | 1992 | "Discover—Read '92" |
| | | 1993 | "Ketchup on Your Reading" |
| | | 1994 | "Go Undercover with Books" |
| | | 1995 | "Saddle Up a Good Book" |
| | | 1996 | "Reading—The Best Game Around" |
| | | 1997 | "Take Us to Your Readers" |
| | | 1998 | "Live Free and Read!" |
| | | 1999 | "Once upon a Summer Reading" |
| | | 2000 | "Reading Cats and Dogs" |
| | | 2001 | "Octopi Your Mind . . . Read!" |

| State | Contact/Web Site | Year | Theme |
|-------|------------------|------|-------|
| | | 2002 | "Lions & Tigers & Books . . . Oh My" |
| | | 2003 | "Reading Rocks the Granite State" |
| | | 2004 | "Check Out a Hero" |
| | | 2005 | *"Camp Wanna Read"* |
| | | 2006 | *No theme reported* |
| New Jersey | Youth Services Consultant New Jersey State Library P.O. Box 520 185 W. State St. Trenton, NJ 08625-0520 www.njstatelib.org | | *No statewide summer programs before 2003* |
| | | 2003 | "Read and Grow @ your library" |
| | | 2004 to 2006 | *Member Collaborative Summer Library Program* |
| New Mexico | Children's Services Consultant New Mexico State Library 1209 Camino Carlos Rey Santa Fe, NM 87507 www.stlib.state.nm.us | 1990 | "Book a Flight" |
| | | 1991 | "Read to Get the Power You Need" |
| | | 1992 | "Be a Super Sleuth" |
| | | 1993 | "Quest for Enchantment—Treasure Reading" |
| | | 1994 | "Wild about Reading" |
| | | 1995 | "Dig in to Books" |
| | | 1996 | "Reading Fiesta!" |
| | | 1997 | "Read the Seven Seas" |
| | | 1998 | "Books Come in All Flavors: Carry-out Available" |
| | | 1999 | "Creature Features" |
| | | 2000 | "Read 'round the World" |
| | | 2001 | "Once upon a Planet" |
| | | 2002 | "READiculous" |
| | | 2003 | "Magical Mystery Tour" |
| | | 2004 | "READiscover New Mexico" |

| State | Contact/Web Site | Year | Theme |
|---|---|---|---|
| | | 2005 | "Talking Books/Los libros nos hablan/Naaltsoos Bahane' hólóní" |
| | | 2006 | *No theme reported* |
| **New York** | Youth Services Consultant<br>New York State Library<br>10C34 Cultural Education Center<br>Albany, NY 12230<br>www.summerreadingnys.org/<br>www.nysl.nysed.gov/libdev/summer/<br>index.html | | *No statewide program before 1992* |
| | | 1992 | "New York Is Reading Country" |
| | | 1993 | "Book Banquet" |
| | | 1994 | "Read around the Clock" |
| | | 1995 | "Read the World Over" |
| | | 1996 | "Read to Win—Team Up with Books" |
| | | 1997 | "Go Wild—Read!" |
| | | 1998 | "Solve It @ the Library" |
| | | 1999 | "Celebrate—Read!" |
| | | 2000 | "Discover2000—Read!" |
| | | 2001 | "2001—A Reading Odyssey" |
| | | 2002 | "Splish, Splash—Read!" |
| | | 2003 | "Picture This, Imagine That—Read!" |
| | | 2004 | "New York is Read, White and Blue" |
| | | 2005 | "Tune In @ Your Library" |
| | | 2006 | *No theme reported* |
| **North Carolina** | Youth Services Consultant<br>State Library of North Carolina<br>4640 Mail Service Center<br>109 E. Jones St.<br>Raleigh, NC 27699-4640 | 1990 | "Book a Trip to Africa" |
| | | 1991 | "Outer Space—Calling All Readers" |
| | | 1992 | "The Whole World in a Book" |
| | | 1993 | "Books Come in All Flavors" |
| | | 1994 | "Dive into a Book" |

| State | Contact/Web Site | Year | Theme |
|---|---|---|---|
| | | 1995 | "Nature Tales and Trails" |
| | | 1996 | "Reading Is the Name of the Game" |
| | | 1997 | "Get Cookin' with Books" |
| | | 1998 | "Go Places . . . Read" |
| | | 1999 | "Rounds and Rounds of Stories at the Library" |
| | | 2000 | "Time to READiscover" |
| | | 2001 | "Books for Seekers and Dreamers at the Library" |
| | | 2002 | "Exercise Your Mind . . . Read!" |
| | | 2003 | "Mission: R.E.A.D." |
| | | 2004 to 2006 | *Member Collaborative Summer Library Program* |
| **North Dakota** | North Dakota State Library 604 E Blvd. Bismarck, ND 58505-0800 http://ndsl.lib.state.nd.us | 1990 to 2006 | *Member Collaborative Summer Library Program* |
| **Ohio** | Library Development Consultant State Library of Ohio 274 E. First Ave., Ste. 100 Columbus, OH 43201 http://winslo.state.oh.us | 1990 | "Read for the Fun of It" |
| | | 1991 | "Hats Off to Books!" |
| | | 1992 | "Ticket to Read: Explore New Worlds" |
| | | 1993 | "Spinning Yarns! Telling Tales!" |
| | | 1994 | "Step into the Spotlight: Read!" |
| | | 1995 | "Rally Round Rugged Readers" |
| | | 1996 | "Read for the Gold" |
| | | 1997 | "Ride a Wild Book" |
| | | 1998 | "Drop Anchor in a Good Book!" |
| | | 1999 | "The Incredible Library Time Machine!" |

| State | Contact/Web Site | Year | Theme |
|-------|------------------|------|-------|
| | | 2000 | "Into Books and out of This World!" |
| | | 2001 | "Where in the World Are You Reading?" |
| | | 2002 | "Your Library: The Greatest Show in Town!" |
| | | 2003 | "Celebrate Ohio!" |
| | | 2004 to 2006 | *Member Collaborative Summer Library Program* |
| **Oklahoma** | Public Library Consultant for Children's Services Oklahoma Department of Libraries 200 N.E. 18th St. Oklahoma City, OK 73105 www.odl.state.ok.us | 1990 | "Discover the World" |
| | | 1991 | "Summer Bookaneers" |
| | | 1992 | "Summer Safari: Make Tracks to the Library" |
| | | 1993 | "Hang Out with Heroes" |
| | | 1994 | "Summer Yummers: Scoop Up a Good Book" |
| | | 1995 | "Knight Alive in '95" |
| | | 1996 | "Pandemonium in Your Library" |
| | | 1997 | "Be a Super Snooper Sleuth at Your Library" |
| | | 1998 | "Books a Magical Madcap Tour" |
| | | 1999 | "Totally Timeless Tales at Your Library" |
| | | 2000 | "Into Books and out of This World: An Adventure in Space" |
| | | 2001 | "Books Ahoy! Sail through the Summer with Stories" |
| | | 2002 | "Dinosuars Galore and More: Join the "DIG" @ Your Library" |
| | | 2003 to 2004 | *No theme reported* |
| | | 2005 to 2006 | *Member Collaborative Summer Library Program* |

| State | Contact/Web Site | Year | Theme |
|---|---|---|---|
| **Oregon** | Youth Services Consultant<br>Oregon State Library<br>250 Winter St. NE<br>Salem, OR 97301-3950<br>www.osl.state.or.us/home | 1990 | "Celebrate Reading! The Party's on Us!" |
| | | 1991 | "Munch a Bunch of Books" |
| | | 1992 | "The Great Summer Escape" |
| | | 1993 | "Wild about Books" |
| | | 1994 | "Catch the Wave" |
| | | 1995 | "Blast Off with Books" |
| | | 1996 | "Everyone's A Winner—READ" |
| | | 1997 | "Celebrate Reading" |
| | | 1998 | "Kids.read@libraries" |
| | | 1999 | "ReadQuest" |
| | | 2000 | "Ticket to Tomorrow" |
| | | 2001 | "Read a Wild Tale" |
| | | 2002 | "Don't Bug Me, I'm Reading" |
| | | 2003 | "Read! Discover! Explore!" |
| | | 2004 to 2006 | *Member Collaborative Summer Library Program* |
| **Pennsylvania** | Youth Services Advisor<br>Office of Commonwealth Libraries<br>Pennsylvania Department of Education<br>333 Market St.<br>Harrisburg, PA 17126-1745<br>www.statelibrary.state.pa.us | | *Statewide programs begin in 1996* |
| | | 1996 | "Pennsylvania Patchwork" |
| | | 1997 | "Grab the Treasure . . . Be a Bookaneer" |
| | | 1998 | "Click on Adventure at the Library" |
| | | 1999 | "Route for Reading: Going Places at the Library" |
| | | 2000 | "Readers 2000: Masters for the Millennium" |
| | | 2001 | "Animal Odyssey" |
| | | 2002 | "Be a STAR" |

| State | Contact/Web Site | Year | Theme |
|---|---|---|---|
|  |  | 2003 | "Get in the Game" |
|  |  | 2004 to 2006 | *Member Collaborative Summer Library Program* |
| **Rhode Island** | Rhode Island Youth Services Consultant<br>Office of Library and Information Services<br>One Capitol Hill, 4th Fl.<br>Providence, RI 02908<br>www.lori.ri.gov/srp | 1990 | "Exercise Your Mind—Read" |
|  |  | 1991 | "Hats Off to Reading" |
|  |  | 1992 | "Go Green at the Library" |
|  |  | 1993 | "Travel the Reading Road" |
|  |  | 1994 | "Reading Is a Magic Trip" |
|  |  | 1995 | "Solve Mysteries—READ" |
|  |  | 1996 | "Get in the Reading MOOOD" |
|  |  | 1997 | "Reach for the Stars—Read!" (in cooperation with Vermont) |
|  |  | 1998 | "Ride the Reading Wave" (in cooperation with Vermont's "Books Ahoy!") |
|  |  | 1999 | "Don't Bug Me—I'm READING" |
|  |  | 2000 | "Chill Out at the Library" |
|  |  | 2001 | "Camp Out with a Good Book" |
|  |  | 2002 | "Once upon a Summertime" |
|  |  | 2003 | "Read Yourself Silly" |
|  |  | 2004 | "Book an Adventure @ the library" |
|  |  | 2005 | "Read Up a Storm @ your library" |
|  |  | 2006 | *No theme reported* |
| **South Carolina** | Library Development Consultant for Youth Services<br>South Carolina State Library<br>P.O. Box 11469<br>Columbia, SC 29211<br>www.state.sc.us/scsl/ | 1990 | "Hurry, Hurry, Hurry to the Library" |
|  |  | 1991 | "The Incredible Dream Machine" |
|  |  | 1992 | "Read, Explore & Discover—South Carolina" |

| State | Contact/Web Site | Year | Theme |
|---|---|---|---|
| | | 1993 | "Plant a Reading Seed" |
| | | 1994 | "Bone Up on Books" |
| | | 1995 | "Catch the Beat. Read a Book!" |
| | | 1996 | "Everyone's A Winner . . . Read!" |
| | | 1997 | "Read around the Clock" |
| | | 1998 | "The Great Book Feast" |
| | | 1999 | "Book Trek" |
| | | 2000 to 2006 | *Member Southern States Summer Reading Cooperative* |
| **South Dakota** | South Dakota State Library Mercedes MacKay Bldg 800 Governors Dr. Pierre, SD 57501-2294 www.sdstatelibrary.com | 1990 to 2006 | *Member Collaborative Summer Library Program* |
| **Tennessee** | Tennessee State Library and Archives 403 Seventh Ave. N. Nashville, TN 37243-0312 www.state.tn.us/sos/statelib | 1990 | "Wild about Reading" |
| | | 1991 | "Mysterious Summer: Case No. 1991" |
| | | 1992 | "Camp Read-a-Lot" |
| | | 1993 | "Star Kids * Mission: Read" |
| | | 1994 | "Dive into Reading!" |
| | | 1995 | "Ticket to Read" |
| | | 1996 | "Celebrate 200! Read across Tennessee" |
| | | 1997 | "Fantastic Readers—Fantastic Worlds" |
| | | 1998 | "Read under the Big Top" |
| | | 1999 | "The Great Time Machine" |
| | | 2001 | "Adventure 2000" |
| | | 2002 to 2006 | *No theme reported* |

| State | Contact/Web Site | Year | Theme |
|---|---|---|---|
| Texas | Continuing Education and Youth Services Consultant<br>Texas State Library & Archives Commission<br>1201 Brazos St.<br>P.O. Box 12927<br>Austin, TX 78711-2927<br>www.tsl.state.tx.us | 1990 | "The Secret Code is . . . Read" |
| | | 1991 | "Camp Wanna-Read" |
| | | 1992 | "Discover the New World of Reading" |
| | | 1993 | "Lions, and Tigers, and Books, Oh My!" |
| | | 1994 | "Familiar Faces, Faraway Places" |
| | | 1995 | "Once upon a Planet . . ." |
| | | 1996 | "Ready, Set . . . Read" |
| | | 1997 | "The Incredible Dream Machine" |
| | | 1998 | "Furry Tails! Funny Tales!" |
| | | 1999 | "Open a Book—On with the Show!" |
| | | 2000 | "Invent the Future—READ!" |
| | | 2001 | "To the Library and Beyond!" |
| | | 2002 | "Read across Texas!" |
| | | 2003 | "Mission Possible: Spy a Book!" |
| | | 2004 | "Color Your World . . . Read!" |
| | | 2005 | "Go Wild . . . Read!" |
| | | 2006 | *No theme reported* |
| Utah | Utah State Library Division<br>250 N. 1950 W., Ste. A<br>Salt Lake City, UT 84116-7901<br>http://library.utah.gov/ | 1990 | "Knights and Dragontails" |
| | | 1991 | "It's Readiculous: Read for the Fun of It!" |
| | | 1992 | "Around the Library in 80 Days: Read and Discover" |
| | | 1993 | "Read and Talk with the Animals at Your Library" |
| | | 1994 | "Start a Read Stampede at Your Library" |
| | | 1995 | "Reading Railroad" |

| State | Contact/Web Site | Year | Theme |
|---|---|---|---|
| | | 1996 | "100 Years of Adventure in Reading" |
| | | 1997 to 2006 | *Member Collaborative Summer Library Program* |
| **Vermont** | Children's Services Consultant<br>Department of Libraries<br>109 State St.<br>Montpelier, VT 05609<br>http://dol.state.vt.us | 1990 | "Celebrate Vermont!" |
| | | 1991 | "Library Laugh-In" |
| | | 1992 | "Great Global Readaway" |
| | | 1993 | "Flights of Fantasy" |
| | | 1994 | "Reading Is a Magic Trip" |
| | | 1995 | "Go Wild! Read!" |
| | | 1996 | "Solve the Mystery . . . Read!" |
| | | 1997 | "Reach for the Stars—Read!" |
| | | 1998 | "Books Ahoy" |
| | | 1999 | "Library Laughs" |
| | | 2000 | "Time Travelers" |
| | | 2001 | "Wild about Reading" |
| | | 2002 | "Travel Far, Pay No Fare" |
| | | 2003 | "Summer Feast" |
| | | 2004 | "Telling Tales" |
| | | 2005 | "Surf Your Library" |
| | | 2006 | *No theme reported* |
| **Virginia** | Children's Services Consultant<br>The Library of Virginia<br>800 E. Broad St.<br>Richmond, VA 23219<br>www.lva.lib.va.us | 1990 | "Catch the Wave" |
| | | 1991 | "Explore Your Library for the Fun of It" |
| | | 1992 | "Reading Is DINO-mite" |
| | | 1993 | "SI for Kids Library Reading Team" |

| State | Contact/Web Site | Year | Theme |
|---|---|---|---|
| | | 1994 | "Peer Amid Books . . . Read" |
| | | 1995 | "Reading Is a Magic Trip" |
| | | 1996 | "Amazing Library Kids" |
| | | 1997 | "Choose Your Own Adventure—READ" |
| | | 1998 | "Visiting Virginia" |
| | | 1999 | "Read around the World" (Children & teens) |
| | | 2000 | "Get Carried Away with Books" (Children) "Say What? Say Read!" (Teens) |
| | | 2001 | "2001, A Reading Odyssey" (Children) "Say What? Say Read!" (Teens) |
| | | 2002 | "Books and Pets: Our Friends for Life" (Children) "Reading Rescue" (Teens) |
| | | 2003 | "Wolfin' Down Books" (Children) "Eye Read" (Teens) |
| | | 2004 to 2006 | *Member Southern States Summer Reading Cooperative* |
| **Washington** | | 2002 to 2006 | *Member Collaborative Summer Library Program* |
| **Wyoming** | | 2004 to 2006 | *Member Collaborative Summer Library Program* |
| **Wisconsin** | Youth and Special Services Consultant Division for Libraries, Technology and Community Learning Wisconsin Department of Public Instruction 125 S. Webster St. P.O. Box 7841 Madison, WI 53707-7841 www.dpi.state.wi.us/dpi/dltcl/pld/youth.html | 1990 | "Wheels, Wings 'n' Words" |
| | | 1991 | "Summer Quest" |
| | | 1992 | "Go Wild! Read!" |
| | | 1993 | "Rock 'n' Read" |
| | | 1994 | "Sportacular Summer" |
| | | 1995 | "Razzle Dazzle Read" |

| State | Contact/Web Site | Year | Theme |
|-------|------------------|------|-------|
|       |                  | 1996 | "Zap into the Past" |
|       |                  | 1997 | "Make Waves: Read!" |
|       |                  | 1998 | "Go Global: Read!" |
|       |                  | 1999 | *No theme reported* |
|       |                  | 2000 | "Zap into the Past" |
|       |                  | 2001 to 2006 | *Member Collaborative Summer Library Program* |

# Appendix B

## Collaborative Summer Library Program Themes by Year with Members

The Cooperative Summer Library Program changed its name to the Collaborative Summer Library program in 2003 when the state of incorporation moved from Minnesota to Iowa.

|      | Children's Theme | Teen Theme | Members |
|------|------------------|------------|---------|
| 1990 | "Wheel 'n' through Summer" | | North Dakota<br>South Dakota |
| 1991 | "Hats Off to Libraries" | | North Dakota<br>South Dakota |
| 1992 | "Library All Stars" | | North Dakota<br>South Dakota |
| 1993 | "Hook a Book" | | North Dakota<br>South Dakota |
| 1994 | "Go Wild for Libraries" | | North Dakota<br>South Dakota |
| 1995 | "The Sky's the Limit" | | Iowa<br>North Dakota<br>South Dakota |
| 1996 | "Get in the Game . . . At Your Library" | | North Dakota<br>South Dakota |
| 1997 | "Thrills and Chills" | | Iowa<br>Minnesota<br>Nebraska<br>North Dakota<br>South Dakota<br>Utah |
| 1998 | "Rock 'n' Read" | | Iowa<br>Minnesota<br>Nebraksa<br>North Dakota<br>South Dakota<br>Utah |
| 1999 | "Treasure Your Library!" | | Kansas<br>Idaho<br>Iowa<br>Minnesota<br>Nebraska<br>North Dakota<br>South Dakota<br>Utah |

| | Children's Theme | Teen Theme | Members |
|---|---|---|---|
| 2000 | "Cosmic Connections" | | Alaska |
| | | | Idaho |
| | | | Iowa |
| | | | Kansas |
| | | | Minnesota |
| | | | Montana |
| | | | Nebraska |
| | | | North Dakota |
| | | | South Dakota |
| | | | Utah |
| 2001 | "Reading Road Trip U.S.A." | | Alaska |
| | | | Idaho |
| | | | Iowa |
| | | | Kansas |
| | | | Michigan |
| | | | Montana |
| | | | Nebraska |
| | | | Nevada |
| | | | North Dakota |
| | | | South Dakota |
| | | | Utah |
| | | | Wisconsin |
| 2002 | "Join the Winner's Circle: READ!" | | Alaska |
| | | | Delaware |
| | | | Idaho |
| | | | Iowa |
| | | | Kansas |
| | | | Michigan |
| | | | Montana |
| | | | Nebraska |
| | | | North Dakota |
| | | | South Dakota |
| | | | Utah |
| | | | Washington |
| | | | Wisconsin |

|      | Children's Theme | Teen Theme | Members |
|------|------------------|------------|---------|
| 2003 | "Laugh It Up at the Library" | | Alaska |
|      |                  |            | Arkansas |
|      |                  |            | Delaware |
|      |                  |            | Idaho |
|      |                  |            | Iowa |
|      |                  |            | Kansas |
|      |                  |            | Michigan |
|      |                  |            | Montana |
|      |                  |            | Nebraska |
|      |                  |            | Nevada |
|      |                  |            | North Dakota |
|      |                  |            | South Dakota |
|      |                  |            | Utah |
|      |                  |            | Washington |
|      |                  |            | Wisconsin |
| 2004 | "Discover New Trails @ Your Library" | "Get Lost" | Alaska |
|      |                  |            | Arkansas |
|      |                  |            | California (various systems and individual libraries) |
|      |                  |            | Colorado |
|      |                  |            | Delaware |
|      |                  |            | Idaho |
|      |                  |            | Illinois – Suburban Chicago System |
|      |                  |            | Iowa |
|      |                  |            | Kansas |
|      |                  |            | Maine |
|      |                  |            | Michigan |
|      |                  |            | Montana |
|      |                  |            | Nebraska |
|      |                  |            | Nevada |
|      |                  |            | New Jersey |
|      |                  |            | North Carolina |
|      |                  |            | Ohio |
|      |                  |            | Oregon |
|      |                  |            | Pennsylvania |

|  | Children's Theme | Teen Theme | Members |
|---|---|---|---|
|  |  |  | South Dakota |
|  |  |  | Utah |
|  |  |  | Washington |
|  |  |  | Wisconsin |
|  |  |  | Wyoming |
| 2005 | "Dragons, Dreams, and Daring Deeds" | "Joust Read" | Alaska |
|  |  |  | Arizona |
|  |  |  | Arkansas |
|  |  |  | California – various systems and individual libraries |
|  |  |  | Colorado |
|  |  |  | Connecticut |
|  |  |  | Delaware |
|  |  |  | Idaho |
|  |  |  | Illinois – Suburban Chicago System |
|  |  |  | Iowa |
|  |  |  | Kansas |
|  |  |  | Kentucky |
|  |  |  | Maine |
|  |  |  | Michigan |
|  |  |  | Montana |
|  |  |  | Nebraska |
|  |  |  | Nevada |
|  |  |  | New Jersey |
|  |  |  | North Carolina |
|  |  |  | Ohio |
|  |  |  | Oklahoma |
|  |  |  | Oregon |
|  |  |  | Pennsylvania |
|  |  |  | South Dakota |
|  |  |  | Utah |
|  |  |  | Washington |
|  |  |  | Wisconsin |
|  |  |  | Wyoming |

| | Children's Theme | Teen Theme | Members |
|---|---|---|---|
| 2006 | "Paws, Claws, Scales, and Tales" | | Alaska |
| | | | Arizona |
| | | | Arkansas |
| | | | California (various systems and individual libraries) |
| | | | Colorado |
| | | | Connecticut |
| | | | Delaware |
| | | | Idaho |
| | | | Illinois (Suburban Chicago) |
| | | | Iowa |
| | | | Kansas |
| | | | Kentucky |
| | | | Maine |
| | | | Michigan |
| | | | Montana |
| | | | Nebraska |
| | | | Nevada |
| | | | New Jersey |
| | | | North Carolina |
| | | | Ohio |
| | | | Oklahoma |
| | | | Oregon |
| | | | Pennsylvania |
| | | | South Dakota |
| | | | Utah |
| | | | Washington |
| | | | Wisconsin |
| | | | Wyoming |

# Appendix C

## Southern States Summer Reading Cooperative Themes by Year with Members

www.vacationreading.org (for children)
www.teenreading.net (for teens)

| Year | Children's Theme | Teen Theme | Members |
|------|------------------|------------|---------|
| 2001 | "Extra! Extra! Read All about It" | | Georgia<br>South Carolina |
| 2002 | "world.wide.reading@your.library" | | Georgia<br>South Carolina |
| 2003 | "Books Ahoy!" | | Alabama<br>Georgia<br>Mississippi<br>South Carolina<br>Virginia |
| 2004 | "Step to the Beat . . . READ!" | "Rock 'n' Read" | Alabama<br>Georgia<br>Mississippi<br>South Carolina<br>Virginia |
| 2005 | "FUNtastic Reading!" | "READiculous!" | Alabama<br>Georgia<br>Mississippi<br>South Carolina<br>Virginia |

# Appendix D

## Outstanding Summer Library Reading Programs

To help with continuous updating of this book, please answer as many of the questions as possible and submit via e-mail to

Carole D. Fiore
cfiore@earthlink.net

or send the information and any sample materials to

Model Summer Library Reading Programs
Carole D. Fiore
c/o Neal-Schuman Publishers, Inc.
100 William Street
Suite 2004
New York, NY 10038

Use additional paper as necessary.

## 1.  Name of Program

## 2.  Name of Library

## 3.  Address

City                          State          Zip
Country

## 4.  Type of library:

- ❑   Public Library – main library of a system
- ❑   Public Library – branch library in a system
- ❑   Public Library – independent library
- ❑   School Library
- ❑   Other – Please specify _____

## 5.  Please provide the name of the parent organization:

## 6.  Name, title, and contact information (phone and e-mail) of person responsible for this program:

Name:
Title:
Phone: (    )      -
Fax: (    )      -
E-mail:

## 7.  Name, title, and contact information (phone and e-mail) of person submitting this nomination if different from above:

Name:
Title:
Phone: (    )      -
Fax: (    )      -
E-mail:

# 8. Please provide the following information about the nominated program:

a. Target Audience: Number of persons reached by this program. If several target groups are reached by this program, please separate patrons reached by groups as indicated below.

| Target Audience | Primary or Secondary<br><br>Mark primary audience with a "P";<br><br>mark secondary audience(s) with "S." | Number of persons reached by this<br><br>program |
|---|---|---|
| Preschool children | | |
| Children in early-elementary grades | | |
| Children in upper-elementary grades | | |
| Middle and high school students | | |
| Special-needs students | | |
| Families | | |

b. When was this program presented? (Month, year, time of day, frequency, etc.)

c. Please provide a summary of this program (do not exceed 300 words):

d. Please tell how this program fits into the long-range or strategic plan of the library sponsoring the program.

e. Please tell how this summer library reading program supports the education of the patrons involved. You may include quotes from users, parents, and/or teachers.

f. Please indicate how this program enhances developmental assets (as developed by the Search Institute) for the individual patrons involved in the program.

g. Please provide a brief budget for this program.

h. Please describe the evaluation methods and instruments that were used to determine the success of this program. If possible, include both outputs and outcomes. If an outcome plan was used, please include. Include sample evaluation instruments if available or forward them via snail mail.

i. Please tell how the target audience and the community at-large were informed about the program. Include samples of promotional materials or media coverage, if available, or forward them via snail mail.

    j.  What changes or improvements would you make in the program?

**9.  Please provide the following information about the library where this program takes place or where it is based:**

    a.  Describe the population in the library's service area:  (size of population, demographic breakdown, educational level, poverty rate, etc.):

    b.  Please describe this library.

        Total number of square feet
        Meeting room(s)
        Children's area
        Young adult area

    c.  Feel free to provide a narrative description of the library. Provide additional information about the library facility or other facility where the program takes place, if appropriate.

    d.  Number and type of (PC or Mac) public-access computers:

    e.  How are computers and the Internet used in this summer library reading program?

    f.  Library's Web address

    g.  Please provide information on partner agencies involved in this program. Use additional space if necessary.

        i.  Name of Agency:
           Contact Person:
           Phone:
           E-mail:
           How was this agency involved in the summer library reading program?

       ii.  Name of Agency:
           Contact Person:
           Phone:
           E-mail:
           How was this agency involved in the summer library reading program?

    h.  Anything else you want to tell us about your program:

Additional documentation, photographs, program fliers, and program samples may be sent via snail mail to

Model Summer Library Reading Programs
Carole D. Fiore
c/o Neal-Schuman Publishers, Inc.
100 William Street
Suite 2004
New York, NY 10038

*Please note: By submitting this form, you are agreeing to allow Carole Fiore to use this information in a book to be published by Neal-Schuman Publishers featuring **Outstanding Summer Library Reading Programs**. Submission of this form does not guarantee inclusion in updates to this book. Also, note that neither the publisher nor the author will be responsible for items lost. When sending additional items via snail mail, please include a copy of this form. Unfortunately, we are unable to return items sent to us.*

# Index

# About the Author

Carole D. Fiore holds a B.S. in early childhood and elementary education from Temple University and an M.S. in library science from Drexel University. She has worked in both school and public libraries in Philadelphia and in various locations in Florida. She is currently a library program specialist/youth services consultant with the State Library and Archives of Florida, where she directs the award-winning Florida Library Youth Program (FLYP). Under her guidance, the FLYP program was awarded a John Cotton Dana Library Public Relations Award and a Davis Productivity Award for "increased performance and added value which enhances the productivity of Florida government and improves the lives of Florida's taxpaying citizens." It was under Fiore's leadership that Florida was the first state to adopt "Born to Read" as a statewide program. She has served as visiting instructor at the School of Library and Information Studies, Florida State University, and has taught children's literature at the College of Education, University of Tampa. Fiore, active in local, state, and national library and youth-serving organizations, is a trainer for the Young Adult Library Services Association's "Serving the Underserved" and for the Public Library Association's "Planning for Results." She is the author of several journal articles and lectures and leads workshops throughout the United States and England. In addition to providing training in emergent literacy, she organizes and presents workshops on many aspects of service to children and teens not only in Florida but across the nation. Fiore is a past president of the Association for Library Service to Children; she has also served that organization as a member of the 1986 Newbery Award Committee and the 1993 Caldecott Award Committee. She was recently appointed to the first Theodore Seuss Geisel Award Committee and to the Steering Committee for the Johns Hopkins Center for Summer Learning on Summer Learning Resource Guide and Training Project.